Daily Readings
In Catholic Classics

Daily Readings
In Catholic Classics

Compiled by

Rawley Myers

IGNATIUS PRESS   SAN FRANCISCO

Cover by Marcia Ryan

Dedicated to
John Griffin, Ph.D.,
educator, scholar, Newman authority,
a Christian gentleman and a good friend

CONTENTS

INTRODUCTION

"Don't read good books—read the best books", Mother Bernadette taught me long ago when I was in high school. These excerpts are from some of the very best Catholic books. We have such a rich heritage as Catholics but in our day many are unaware of this. They are led to believe, as TV constantly tells us (to sell products), that the "latest is best". May this book introduce you, not to mediocre Catholic writing, but to our great Catholic authors. They enlighten our minds and inflame our hearts and strengthen our souls. They give us wonderful inspiration and faith-filled new hope.

Rawley Myers

SOURCES

Karl Adam. *Spirit of Catholicism.* New York, Macmillan.

Saint Ambrose.

Saint Augustine. *Confessions.*

Hilaire Belloc. *The Question and the Answer.* Milwaukee: Bruce.

Saint Bernard of Clairvaux.

Orestes Brownson. *Selected Essays.* Chicago: Henery Regnery.

Abbot John Chapman. *Selected Letters.* London: Sheed and Ward.

G. K. Chesterton. *Orthodoxy.* In *The Collected Works of G. K. Chesterton,* vol. 2. San Francisco: Ignatius Press, 1986. *The Thing: Why I Am Catholic.* In *The Collected Works of G. K. Chesterton,* vol. 4. San Francisco: Ignatius Press, 1990.

Yves Congar. *Jesus Christ.* Herder and Herder.

Martin D'Arcy. *Dialog with Myself.* New York: Trident Press, 1966.

Henri Daniel-Rops. *The Life of Our Lord.* New York: Hawthorn. *The Lord.* Chicago: Henry Regnery.

Christopher Dawson. *Essays in Order.* London: Sheed and Ward.

Walter Farrell, O.P. *Only Son.* London: Sheed and Ward.

Saint Francis de Sales. *Sermons on Our Lady.* Rockford, Ill.: Tan Books.

Dom Aelred Graham, O.S.B. *The Love of God.* New York: Longmans, Green.

Romano Guardini. *Jesus Christ.* Chicago: Henry Regnery.

Cardinal Basil Hume. *To Be a Pilgrim.* Boston: St. Paul Publications.

Thomas à Kempis. *The Imitation of Christ.*

Ronald Knox. *A Spiritual Aeneid.* London: Burns and Oates. *In Soft Garments.* London: Burns and Oates. *The Hidden Stream.* New York: Sheed and Ward. *The Layman and His Conscience.* New York: Sheed and Ward.

C. S. Lewis. *A Case for Christianity.* New York, Macmillan.

Arnold Lunn. *Within That City.* London: Sheed and Ward.

Vincent McNabb, O.P. *In Our Valley.* London: Burns and Oates.

Jacques Maritain. *Peasant of Garonne.* New York: Macmillan.

Abbot Marmion. *Growth in Christ.* B. Herder.

C. C. Martindale. *Creative Love.* London: Sheed and Ward.

Thomas Merton. *Thoughts in Solitude.* New York: Farrar, Straus, Giroux.

Thomas More. *The Essential Thomas More.* Mentor-Omega.

Malcolm Muggeridge. *The End of Christendom.* Grand Rapids, Mich.: William B. Eerdmans.

Cardinal John Henry Newman. *Prayers, Meditations and Devotions.* San Francisco: Ignatius Press, 1989.

Blaise Pascal. *Pensées.*

Karl Rahner, S.J. *The Mother of the Lord.* New York: Crossroad.

Frank J. Sheed. *To Know Christ Jesus.* London: Sheed and Ward.

Archbishop Fulton J. Sheen. *Life of Christ.* New York: McGraw-Hill. *Preface to Religion.* New York: P. J. Kenedy. *Philosophy of Religion.* New York: Appleton Century Crofts.

Saint Thérèse of Lisieux. *The Story of a Soul.*

Saint Teresa of Avila.

Cardinal John Wright. *Mary Our Hope.* San Francisco: Ignatius Press, 1984. *The Saints Always Belong to the Present.* San Francisco: Ignatius Press, 1985.

BIOGRAPHICAL NOTES

Karl Adam (1876–1966) was a German priest of gifted mind. A theologian, he taught in outstanding universities and wrote a number of noteworthy books; one of the most widely read was *The Spirit of Catholicism,* which has appeared in almost every European language as well as Japanese. His writing is clear, exact and compact.

Saint Ambrose was the famous bishop of Milan in the fourth century. He was an outstanding orator and it was he with his sermons who moved St. Augustine to repent his sins. Ambrose was a Roman governor so popular with the people of Milan that they acclaimed him their bishop.

Saint Augustine (354–430) is a Father of the Church. Few have thought so clearly or have written so beautifully. He led a pagan life as a youth, a life of sin and carnality, but as an adult he turned to Christ and found peace for his restless heart. In time he became a priest and then Bishop of Hippo in North Africa; he died in the city during its siege by the Vandals. This great man was the greatest Christian influence for a thousand years and still is very widely read and loved.

Hilaire Belloc (1870–1953) was blessed with a keen and brilliant mind and abounding energy. He was tireless in defending the faith. He was English and served in the House of Commons; he spoke often for the Church, and gave lectures in America.

Saint Bernard of Clairvaux (1091–1153) was a great reformer of the Church in the Middle Ages. As an abbot he was the most influential preacher of his time. He renewed monasteries and brought countless Christians back to Christ.

Orestes Brownson (1803–76) was a Presbyterian and Unitarian minister before he became a Catholic. His *Quarterly Review* was the first great venture in American Catholic intellectual journalism. Gifted with an excellent mind, Brownson engaged in constant debate against those who attacked the Church, and at times argued on philosophical matters with some within the Church.

Abbot John Chapman (1865–1933) was an English Benedictine and Abbot at Downside. Educated at Oxford he won a First in Greats. Abbot John was noted for his sermons and retreats and was the author of well written, lucid religious books.

G. K. Chesterton (1874–1936) was a great thinker, Catholic apologist, humorist, author and poet. He was a convert to Catholicism. GKC, as he was called, wrote extensively, including his outstanding books on religion, in particular "Orthodoxy" and "The Everlasting Man", and beautiful biographies of Saint Francis and Thomas Aquinas.

Yves Congar, O.P. (1904–   ) is a French Dominican. Few theologians have had an impact on the Church that can compare to his. He is a distinguished ecclesiologist and a spiritual writer of the first rank.

Henri Daniel-Rops (1901–65) was a distinguished, widely-recognized French ecclesiastical historian. His books, which have had a vast audience, are scholarly but readable. He wrote Church history in an interesting way. In 1955 he was elected to the French Academy for his thoughtful research.

Martin D'Arcy, S.J. (1888–1976) was one of the eminent Catholic philosophers in the world in his day. He was an English Jesuit. At Oxford he took first class honors in Humanities, and won a number of prestigious prizes. Much in demand as a preacher of thought and wisdom, he served as a university professor in England and the United States. His excellent books are philosophical and spiritual treasures.

Christopher Dawson (1889–1970) was a well known English historian. He attended Oxford and his reading of the lives of the Catholic mystics and saints led him into the Church.

He was twenty-five when he embraced Catholicism. He wrote many brilliant religious histories.

Walter Farrell, O.P. (1902–51) was an American Dominican. He gave himself to Thomistic studies. He wrote a four-part guide to the *Summa* of Saint Thomas as well as other excellent volumes. He was a professor of theology.

Saint Francis de Sales (1567–1622) was Bishop of Geneva. He was an outstanding preacher and writer. The patron saint of writers, he with Saint Jane Frances de Chantal founded the order of the Visitation Sisters.

Dom Aelred Graham, O.S.B. (1907–84) was English. He became a monk of Ampleforth Abbey, York, in 1930, attended Oxford and was professor of dogmatic theology at his monastery. He came to America and was prior of the Benedictine Community in Portsmouth, Rhode Island. He was the author of a number of noted spiritual books.

Romano Guardini (1885–1968) was one of the foremost German leaders in reviving religion. He was born in Italy but grew up in Germany and became a priest, a professor, and an outstanding religious author. His books are wonderful reading.

Cardinal Basil Hume (1923–) is the Archbishop of Westminster in England. Prior to that he was Abbot of Ampleforth. He has a gifted mind and is an excellent writer.

Thomas à Kempis (c.1379–1471) spent his years in the monastery of St. Agnes in the Netherlands. He is customarily designated as the author of one of the most beautiful books in religious literature, *The Imitation of Christ.*

Ronald Knox (1888–1957) was an English Anglican priest who became a Catholic priest. He was the son of a bishop in the Church of England. Brilliant, witty, gifted he won many prizes and honors while a student at Oxford. In studying the subject of authority in the Church he came to see he must submit to Rome. As a Catholic priest he served as chaplain at Oxford for many years. He is the only person to ever translate by himself the whole Bible into English. His books, logical and clear, with a wonderful style, are among the greatest religious volumes in this century.

C. S. Lewis (1898–1963) wrote many books on Christian apologetics. His *Screwtape Letters* achieved worldwide fame. He was an Anglican and a professor at both Oxford and Cambridge. His gift was to make religion come alive for modern man. While a student he lost his faith, but in time reason convinced him, "We are in God's hands or nowhere", as the poet W. H. Auden wrote.

Arnold Lunn (1888–1974) was another English convert writer. He attended Oxford, was secretary of the Oxford Union and editor of the university literary publication, *Isis*. After becoming a Catholic most of his writing was controversial, showing the logic of Catholicism to an increasingly agnostic world. Reason forced him to enter the Church.

Vincent McNabb, O.P. (1868–1943) was of an Irish family who spent his years as a Dominican in England. "Nobody who ever met or saw or heard Father McNabb ever forgot him", wrote his friend G. K. Chesterton. He served the poor, preached frequently and every Sunday he spoke at the Preacher's Corner at Hyde Park, London, amid heckling of all kinds; this for more than forty years.

Jacques Maritain (1882–1973) was one of the outstanding philosophers in this century, some say the greatest. Born in France, Maritain entered the Catholic Church as an adult. He taught in France and at Columbia and Princeton and Notre Dame in this country. He wrote a number of outstanding philosophical books. He was ambassador for France to the Vatican.

C. C. Martindale, S.J. (1879–1963) was an English Jesuit; another of a long list of distinguished and highly intelligent converts to the faith. He had a keen mind and a swift pen and he was a zealous priest. He was a brilliant student at Oxford. As a priest, he constantly wrote about the faith. He was a chaplain in the trenches in World War I and being in Denmark at the time of the Nazi invasion in World War II became a prisoner.

Abbot Marmion, O.S.B. (1858–1923). Born in Ireland where he became a parish priest and professor of philosophy at the seminary, he later entered the Benedictine monastery in Belgium, and became Abbot. He is recognized as a master of the spiritual life; his writings have been popular in many countries for those who are serious in growing spiritually.

Thomas Merton (1915–68) was an American convert to the faith. Educated in Europe and at Columbia University in New York City, he became a Trappist monk at Gethsemani in Kentucky. He was the author of many books on religious topics and his autobiography, *Seven Storey Mountain,* is an American religious masterpiece.

Malcolm Muggeridge (1903–90) was, in his old age, a convert to the Church. He was greatly influenced by Mother Teresa of Calcutta. He was a well-known English journalist, editor of *Punch,* the popular English humor magazine. He went from atheism to skepticism to agnosticism, to socialism, and he once tried to commit suicide, before he turned to Christ. An able and gifted writer he realized at last that cynicism led nowhere. In the end he found Jesus and peace. An observer and commentator in the press, on radio and TV, he saw that materialism leads to selfishness, pessimism and despair.

Cardinal John Henry Newman (1801–90) was one of the most famous preachers and religious writers in modern times. An Anglican priest and rector of the university church, St. Mary Virgin, at Oxford, crowds came from all over England to hear him speak, and his writings were read everywhere. But his constant study of the early Church made him realize he must be a Catholic. This meant to give up everything he loved, for England turned against him, and he was the most English of Englishmen. He was forty-five years old when he turned his back on fame and became a Catholic. He was ordained a Catholic priest and founded and served at the Oratory in Birmingham for the rest of his life. He is the greatest modern Catholic writer. The story of his conversion, *Apologia Pro Vita Sua,* is an all-time masterpiece.

Blaise Pascal (1623–62) was a French mathematical genius. He was deeply religious and wrote most thoughtful books.

Karl Rahner, S.J. (1904–84) was a professor of dogmatic theology at the University of Innsbruck in Austria and one of the most influential postconciliar theologians in the Church. His numerous books are highly esteemed by Catholics and in scholarly circles outside the Church.

Frank J. Sheed (1897–1981) was born in Australia and went to England where he became a noted Catholic publisher. He and his wife, Maisie Ward, founded Sheed & Ward, a publishing company which was known for printing outstanding Catholic books. He himself wrote a series of fine books on the faith.

Archbishop Fulton J. Sheen (1895–1979). Bishop Sheen, as he was popularly known, was for years the foremost preacher of religion in America, first on radio and then on television. Millions tuned in to hear his clear presentation of the Catholic Church. He was admired everywhere. His books sold in the hundreds of thousands. Before becoming a bishop he was a famous professor of philosophy at the Catholic University of America, Washington, D.C.

Saint Teresa of Avila (1515–82), a Doctor of the Church, was a Spanish mystic and great religious reformer; she was a masterful religious superior in the Carmelite Order. Her *Autobiography* is one of the noblest books in Spanish literature.

Saint Thérèse of Lisieux (1873–97) was a young French Carmelite nun of great but childlike sanctity. She is called "The Little Flower". She died in her early twenties and said she would spend her eternity in Heaven showering spiritual roses upon the people of the world.

Saint Thomas Aquinas (1225–74) is one of the greatest thinkers in all of Christianity. He was born in Italy and became a Dominican priest and studied under St. Albert the Great. He taught at the University of Paris and gained a reputation as a skillful and inventive thinker, yet he was a very humble friar whose prayers were childlike. He "baptized" Aristotle, adapting the noble Greek philosopher to Catholic thought. Thomas has the title in the Church of Angelic Doctor. His *Summa Theologica* is the most systematic philosophical-theological work ever written. It is breathtaking in depth and extent.

Saint Thomas More (1478–1535) was Chancellor of England during the infamous reign of King Henry VIII. A man of conscience and courage, Thomas More opposed the king, who had begun to defy the Church. For resistance to the king's divorce of Queen Catherine and his marriage to Anne Boleyn, More was imprisoned in a horrible dungeon in the Tower of London and then publicly executed. He was one of the great literary figures of his time.

Cardinal John Wright (1909–79) was intellectually the shining light of the American hierarchy. With a magnificent mind he spoke and wrote extensively, as auxiliary Bishop of Boston, Bishop of Worcester, Bishop of Pittsburgh and a Cardinal in Rome.

ACKNOWLEDGMENTS

The compiler and publisher gratefully acknowledge the following permissions to reprint previously published material.

Burns and Oates, Ltd., Tunbridge Wells, Kent, England, for permission to reprint from *In Our Valley* by Father Vincent McNabb, O.P.

Confraternity of Christian Doctrine, Washington, D.C., for permission to use verses from their edition of the New Testament.

Crossroad/Continuum, New York, for permission to reprint from *Mother of the Lord* by Karl Rahner and *Jesus Christ* by Yves Congar.

Doubleday, a division of Bantam, Doubleday, Dell Publishing Group, Inc., New York, for permission to reprint from *The Life of Christ* by Bishop Fulton Sheen.

Farrar, Straus and Giroux, Inc., New York, for permission to reprint from *Thoughts in Solitude* by Thomas Merton. © 1958 by The Abbey of Our Lady of Gethsemani. Renewal © 1986 by the Trustees of the Thomas Merton Legacy Trust.

Harper Collins, London, for permission to reprint from *The Case for Christianity* by C. S. Lewis.

Macmillan Publishing Company, New York, for permission to reprint from *Preface to Religion* by Bishop Fulton J. Sheen. © 1946 by P. J. Kenedy and Sons.

Saint Paul Publications, Langley, Slough, England, for permission to reprint from *To Be a Pilgrim* by Cardinal Basil Hume, O.S.B. Published in the U.S. in 1984 by Harper and Row, Inc.

Simon and Schuster, New York, for permission to reprint from *Dialogue with Myself* by Martin D'Arcy. © 1966 by Martin D'Arcy.

Tan Books, Rockford, Ill., for permission to reprint from *Sermons on Our Lady* by Francis de Sales.

A. P. Watt, Ltd., London and Burns and Oates, Ltd., London, for permission to use material from two books by Ronald Knox: *A Spiritual Aeneid* and *In Soft Garments*.

Daily Readings

Mary, Mother of God

Mary is the *Virgin Most Prudent,* the *Seat of Wisdom,* the *Queen of the Patriarchs, Prophets,* and *Apostles*—but few, indeed, are the great shrines dedicated to these venerable qualities. We are prone to cultivate fame and those who possess it. Mary is the *Virgin Most Renowned,* the *Vessel of Honor,* of *Singular Devotion,* the *Queen of All Saints*—yet no common instinct impels us to hail her under these proud titles of acclaim. We are a nation avid for power. Mary is the *Virgin Most Powerful,* the *Tower of David,* the *Strength of the Weak,* the *Help of Christians;* the liturgy speaks of her as being of strength, a strength commanding like that to an army, unconquerable and compact—and yet, save in the time of affliction and of great need, we do not seem to pay tribute to Mary in terms of her power. Always we are preoccupied by her *purity.* Of all her attributes this most haunts us; of all her qualities this most causes us to hush, to bow our heads in prayer, alike of petition and of praise. *Mother Most Pure!* So under every sky the believing breathe to her their love and need. *Ave Maria*—undefiled! *Ave Maria*—stainless styled! So even the unbelieving cry. *Mother Fairest, Mother Purest, Virgin Most Pure*—this the constant song of those who love her most.

Why does her purity so preoccupy our minds, so silence our speech, so inflame our hearts? Perhaps it is because in no wise are we so pathetically alien to her. Wisdom we have in part; knowledge—alas! sometimes we are surfeited with it. Power we have of a kind; and fame is the food on which we grow fat. With all her other qualities, we can make some show of kinship. But the most strong, the most wise, the most fair, the most renowned of us must bow our heads whenever there is mention of the *purity* of the Mother of God!

—Cardinal John Wright

Are You Happy?   *January 2*

If you saw hordes of people tramping the fields, with axes in their hands and pans strapped to their shoulders, you would conclude that those people had not found all the gold they wanted. If you saw armies of nurses and doctors riding ambulances, or carrying cots, you would conclude that health had not been found. When you see people crowding into theaters, charging cocktail bars, seeking new thrills in a spirit of restlessness, you would conclude that they have not yet found pleasure, otherwise they would not be looking for it.

The very fact that you can conceive of greater happiness than you possess now is a proof that you are not happy. If you were perfect, you would be happy. There is no doubt that at one time or another in your life you attained that which you believed would make you happy, but when you got what you wanted, were you happy?

—Archbishop Fulton J. Sheen

You Are Dust   *January 3*

Ash Wednesday is the occasion of a ceremony which enjoys a curious popularity among Catholics. Having ashes smeared on your forehead is not meant to be a particularly enjoyable thing; rather the contrary; it is the outward symbol of penance, which was probably used in the reconciling of notorious sinners before it ever came to be applied, on this one day, to the faithful at large. We humiliate ourselves, disfigure ourselves—just what, in the ordinary way, we least like doing. And yet, as I say, I think there is something curiously attractive to most Catholics about this ceremony. Perhaps it takes us back to our childish days when we liked getting dirty for its own sake, and Ash Wednesday was the one day in the year on which we were allowed to get dirty without being sent upstairs to wash. Dust and ashes; let us give them a few minutes' consideration. Of course it sounds rather too obvious a thing to deserve much attention; but really we are getting into such a complicated frame of mind nowadays that the obvious things are coming into their own again. You open your newspaper and find an advertisement which suggests that you should eat bread; or another which asks you whether you have ever tried burning coal on your fire.

I don't think it's necessary to suppose that we are being informed of anything we couldn't have found out for ourselves. The fact is that this universe which is made up of irrational dust bears, nevertheless, the stamp of reason marked upon it; and that man, unique among the creatures, has a reasoning faculty which is akin, evidently, to that higher and immaterial order. Alone among the creatures, man can look back upon himself and become the object of his own thought; can distinguish the world he knows from himself as knowing it. And in the exercise of that faculty, at however low a level, he transcends the limits of mere matter and makes himself one with that higher order of which matter is only the inadequate expression.

—Msgr. Ronald Knox

Body and Soul   *January 4*

[Man] is dust. This body of yours *is you*. No good to talk, Eastern-fashion, as if the body were a cage in which your soul is imprisoned, or a garment which your soul wears and can slip off at any time. It is all very well as a matter of rhetoric to talk about your body as a garment of dust. But if somebody jabs a pin into you, it is no use telling yourself that it is going into your garment of dust; it goes into you. The liaison, whatever it be, between your body and your soul is something quite unique; we have no comparison, in the whole of our experience, which would begin to make it clearer to us. We are, as a matter of fact, intellectual souls; and those souls, our religion assures us, are immortal. But once we begin to think about ourselves as immortal souls, we are inclined to grow self-important and put on airs about it. So the first way in which we are encouraged to humiliate ourselves, . . . is to remember (what is quite equally true) that we are dust—lumps of matter lying about for no very obvious reason in a world which is as material as ourselves.

—Msgr. Ronald Knox

Why Rules? *January 5*

Every one has heard people quarrelling. Sometimes it sounds funny and sometimes it sounds merely unpleasant; but however it sounds, I believe we can learn something very important from listening to the kind of things they say. They say things like this: "That's my seat, I was there first"—"Leave him alone, he isn't doing you any harm"—"Why should you shove in first?"—"Give me a bit of your orange, I gave you a bit of mine"—"How'd you like it if anyone did the same to you?"—"Come on, you promised." People say things like that every day, educated people as well as uneducated, and children as well as grown-ups.

Now what interests me about all these remarks is that the man who makes them isn't just saying that the other man's behaviour doesn't happen to please him. He is appealing to some kind of standard of behaviour which he expects the other man to know about. And the other man very seldom replies, "To hell with your standard." Nearly always he tries to make out that what he has been doing doesn't really go against the standard, or that if it does, there is some special excuse. He pretends there is some special reason in this particular case why the person who took the seat first should not keep it, or that things were quite different when he was given the bit of orange, or that something has turned up which lets him off keeping his promise. It looks, in fact, very much as if both parties had in mind some kind of Law or Rule of fair play or decent behaviour or morality or whatever you like to call it, about which they really agreed. And they have. If they hadn't, they might, of course, fight like animals, but they couldn't *quarrel* in the human sense of the word. Quarrelling means trying to show that the other man's in the wrong. And there'd be no sense in trying to do that unless you and he had some sort of agreement as to what Right and Wrong are; just as there'd be no sense in saying that a footballer had committed a foul unless there was some agreement about the rules of football.

—C. S. Lewis

The Epiphany *January 6*

Our Savior said to the woman of Samaria, "the hour comes, when you shall neither in this mountain, nor yet at Jerusalem, worship the Father." And upon today's feast I may say to you in his words on another occasion, "This day is this scripture fulfilled in your ears." This day we commemorate the opening of the door of faith to the Gentiles, the extension of the Church of God through all lands, whereas, before Christ's coming it had been confined to one nation only [the Jews]. This dissemination of the Truth throughout the world had been the subject of prophecy.

The characteristic blessing of the Church of Christ, its Catholic nature, is a frequent subject of rejoicing with St. Paul, who was the chief instrument of its propagation. In one Epistle he speaks of Gentiles being "fellow heirs" with the Jews, "and of the same body, and partakers of His promise in Christ by the Gospel." In another he enlarges on "the mystery now made manifest to saints," viz., "Christ among the Gentiles, the hope of glory."

The day on which we commemorate this gracious appointment of God's Providence, is called the Epiphany, or bright manifestation of Christ to the Gentiles; being the day on which the wise men came from the East under guidance of a star, to worship him, and thus became the first-fruits of the heathen world.

When Christ's Church, built upon the Apostles, wonderfully branched out from Jerusalem as a center into the heathen world round about, and gathering into it men of all ranks, languages, and characters, moulded them into one pattern, the pattern of their Savior, in truth and righteousness.

The Gospel is to be preached in all lands, before the end comes: "This Gospel of the Kingdom shall be preached in all the world for a witness unto all nations; and then shall the end come."

Let us then work with zeal, but as to the Lord and not to me; recollecting that even Apostles saw the sins of the churches they planted; that St. Paul predicted that "evil men and seducers would wax worse and worse"; and that St. John seems even to consider extraordinary unbelief as the very sign of times of the Gospel, as if the light increased the darkness of those who hated it.

Therefore we will seek within for the Epiphany of Christ. We will look towards his Holy Altar, and approach it for the fire of love and purity which there burns. We will find comfort in the illumination which Baptism gives. We will rest and be satisfied in his ordinances and in his word. We will bless and praise his name, whenever he vouchsafes to display his glory and we will ever pray him to manifest it in our own souls.

—*Cardinal John Henry Newman*

Too Modest   *January 7*

We are on the road to producing a race of men too mentally modest to believe in the multiplication table. We are in danger of seeing philosophers who doubt the law of gravity as being a mere fancy of their own. Scoffers of old time were too proud to be convinced; but these are too humble to be convinced. The meek do inherit the earth; but the modern sceptics are too meek even to claim their inheritance. It is exactly this intellectual helplessness which is our . . . problem.

. . . What peril of morbidity there is for man comes rather from his reason than his imagination. It was not meant to attack the authority of reason; rather it is the ultimate purpose to defend it. For it needs defence. The whole modern world is at war with reason; and the tower already reels.

—*G. K. Chesterton*

All Creatures Are Good

Now every creature of God is good [1 Tim 4:4] and every man, in so far as he is a man, is a creature—but not by virtue of the fact that he is a sinner. So, God is the Creator of both human body and soul. Neither of these is evil, nor does God hate either of them: for He hates none of the things that He has made. But the conscious soul (*animus*) is better than the body; while God, the Maker and Founder of both, is still more excellent and He hates nothing in man except sin. Sin for man is a disorder and perversion: that is, a turning away (*aversio*) from the most worthy Creator and a turning toward (*conversio*) the inferior things that He has created.

—*Saint Augustine*

A Masterpiece   *January 8*

"What a piece of work is a man! how noble in reason! how infinite in faculty! in form and moving how express and admirable! in action how like an angel! in apprehension how like a god! the beauty of the world! the paragon of animals!" So Shakespeare, through the mouth of Hamlet, expressing no doubt the mood of the Renaissance, proclaims man's confidence in his own worth. It is permissible to think that St Thomas himself, notwithstanding his acknowledgement of original sin and the fall, would have had but little qualification to make of this eulogy of man.

The conception of human nature preserved by the Christian philosophical tradition can be stated quite simply: man is a rational animal. He is a being sharing with the animals many of their activities: he is born by the processes of physical generation and dies from physical decay; he enjoys a life of the senses and imagination; the need for food, susceptibility to heat and cold, the effects of environment and heredity, of changes of time and place—in all these he is subject to much the same laws as the animal world. He is nevertheless outside that world by reason of a vital unifying principle which places him nearer to the angels than to the brute creation. He possesses a spiritual soul. Or, to be more exact, he *is* a spiritual soul informing and giving substance to a material body. His body is not an animal body indwelt by an alien substance which we call the soul; it is a human body, designed by nature to be united to, and vivified by, a principle of undying life. We speak commonly of the body possessing the soul, of the soul being within the body, but a more accurate description is the reverse of this: the soul is the rightful master of the body, the body is within the soul—not indeed spatially, but in virtue of its relation to it as instrument.

—*Dom Aelred Graham*

Does God Speak to Us?   *January 9*

The second great and abrupt step in the process of reasoning by which we are seeking to answer the question, "What am I?" is an approach to the problem, "Has there been a revelation of God to man?"

When, or if, we establish to our satisfaction that man is such and such; that he finds himself to be, by the use of his senses and by the use of his reason, created by an omnipotent God Who is the end of his being, to Whom he is responsible for his actions, from Whom he derives his moral sense and to Whom he must account for his use or abuse of that sense; when we have given Man and his life at least *so* much meaning, we have established what is well called "natural religion."

Man so far comprehended by himself, so far aware of what he is, in such a degree able to answer the Great Question and the questions that derive from it, worships, prays, manifests indignation at evil, confesses (if only to himself) his own wrongdoing, knows that he should strive against the tendency to wrongdoing; and he expresses all this in some form of action. In other words, man is possessed of natural religion (as much the most of mankind have been for much the most of the periods and places open to our inspection).

—*Hilaire Belloc*

God's Help   *January 10*

God created man, who had no coherence, no life save in his Creator. Then man sinned; he attempted to free himself from this fundamental truth of his existence; attempted to be sufficient unto himself. And he fell away from God—in the terrible, literal sense of the word. He fell from genuine being towards nothingness—and not back to the positive, creative pure nothingness from which God had lifted him, but towards the negative nothingness of sin, destruction, death, senselessness and the abyss. Admittedly, he never quite touches bottom, for then he would cease to exist, and he who has not created himself is incapable of cancelling his existence.

God's mysterious grace could not leave man in such forlornness; it desired to help him home. It is not for us to discuss how he might have accomplished this. Our task is to hold to the text that accounts how it actually was done: in a manner of such sacred magnanimity and power, that once revealed to us, it is impossible to conceive of any other: in the manner of love.

—Romano Guardini

Valuable   *January 11*

Everybody feels he is envalued by love. "Nobody loves me" is the equivalent of being valueless. It is love that confers value, and the more important the person who loves you, the more precious is your value. You are infinitely precious because you are loved by God, but God is not infinite because you love Him.

God thirsts for you, not because you are His waters of everlasting life, but because you are the thirst, He the waters. He needs you only because you need Him. Without Him you are imperfect; but without you He is Perfect. It is the echo that needs the Voice, and not the Voice that needs the echo. "In this is charity: not as though we had loved God, but because he hath first loved us, and sent his Son to be a propitiation for our sins" (I Jn 4:10).

Never think that, in giving glory to God, you are giving

something without which He would be unhappy, and with which He becomes a dissatisfied dictator. What is glory? Glory is *clara notitia cum laude:* a clear understanding of the worth of another which prompts us to praise. Glory is the result of knowledge and love.

—Archbishop Fulton J. Sheen

A Person Must Think   *January 12*

It is very difficult for us sometimes to make up our minds. On this or that point we may never have been able to make up our minds. Even in the matter of ordinary thinking, some people do not quite easily follow out the workings of their own intelligence. It is fatiguing. In Mathematics or Euclid some people can't get on because it is a little hard for them to keep their minds on it. Sometimes people get a reputation for being very intelligent when they are not really very intelligent, but persevering. A great number of people do not make up their minds because they won't take the trouble of thinking things out. Even in tidying up a room, they won't take the trouble to think, or they would see they are pushing all the dust into the air—merely distributing it. Or sometimes people make up their minds in the wrong way. They will not be taught. They are not teachable. To be taught, in about ninety-nine per cent of things, is the quickest way.

If you and I neglect thinking on important things because it is hard, we do not "bring forth our firstborn." We do not arrive at anything. Some people will not think, because they know it will mean their doing disagreeable things.

—Vincent McNabb

Human Dignity

"O God," exclaims St Augustine in a memorable phrase, "Who art loved knowingly or unknowingly by everything capable of loving." There is indeed a sense in which all things can be said to love God. As we have seen, everything depends on Him for its existence, and this law of dependence permeates the universe. From this viewpoint the whole of nature is to be conceived as loving God, stretching out its hands towards the Creator in silent acknowledgement of His act of creation. Man also, being a part of the cosmos, tends towards God in this way. In this chapter, however, we shall attempt to state certain truths about man's nature which throw light upon a capacity for a love-union with God which belongs to him alone.

In the first place it is well to insist on human dignity. It is an error to suppose that we glorify God by belittling His creation. Not a few of the expressions of the masters of spirituality, and even of the saints, if taken too literally, could lead us astray in this respect. The essence of the virtue of humility lies not in self-depreciation but in a practical realization of our complete dependence on God. " . . . What hast thou that thou hast not received? And if thou hast received, why dost thou glory as if thou hadst not received?" asks St Paul. Truly. But we are not thereby justified in denying the worth of what we have in fact received. "Acknowledge, O Christian, thy dignity," writes the great St Leo, "and, being made sharer in the divine nature, do not fall back into thy former degeneracy." But even the lowly state from which we have been uplifted denotes a weakness in action, in our capacity to know what is true and do what is good, rather than essential corruption. Grace does not destroy but perfects nature and the supernatural life is built upon a natural structure that is fundamentally sound.

—Dom Aelred Graham

But we must now contemplate the rich and countless blessings with which the goodness of God, who cares for all He has created, has filled this very misery of the human race, which reflects His retributive justice. . . . He alone, coupling and connecting in some wonderful fashion the spiritual and corporeal natures, the one to command, the other to obey, makes a living being. And this work of His is so great and wonderful, that not only man, who is a rational animal, and consequently more excellent than all other animals of the earth, but even the most diminutive insect, cannot be considered attentively without astonishment and without praising the Creator.

It is He, then, who has given to the human soul a mind, in which reason and understanding lie as it were asleep during infancy, and as if they were not destined, however, to be awakened and exercised as years increase, so as to become capable of knowledge and of receiving instruction, fit to understand what is true and to love what is good. It is by this capacity the soul drinks in wisdom, and becomes endowed with those virtues by which, in prudence, fortitude, temperance, and righteousness, it makes war upon error and the other inborn vices, and conquers them by fixing its desires upon no other object than the supreme and unchangeable Good. And even though this be not uniformly the result, yet who can competently utter or even conceive the grandeur of this work of the Almighty, and the unspeakable boon He has conferred upon our rational nature, by giving us even the capacity of such attainment? For over and above those arts which are called virtues, and which teach us how we may spend our life well, and attain to endless happiness—arts which are given to the children of the promise and the kingdom by the sole grace of God which is in Christ—has not the genius of man invented and applied countless astonishing arts, partly the result of necessity, partly the result of exuberant invention, so that this vigor of mind, which is so active in the discovery not merely of superfluous but even of dangerous and destructive things, betokens an inexhaustible wealth in the nature which can invent, learn, or employ such arts? What wonderful—one might say stupefying—advances has human industry made!

— *Saint Augustine*

What Is Man? *January 15*

If one were to ask of the New Testament: What is Man? it would reply with the words of the apostle John: That creature whom God "so loved . . . that he gave his only-begotten Son . . . " (3:16). The answer immediately evokes a second: Man is that creature who dared to slaughter the Son God sent him. He who retorts: What have I to do with Annas and Caiphas? is still ignorant of the collective guilt that binds all men. Already on the historical plane one stands for all, and all have to bear the consequences of the deeds of the one; how much more so here where it is question of the great collectivity of deicide and redemption. Then Scripture gives still a third answer to the question: Man is that creature who now lives upon the destiny of Christ; him on whom God's love still rests, but also the responsibility for driving that love to death.

— *Romano Guardini*

We Are Not Angels *January 16*

I always recall that wonderful phrase of St. Paul, "This is the will of God, your sanctification" (I Th 4:3). That is one of the great phrases you can turn about. It does not only mean it is God's Will we should be holy, but that our holiness will be the doing of His Will.

God's Will is shown to us in many ways. We are born into this world, and the Will of God is around us—even before our birth! Round about us lies the Will of God. Round about us are so many people, so many things. We are born of this or that parent, in this or that hamlet, or city; under this or that sky; at this time or the other; under the patronage of some saint—and never till we reach heaven shall we know all that that Saint has done for us. We are born surrounded by the Will of God, and that Will now is going to be our sanctification.

God's Will is manifested to us even by what we are ourselves. We are not angels. Had we been angels our eternity would have been settled by one act. We are human beings, with that strange wedlock between body and soul. That is the Will of God. Our very body is the Will of God, and our sanctification depends on our accepting the Will of God with regard to our body and our soul. Some are born with weakly bodies, some with strong. That is the Will of God.

Do not think, dear children in Jesus Christ, do not think it is always easy to do the Will of God. Those who have strength of body must not think that is given them that they may enjoy it. God has not given it for enjoyment, but for work. Not even the sun and the moon are given to us merely to enjoy, but that by them we may see to work. That is the Will of God—not that we should just sing "Te Deums" that we have healthy bodies and are enjoying good health. The Will of God consists in our taking that strength of body and working with it.

—*Vincent McNabb*

The Battle Within   *January 17*

The psychological explanation attributes this tension within you to something peculiar to you as an individual, e.g., to your erotic impulses, for example, because you were frightened by a mouse in a dark closet during a thunderstorm while reading a book on sex.

This hardly fits the facts because you are not the only one who is "that way;" everyone is. There is nothing queer about *you*. But there is something queer about *human nature*. Do not think that basically you are any different from anyone else in the world, or that you have a monopoly on temptations, or that you alone find it hard to be good, or that you alone suffer remorse when you do evil. It is human nature that is queer, not you.

Your soul is the battlefield of a great civil war. The law of your members is fighting against the law of your mind. Your name is "legion"—you have no unifying purpose in life; there is only a succession of choices, but there is no one over-all goal to which everything is subordinated. You are split into many worlds: eyes, ears, heart, body and soul.

—Archbishop Fulton J. Sheen

Decency

Taking the race as a whole, [the earlier thinkers] thought that the human idea of Decent Behaviour was obvious to every one. And I believe they were right. If they weren't, then all the things we say about this war are nonsense. What is the sense in saying the enemy are in the wrong unless Right is a real thing which the [Nazis] deny.

Think of a country where people were *admired* for running away in battle, or where a man felt *proud* for double-crossing all the people who had been kindest to him. You might just as well try to imagine a country where two and two made five. Men have differed as regards what people you ought to be unselfish to— whether it was only your own family, or your fellow countrymen, or every one. But they have always agreed that you oughtn't to put yourself first. Selfishness has never been admired. Men have differed as to whether you should have one wife or four. But they have always agreed that you mustn't simply have any woman you liked.

But the most remarkable thing is this. Whenever you find a man who says he doesn't believe in a real Right and Wrong, you will find the same man going back on this a moment later. He may break his promise to you, but if you try breaking one to him he'll be complaining "It's not fair" before you can say Jack Robinson. A nation may say treaties don't matter; but then, next minute, they spoil their case by saying that the particular treaty they want to break was an unfair one. But if treaties don't matter, and if there's no such things as Right and Wrong—in other words, if there is no Law of Nature—what is the difference between a fair treaty and an unfair one?

—C. S. Lewis

What Are You Like?

Either God created you the way you are now, or else you are fallen from the state in which God created you. The facts support the second view: the present tension and inner contradiction within us is due to some fault subsequent to the creation of human nature.

An unequivocal voice in your moral consciousness tells you that your acts of wrong-doing are abnormal facts in your nature. They ought not to be. There is something wrong inside of us. God made us one way; we made ourselves, in virtue of our freedom, another way. He wrote the drama; we changed the plot. You are not an animal that failed to evolve into a human; you are a human who rebelled against the Divine. If we are a riddle to ourselves, the blame is not to be put on God, but on us.

The fact remains: whatever you are, you are not what you ought to be. You are not a depraved criminal, but you are weak; you are not a mass of irremediable corruption for you bear within yourself the image of God. You are like a man fallen into a well. You know you ought not to be there, and you know you cannot get out by yourself.

This is a roundabout way of saying that you need religion, but not a religion with pious platitudes. You want healing; you want deliverance. . . .

Analyzing your soul you discover it to be like an auto that has run out of gas, and you are not quite sure of the right road. Hence, you need someone not only to give you some fuel for your tank, but also someone to point out your destination. If you have no religion at the present time, it may be because you rightly reacted against those bland assumptions that a few moral exhortations on Sunday will transform the world into the Kingdom of God.

—*Archbishop Fulton J. Sheen*

You Couldn't Have Guessed *January 20*

Reality, in fact, is always something you couldn't have guessed. That's *one* of the reasons I believe Christianity. It's a religion you couldn't have guessed. If it offered us just the kind of universe we'd always expected, I'd feel we were making it up. But, in fact, it's not the sort of thing anyone would have made up. It has just that queer twist about it that real things have. So let's leave behind all these boys' philosophies—these over-simple answers. The problem isn't simple and the answer isn't going to be simple either.

What is the problem? A universe that contains much that is obviously bad and apparently meaningless, but containing creatures like ourselves who know that it is bad and meaningless. There are only two views that face all the facts. One is the Christian view that this is a good world that has gone wrong, but still retains the memory of what it ought to have been. The other is the view called Dualism. Dualism means the belief that there are two equal and independent powers at the back of everything, one of them good and the other bad, and that this universe is the battlefield in which they fight out an endless war. I personally think that next to Christianity Dualism is the manliest and most sensible creed on the market. But it has a catch in it.

The two powers, or spirits, or gods—the good one and the bad one—are supposed to be quite independent. They both existed from all eternity. Neither of them made the other, neither of them has any more right than the other to call itself God. Each presumably thinks it is good and thinks the other bad. One of them likes hatred and cruelty, the other likes love and mercy, and each backs its own view. Now what do we mean when we call one of them the Good Power and the other the Bad Power? Either we're merely saying that we happen to prefer the one to the other—like preferring beer to cider—or else we're saying that, whatever *they* say about it, and whichever *we* happen to like, one of them is actually wrong, actually mistaken, in regarding itself as good. Now if we mean merely that we happen to prefer the first, then we must give up talking about good and evil at all. For good means what you ought to prefer quite regardless of what you happen to like at any given moment. If "being good" meant simply joining the side you happened to fancy, for no real reason, then good wouldn't *be* good. So we must mean that one of the two powers is actually wrong and the other actually right.

—*C. S. Lewis*

Happiness

"The end of man is happiness." I say that this is an axiom which cannot be disputed. If anyone cares to dispute it, he has but to look about for some other end to man's activities. He will not find it. We may be mistaken as to where the greatest good or the greatest happiness lies; along what lines, in the long run and taking the thing as a whole, the maximum of happiness or the minimum of unhappiness will be discovered. But the idea that greater happiness or lesser unhappiness is obtainable by a particular action is and must be connected with all human action whatsoever.

This truth which I have called self-evident is sometimes obscured by the association of certain words with certain experiences. Thus we can say, talking loosely, "Such and such a man is so noble that he sacrificed all his chances of happiness for the good of those whom he loved." But, accurately speaking, what we mean is that he would have found a greater misery had he allowed himself to fail in his duty, or that he sacrificed an immediate happiness for a distant and greater happiness.

—*Hilaire Belloc*

The Great Question

Well, since the end of man and of all his actions is happiness, the answer to the Great Question, "What am I?" must be of supreme moment, for two reasons. In the first place, upon arriving at such answer the power of establishing a true scale in happiness depends. In the second place, the limitations of extent in the matter of happiness can only be discovered by our answers to that main question, "What am I?"

These are the two lines of thought which compel us to acknowledge the answer to the Great Question as being of supreme moment.

Unless we know our own nature and its destiny, where we stand in the universe, to what we are responsible, we cannot establish a true scale of values in the matter of happiness. We may find this or that very pleasant, not knowing that its ultimate consequences are so exceedingly unpleasant that the immediate enjoyment will be quite outweighed by the future penalty. We may miss some very great hidden happiness by seeking in our ignorance some lesser obvious happiness.

Also, unless we can answer the Great Question, "What am I?" we are ignorant of extent as well as of value in happiness. For how long will such and such a good endure? At what length of range do the results of our actions bear fruit? To take the most familiar instance of all; is a lifelong good—say, a large income—procured at the expense of injustice well worth having (because there can be no happiness beyond death); or is it well worth foregoing . . . ?

—Hilaire Belloc

Man Must Be Humble to Be Happy   *January 23*

Well, dear children in Jesus Christ, we are just going to think of Our Lady and especially of her great Humility.

I think here, in this very passage, we have an example of her wonderful humility. She, being the Mother of God, takes after her Divine Son. Her humility is a fore-ray of that perfect humility of the Word Made Flesh. There is not only her intense humility in placing her husband higher than herself. (For the moment St. Joseph represented the authority of God. She would no more think of lessening that than she would think of breaking her union with her husband. In every other sphere she was far above St. Joseph. Yet, in the ordinary sphere of domestic life, he represented the authority of God to her.) I think there is another wonderful example of her humility in the fact that "she kept all these things, pondering them in her heart." The shepherds had told her the tale of what they had seen and heard. She adds: "I kept it all, thinking it over in my heart." I wonder if there is any greater evidence of her humility than that. These poor old men, unfitted for any work by day, could only look after the new-born sheep by night. Our Lady thought it worth while to think over what they said to her. It was only nine months since she had had a glorious Ambassador from heaven. But here is something told her by quite simple folk. You would think she would only ponder over some marvellous communication from Almighty God. For nine months she had been in communion with the Word Made Flesh. That would have given her food for the deepest meditation. Yet here she is meditating on the words of some simple folk. I ventured to suggest we would find more wisdom in a group of night watchmen than in a group from any University.

—*Vincent McNabb*

The Humble Virgin   *January 24*

The words of [the] shepherds were not merely stored in Our Lady's memory, but she conned them over with deep meditation. Perhaps she remembered that, when Moses, fresh from the University, started his social reform by assassination, he had to be made wise by an old shepherd.

Now Our dear Lady stores up the wisdom of these simple people as if she herself was not a Seat of Wisdom. We can think of Our dear Lady's humility and try to catch it. Of all the virtues, humility is the most indescribable; and the most necessary for all the others. No other virtue can be a virtue—hardly more than a mask, a gesture—if there is no humility; real, true humility that accepts the place where God has set us in His wisdom and in His love.

God set Our dear Lady to be Queen and Mother. It was of course part of her humility to know who had set her in that position. Her own people had always had at least that humility—

44

the humility of knowing that they were chosen, but of never thinking they were chosen for anything in themselves. What was in them was the effect of God's choice. They could only deny His choice by their own unworthiness and constant failure. Our dear Lady could not confess to any sin, because she had none, but in her soul there was something deeper than contrition—the acknowledgement that mankind had done something wrong.

In her reply to the Archangel and in the Magnificat she calls herself the Handmaid of the Lord, Ancilla Domini, one of God's least little servants.

—Vincent McNabb

What Am I? *January 25*

We human beings are faced with a question manifestly greater than any other. That question is, "What am I?"

We are insistently faced with problems which, as they concern our very being, are of a different sort and indefinitely more momentous than any other problems whatsoever. "Whence do we come?" "Whither do we go?" "Of what duration is our lease of existence?" "What is its very essence?" "In what shall consist its fulfillment?" "At what must we aim for happiness?—that is, for the fullness of being." All these questions are contained in the master-question, "What am I?"

Next, as necessarily attached to such a group of questions, comes the further group dealing with method. In what way can we attain secure answers? Upon what authority shall we accept those answers so as to be certain that we have the right ones? If such an authority exists, how shall we know it for what it is? Does such an authority even exist?

All of these, I say, and every cognate question of whatsoever form you may devise, comes back to that primal comprehensive question, *"Quid sum?"* "What am I?"

—Hilaire Belloc

We Can Reason

There is a sense in which we know the answer [to the question "What am I?"], if we use the word *know* in a manner highly restricted and quite unsatisfactory. We know that we are. We have experience of our own emotions. We discover ourselves to be of a certain sort, called mankind. We perceive all about us the process whereby our fellows move through the phases of manifest existence. We see very well that we are living animals, which, like all other living animals, are born and pass through a hardly conscious immature phase, getting more mature up to a topmost phase of complete maturity when we enjoy the most of our powers and seem to be most fully ourselves. We know that after this period a man declines and that at last he dies. In whichever phase we stand when we begin to ask ourselves these questions, we know that the further phases will successively follow: the young man knows that if he lives he will grow old: the old man knows that he will die. We also know what are common human appetites and enjoyments, weaknesses and powers. So much at least we can all securely reply to the Great Question. We can say that we are beings with such and such senses and powers of enjoyment and suffering.

We can also say securely that we have in us, as part of our nature, a strange power of standing *outside* our own intelligences, and considering and analyzing our own thoughts, motives, and actions. We can further securely answer that we are possessed of Reason, an instrument so fashioned that it enables us to proceed from the known to the unknown. We know, therefore, that we are beings who can come to some wider knowledge than that which we obtain immediately through the senses.

—Hilaire Belloc

Remarkable Faculties

We know ... that we have in us four chief and remarkable faculties besides this faculty of reason.

First, we have the faculty of love and hate, beyond the mere attraction to and repulsion from physical pleasure and physical pain, or from mere habit and association. We like or dislike and, at the most active, love or hate, not only persons and objects, but ideas.

Second, we have a permanent sense of "ought"; that is, we are conscious of right-doing and wrongdoing and know that certain sensations follow upon each, sensations not physical but just as real as any physical pleasure or pain.

Third, we are aware—and this is very important—that at any particular stage in the inquiries of our reason we can distinguish between what we securely know and what we do not know but merely guess or find probable; we are conscious of our own ignorance. And we can further securely lay down, when we are honest with ourselves, the limits between what we do know and what we do not know.

—Hilaire Belloc

What Is God Like? *January 28*

How do you think of God? Do you think of God as Someone on a throne who sulks and pouts and becomes angry if you do not worship and glorify Him? Do you think you make Him unhappy when you do not give Him attention, or do you imagine Him as One who will punish you if you do not praise Him, or go to Church?

Or do you think of God as a benevolent grandfather who is indifferent to what you do; who likes to see you go places and do things, and does not care whether you have a good time by doing good things, or a good time by doing bad things, so long as you enjoy yourselves? Do you think of God in time of crisis as a vague ideal or a morale builder; and in time of peace as a silent partner whose name helps draw trade, but who has nothing to say about how the business shall be conducted?

If you hold either of these two views of God, you cannot

understand either why you should worship God, or how God can be good if He does not let you do as you please.

—Archbishop Fulton J. Sheen

Why Worship God?   *January 29*

The word, "worship," is a contraction of "worth-ship." It is a manifestation of the worth in which we hold another person. Worship is a sign of value, the price we put on a service or a person. When you applaud an actor on the stage, or a returning hero, you are "worshipping" him in the sense of putting a value on his worth. Every time a man takes off his hat to a lady, he is "worshipping" her. Now to worship God means to acknowledge in some way His Power, His Goodness and His Truth.

If you do not worship God, you worship something, and nine times out of ten it will be yourself. If there is no God, then you are a god; and if you are a god and your own law and your own creator, then we ought never to be surprised that there are so many atheists.

The basic reason there is so little worship of God today is because man denies he is a creature. Without a sense of creatureliness, or dependence, there can be no worship.

—Archbishop Fulton J. Sheen

The Creator   *January 30*

O God, Framer of the universe, grant me first rightly to invoke Thee; then to show myself worthy to be heard by Thee; lastly, deign to set me free. God, through whom all things, which of themselves were not, tend to be. God, who withholdest from perishing even that which seems to be mutually destructive. God, who, out of nothing, hast created this world, which the eyes of all perceive to be most beautiful. God, who dost not cause evil, but causest that it be not most evil. God, who to the few that flee for refuge to that which truly is, showest evil to be nothing. God, through whom the universe, even taking in its sinister side, is perfect. God, from whom things most widely at variance with Thee effect no dissonance, since worse things are included in one plan with better. God, who art loved, wittingly or unwittingly, by everything that is capable of loving. God, in whom are all things, to whom nevertheless neither the vileness of any creature is vile, nor its wickedness harmful, nor its error erroneous. God, who hast not willed that any but the pure should know the truth. God, the Father of truth, the Father of wisdom, the Father of the true and crowning life, the Father of blessedness, the Father of that which is good and fair, the Father of intelligible light, the Father of our awakening and illumination, the Father of the pledge by which we are admonished to return to Thee.

— Saint Augustine

The First Principle   *January 31*

As [Aristotle] relates, some ancient philosophers, namely, the Pythagoreans and Speusippus, did not predicate *best* and *most perfect* of the first principle. The reason was that the ancient philosophers considered only a material principle; and a material principle is most imperfect. For since matter as such is merely potential, the first material principle must be absolutely potential, and thus most imperfect. Now God is the first principle, not material, but in the order of efficient cause, which must be most perfect. For just as matter, as such, is merely potential, so an agent, as such, is in a state of actuality. Hence, the first active principle must needs be most actual, and therefore most perfect; for a thing is said to be perfect in proportion to its actuality, because we call that perfect which lacks nothing of the mode of its perfection.

— Saint Thomas Aquinas

God's Book

Some people read books in order to find God. Yet there is a great book, the very appearance of created things. Look above you; look below you! Note it; read it! God, whom you wish to find, never wrote that book with ink. Instead, He set before your eyes the things that He had made. Can you ask for a louder voice than that? Why, heaven and earth cry out to you: "God made me!"

— Saint Augustine

Is God with Us?   *February 1*

God is not only transcendent to the world, He is also immanent in it. In addition to the preceding arguments for transcendence, it might also be added that creation implies transcendence, for creation made the universe an effect of the creative activity of God. But every effect must differ from a cause, because no cause can communicate its identity. If it did, it would be different by the very reason that it is a twin, as the cause was not. Because the effect does not completely equal the cause, there will be some dissimilarity. The heat of the sun is possessed by objects on the earth, but not in the same way that the sun possesses the heat.

But at the same time, every being acts according to its nature. Hence, something like the cause will be found in the thing produced. There will be something like God in creation, but also something different. In every effect there is something in which an effect resembles a cause, and something in which it differs. In the statue there is the artist's idea which is produced in the marble. But there is one thing the artist did not give, and that is the marble. In creation the same is true. The world made from nothingness will always retain the stigma of its parentage. Yet the universe will be like God inasmuch as it possesses similitude of being.

But the human mind is not content with the bare knowledge that God made this universe; the legitimate curiosity of the mind strives to learn just what relation God bears to His masterpiece. Is He just an architect who designs an edifice but who is not necessary for its continued existence? Or if He is not disinterested in His work once it is produced, is He transformed into His creation as water becomes transformed into steam? The question arises, *how* God is present in the universe which He has created. It is one thing to say God made the world, but it is quite another thing to inquire about the relation between His work and Himself.

—Archbishop Fulton J. Sheen

The Presentation   *February 2*

And when the days of her purification were fulfilled according to the Law of Moses, they took him up to Jerusalem to present him to the Lord—as it is written in the Law of the Lord,

> "Every male that opens the womb shall be
> called holy to the Lord"—

and to offer a sacrifice according to what is said in the Law of the Lord, "a pair of turtledoves or two young pigeons."

And behold, there was in Jerusalem a man named Simeon, and this man was just and devout, looking for the consolation of Israel, and the Holy Spirit was upon him. And it had been revealed to him by the Holy Spirit that he should not see death before he had seen the Christ of the Lord. And he came by inspiration of the Spirit into the temple. And when his parents brought in the child Jesus, to do for him according to the custom of the Law, he also received him into his arms and blessed God, saying,

> "Now thou dost dismiss thy servant, O Lord,
>   according to thy word, in peace;
> Because my eyes have seen thy salvation,
>   which thou hast prepared before the face of
>   all peoples:
>   A light of revelation to the Gentiles,
>   and a glory for thy people Israel."

And his father and mother were marvelling at the things spoken concerning him. And Simeon blessed them, and said to

Mary his mother, "Behold, this child is destined for the fall and for the rise of many in Israel, and for a sign that shall be contradicted. And thy own soul a sword shall pierce, that the thoughts of many hearts may be revealed."

— Saint Luke

The Simplicity of God   *February 3*

The absolute simplicity of God may be shown in many ways. First, from the previous articles of this question. For there is neither composition of quantitative parts in God, since He is not a body; nor composition of form and matter; nor does His nature differ from His *suppositum;* nor His essence from His being; neither is there in Him composition of genus and difference, nor of subject and accident. Therefore, it is clear that God is in no way composite, but is altogether simple. Secondly, because every composite is posterior to its component parts, and is dependent on them; but God is the first being, as has been shown above. Thirdly, because every composite has a cause, for things in themselves diverse cannot unite unless something causes them to unite. But God is uncaused, as has been shown above, since He is the first efficient cause. Fourthly, because in every composite there must be potentiality and actuality (this does not apply to God) for either one of the parts actualizes another, or at least all the parts are as it were in potency with respect to the whole. Fifthly, because nothing composite can be predicated of any one of its parts. And this is evident in a whole made up of dissimilar parts; for no part of a man is a man, nor any of the parts of the foot, a foot. But in wholes made up of similar parts, although something which is predicated of the whole may be predicated of a part (as a part of the air is air, and a part of water, water), nevertheless certain things are predicable of the whole which cannot be predicated of any of the parts: for instance, if the whole volume of water is two cubits, no part of it can be two cubits. Thus in every composite there is something which is not it itself. But, even if this could be said of whatever has a form, viz., that it has something which is not it itself, as in a white object there is something which does not belong to the essence of white, nevertheless, in the form itself there is nothing besides itself. And so, since God is absolute form, or rather absolute being, He can be in no way composite. Hilary touches upon this argument when he says: *God, Who is strength, is not made up of things that are weak; nor is He, Who is light, composed of things that are dark.*

— Saint Thomas Aquinas

Desirable

God is subsistent being. The formula: "I am Who am", in which this truth is expressed, though itself revealed by God, is recognized by reason alone to do Him least injustice. It expresses in ultimate terms, better than the imagery of the poets, better even than the rhapsodies of the mystics, God's infinite ontological richness. The things we know and feel to be desirable exist in Him with a higher reality, a greater desirability, than in their own mode of being. From this there follows the immense lovableness of God. And we must add also that He has the dignity of being a Person; He is not a vague amorphous entity, a "spirit of the universe," but vitally, uniquely, a Person — or rather, a Trinity of Persons identical in their nature. And finally, the divine Personality has been manifested to the world through the Incarnation; not that thereby God might become more lovable, for that were impossible, but in order to draw us to Himself in a way that should make any rejection of Him inexcusable. We should need no threats or moral exhortations to lead us to love God. We have only to realize what He is.

— Dom Aelred Graham

God Is a Person

Now, consciousness and intelligence are functions of personality. That is what, *at the least,* we mean by a person—that there are present in it consciousness and intelligence. Hence, so far, a conscious and intelligent God.

But there is something more. Personality is recognized also by will. Personality, our own and that of our fellows, we know by experience to be. We are equally informed that it cannot be without a will. Our wills, like our consciousness and intelligence, are manifestly imperfect. It may even be argued (correspondingly) that, as they are derivative, they have no independent existence and that our will is not free—and so not a true will. But, like consciousness and intelligence, it came from that which can so provoke such an increment, and argues the Infinite Person Who has Infinite Consciousness and Intelligence and Infinite Will. There is at *least* one Will, as there is one Personality of this kind; if it were not so, then will, like consciousness and intelligence, would not even be present as an addition to the rest of being.

—Hilaire Belloc

God Is Changeless

Immutability we attribute to God; unlike anything in our experience, it arises from the fact that He is actually all that He can be and potentially nothing whatever. To realize what this means must bring solace to the mind grown weary of watching in a distracted world the mere sequence of events—"the moving image of eternity," as Plato called it. By nature we wish for greater stability than is compatible with the order of time. For the *nunc fluens* in which we are immersed so faintly represents the *nunc stans* of the divine changelessness. Eternity, in the great definition of Boethius, is the "simultaneously full and perfect possession of interminable life." This is to be the reward of those who see the face of God.

Such reflections as these bring home to us that God must be the fulfilment of all creaturely desire. There is nothing to be wished for which is not contained in Him; which is but another way of saying that He is intrinsically lovable. Add to what has been said the truth that He is also a Person, "the most perfect thing in all nature," *id quod est perfectissimum in tota natura.* We know indeed from revelation that the divine nature superabounds mysteriously in a Trinity of persons; but reason alone could satisfy itself that God must, of His nature, be endowed with the perfection of personality.

— *Dom Aelred Graham*

The Supreme Being   *February 7*

The argument for the infinity of God is not drawn exclusively from the finiteness of the universe, but also from the nature of purpose itself. The human mind cannot rest in composition as an ultimate. Creatures are finite because compounded. God is infinite because One, and He is One because anything short of perfect unity in which Essence and Existence are identical would not be sufficient explanation. The Infinity of God is the necessary correlation of all being and all thought. If there were a single emergent in the Divine Mind, as reasonable beings, we would have to inquire what made that emergent emerge; how did it fit into the composition of God's imperfect nature; and to what end is it a means? We cannot go back infinitely in a series of dependent causes. We must come to a First Unity which is Perfect and distinct from the world, and that being we call God, Who directed all things toward the proper ends.

This perfect Being is *Life,* for life is immanent activity, and in Him is perfect activity because His mind has no object outside Himself, and because it has no need of being aroused by anything outside of self. The perfect Life of God is a consequence of His perfect Intellect in which there is no potentiality, no composition of knower and thing known. In God, Being and Thought are identical. Pure Thought is Pure Being.

— *Archbishop Fulton J. Sheen*

'A Man who undertakes to praise God', observes St Augustine, 'and yet will not exalt his mercy above all else, had better keep silent.'[2] There is no motive for prayer more authentic, none more surely answered than an appeal to God's mercy in view of the wretchedness of man. The relationship which religion implies receives here its perfect expression: on our side, nothingness and absolute need; on God's the utmost regality and divine power.

The revelation of God's mercy is inseparable from that of his holiness and his transcendent majesty. Whenever, in Scripture, he is revealed as 'the Holy', at an infinite distance from us, supremely above all things, he is at the same time revealed as near us, turning towards us, communicating with us through a gift. From all the passages that illustrate this we shall select two only, those great verses in Exodus (33:18–34:10), that record the two encounters, or rather, the two stages of the single encounter between Moses and God on Sinai.

To begin with Moses comes to Sinai after he had killed an Egyptian soldier who was ill-treating one of his fellow Hebrews. The killing had been seen and he was obliged to hide, in fact to leave the country, and, as we should say, go underground. He found shelter in the Sinai peninsula, where he married. It was during this time, while he was looking after his father-in-law's sheep, that he had the vision of the burning bush, in consequence of which he received God's call to deliver his people from Egypt. Moses replied to God, 'Very good: I will go to the children of Israel and say to them, "The God of your fathers has sent me to you!" But if they ask what his name is, what shall I tell them?' Then God said to Moses, 'I am who I am' (3:13–14).

— Yves Congar

God Speaks to Moses

The revelation of the burning bush is first of all a revelation of God in his supreme power, in the transcendency of his life above and beyond all human estimate and foresight. From the midst of the bush God said, "Do not come near: take off your shoes." God is the Eternal, he who abides while all else comes to be and passes away. God is the mysterious One, his name cannot be uttered, cannot be communicated. He is the Living God whom we meet and know in his overriding initiatives, who makes himself known in his deeds. But now a note of graciousness or mercy is added to the affirmation of transcendent holiness. God, who holds Moses at a distance, speaks to him and calls him, turns towards his people, has pity on them, takes the first step towards their deliverance. Who will he be? The answer will become evident first of all in a fact: He will be the God-who-will-bring-his-people-out-of-Egypt.

But this revelation of God's mystery needed deepening through the experience of sin, or of its consequences. This was, in fact, the development we can observe throughout the course of this revelation in the Old Testament. David only reached the heart of his understanding of God after he had sinned. The people themselves only came to realise that their God was their redeemer after they had been reduced to misery and captivity as a result of their sins. In fact they were really able to grasp it fully only when God himself became the suffering servant, foretold by the Isaiah of the exile, when in Jesus Christ he formed the new alliance with his people (Is 42:6): an alliance maintained and renewed for *sinners,* therefore a redemption! Of course the people of Israel did not have to wait for the exile in order to experience sin, nor Yahweh-God have to wait for Isaiah in order to reveal his mystery more completely with that experience as his starting point. It is all too clear that precisely when the alliance was being contracted between God and his people on Sinai it was being violated and broken at the very foot of the mountain by the disloyalty of those who asked for a "god who walks before them", such as the other nations had, and who were amusing themselves before the statue of a young bull made for them by Aaron (Ex 32).

— Yves Congar

After [the idol worship] event, had God been holiness and nothing else, he could not have remained among his people nor led them: "If I came up into the midst of thee in a moment I should consume thee" (Ex 33:5). But he willed to be gracious. The dialogue he held with Moses' soul emboldened Moses to ask. "Allow me to see thy glory!" He had been told the mysterious name and now he sought deeper knowledge. His petition was granted, at least so far as it could be granted to a man without involving his death. But when Yahweh passed before him, not allowing himself to be really seen but sensed, Moses cried, "Yahweh, Yahweh, God, merciful and gracious, long-suffering and abundant in goodness and truth . . . " (34:6). This is the second revelation of his name and nature that God made. He is not only the Eternal, not only the One who does not tell his name, the Mysterious One, or he who will be revealed as the Living God through the progress of his actions for his people. Not only all this, but now he is revealed as the Merciful.

This revelation remained vivid in Israel's memory: the text itself is literally reproduced at least six or eight times. When David had satisfied his vanity by having a census taken of the people he had to choose between three punishments, a famine of seven years, a seven-month flight from his enemies, or a three-day plague. He chose the plague, and said, "Let us fall into the hand of the Lord, for his mercies are great, and let me not fall into the hand of man" (2 Kings 24:14).

— Yves Congar

One thinks of Mary, tender and touching, as he walks about the sacred *domaine de la grotte* during a pilgrimage to Lourdes. Rome is assuredly the city of Christ, the head of the Church, whose vicar dwells there and whose truth is there defined and defended. As in 1854, so now and always, we look to Rome to learn whatever

Christ has revealed concerning Himself, His Church, His Mother, or ourselves. But, in the present Age of Mary at least, there is no denying the preeminent degree to which Lourdes, the land of the rosary, has become the heart of the praying Catholic world. Mary, the Mother of Christ and of all the redeemed, is unmistakably there; and there in 1958, as in 1858, one finds love confirming at the Grotto of Lourdes what truth defines at Rome.

Every Catholic understands the sense in which these things are true. The presence of Christ at Rome in special and surpassing fashion does not exclude the presence of Mary, His Mother. She is necessarily present wherever He is present to whom she gave flesh and blood as well as, humanly speaking, the breath of life itself. The love of her is also present wherever He rules, Himself or through His vicar. She is present, acknowledged, and loved in the Roman catacombs. She is paid homage in Roman basilicas, supremely, of course, in the regal temple which is *Major* of all the churches which bear the name of Saint Mary. She is remembered at almost every Roman corner where the *madonnelle* of the street shrines bring the Queen of Heaven so close to the life of Rome's very alleyways. She is lifted in triumphant glory atop her column in the Spanish Square, and Michelangelo gave her an exquisite corner and the best of his genius in the Pietà, which adds a touch of humane simplicity to the staggering majesty of Saint Peter's. But Rome is the city of Peter and therefore of Christ, Peter's Lord, Master, and Principal. There is never the slightest doubt about the claims of Peter or the authority of Christ at any point in Rome to which the pilgrim turns.

Lourdes, land of the rosary, is the city of Mary. Again, her priority of presence at Lourdes excludes neither Christ nor, for that matter, Peter. Christ is necessarily present wherever she is loved to whom He gave meaning and vocation, together with every privilege and power which is hers. Christ is present at Lourdes in the stations of the cross, the dramatic markings of the stages of His Passion, in following which the Lourdes pilgrim climbs even higher than the grotto of the shrine. He is present, glorious and full of mercy, in the Blessed Sacrament, enshrined in the Rosary Basilica or carried among the sick on the terrace of tears and hopes where His name is so passionately invoked in the traditional Lourdes prayers. Christ is certainly present authoritatively in the prelates and priests who officiate in the shrine ceremonies; He is present mystically in the masses of the poor, the sick, the halt, lame, and blind who crowd about the sacred springs.

—*Cardinal John Wright*

God Is Goodness   *February 12*

The Creator has not the defects which so often accompany good qualities. In human affairs a capacity for large views, administrative skill, having to take account of many factors at once, not seldom implies insensibility and even ruthlessness in dealing with the individual; contrariwise, due consideration for the personality of each, the endeavour to respect and legislate for the peculiar needs of every member of the community, may well involve real inefficiency and a breakdown in practical government. The limitations of human nature being what they are, this dilemma is almost unavoidable. But with God it is not so. In His Kingdom the individual has not to be sacrificed for the good of the community nor the community rendered ineffective for the benefit of the individual. Divine wisdom knows how to compass the good of the whole without detriment to the perfection of each part. No truth of Christian philosophy is better calculated to encourage than this, that providence extends to things not as classes but as individuals. God deals not with humanity but with man.

Thus the reality behind our innocent passing joys, the good humour which breaks the tedium of every-day life, the pleasures of friendship and human intercourse, these also have in Him their true reality. We speak of heaven as our homeland and no word could be more accurate. The theologians, absorbed in their abstractions, fail perhaps to show the attractiveness of God to those who cannot think theologically. And yet we have only to deduce the consequences of their own principles. How often does it occur to us that the sense of good health and physical well-being, the felicities of family life, such things as the warmth of winter firesides, the thrill of reunions after long absence, the uniqueness of love between man and woman, all have their cause in God and therefore are to be found in Him, not attenuated by their spiritual mode of being, but heightened and intensified beyond description?

—*Dom Aelred Graham*

The Highest Good

The highest good, than which there is no higher, is God, and consequently He is unchangeable good, hence truly eternal and truly immortal. All other good things are only from Him, not of Him. For what is of Him, is Himself. And consequently if He alone is unchangeable, all things that He has made, because He has made them out of nothing, are changeable. For He is so omnipotent, that even out of nothing, that is out of what is absolutely nonexistent, He is able to make good things both great and small, both celestial and terrestrial, both spiritual and corporeal. But because He is also just, He has not put those things that He has made out of nothing on an equality with that which He begat out of Himself. Because, therefore, no good things whether great or small, through whatever gradations of things, can exist except from God; but since every nature, so far as it is nature, is good, it follows that no nature can exist save from the most high and true God: because all things even not in the highest degree good, but related to the highest good, and again, because all good things, even those of most recent origin, which are far from the highest good, can have their existence only from the highest good. Therefore every spirit, though subject to change, and every corporeal entity, is from God, and all this, having been made, is nature. For every nature is either spirit or body. Unchangeable spirit is God, changeable spirit, having been made, is nature, but is better than body; but body is not spirit, unless when the wind, because it is invisible to us and yet its power is felt as something not inconsiderable, is in a certain sense called spirit.

—*Saint Augustine*

Indescribably Rich February 14

Transferred to God the notion of personality is indescribably rich. Development here is out of the question. He is all that He can be. Vitality, understanding, generosity, magnanimity, those character-istics we associate with the highest type of personality, are there in an infinite degree. In the light of the Incarnation the significance for mankind of this truth is heightened beyond measure. Space and the selected method of treatment forbid more than an indication of what might form the subject of a volume. The unique fact about Christ Our Lord is that He is God. All that He did and continues to do through His Church and by the instrumentality of the sacraments takes its value from His Godhead. Of the grace and redemption that pour out upon the world the sacred humanity of Christ is truly the instrument (*instrumentum conjunctum*), but it is the divinity that is the origin and cause. *Deum de Deo, lumen de lumine, Deum verum de Deo vero.* These words of the Creed proclaim the ancestral faith of Christians. To reject them means the rejection of Christianity.

All then that can be said of God can be said of the Person of Jesus Christ. In His humanity He was subject to limitations but not in His Godhead. The hypostatic union, the unity which is so close as to permit of only one personality, and that divine, while excluding any confusion between the two natures, is the richest and most consoling mystery of our faith.

—*Dom Aelred Graham*

The Supreme Lover February 15

The Goodness of God means that God gives us what we *need* for our perfection, not what we *want* for our pleasure and sometimes for our destruction. As a sculptor, He sometimes applies the chisel to the marble of our imperfect selves and knocks off huge chunks of selfishness that His image may better stand revealed. Like a musician, whenever He finds the strings too loose on the violin of our personality, He tightens them even though it hurts, that we may better reveal our hidden harmonies.

As the Supreme Lover of our soul, He does care how we act and think and speak. What father does not want to be proud of his son? If the father speaks with authority now and then to his son, it is not because he is a dictator, but because he wants him to be a worthy son. Not even progressive parents, who deny discipline and restraint, are indifferent to the progress of their children. So long as there is love, there is necessarily a desire for the perfecting of the beloved.

That is precisely the way God's goodness manifests itself to us. God really *loves* us and, because He loves us, He is not disinterested. He no more wants you to be unhappy than your own parents want you to be unhappy. God made you not for His happiness, but for yours, and to ask God to be satisfied with most of us as we really are, is to ask that God cease to love.

—*Archbishop Fulton J. Sheen*

Pain For a Purpose   *February 16*

God could never let you suffer a pain, or a reversal, or experience sadness, if it could not in some way minister to your perfection. If He did not spare His own Son on the Cross for the redemption of the world, then you may be sure that He will sometimes not spare your wants, that you might be all you *need* to be: happy and perfect children of a loving Father. He may even permit us to wage wars as a result of our selfishness, that we may learn there is no peace except in Goodness and Truth.

—*Archbishop Fulton J. Sheen*

God Is Spiritual

The fact that God is a spirit suggests not only that we should worship Him, but also think about Him, in spirit and in truth. Any approach towards an understanding of Him requires an intellectual as well as a moral purification. Unhappily contemporary culture and modern methods of instruction are unfavourable to concentration upon the great realities. Linguistic versatility and cultivated eclecticism, the fairest fruits of our present-day educational system, engender habits of mind little adapted to the contemplation of universal ideas. Indeed contemplation—by which, for the moment, no more is meant than thoughtfulness and reflection—is only to be achieved at a price which few can be induced to pay. The times in which we live cry out for such an effort but no other encouragement is offered. Yet if we are to approach God in thought, and such is an indispensable preliminary to our approaching Him in love, the effort must be made.

—Dom Aelred Graham

God Is Truth *February 17*

Thee I invoke, O God, the Truth, in whom and from whom and through whom all things are true which anywhere are true. God, the Wisdom, in whom and from whom and through whom all things are wise which anywhere are wise. God, the true and crowning Life, in whom and from whom and through whom all things live which truly and supremely live. God, the Blessedness, in whom and from whom and through whom all things are blessed which anywhere are blessed. God, the Good and Fair, in whom and from whom and through whom all things are good and fair which anywhere are good and fair. God, the intelligible Light, in whom and from whom and through whom all things intelligibly shine which anywhere intelligibly shine. God, whose kingdom is that whole world of which sense has no ken. God, from whose kingdom a law is even derived down upon these lower realms. God, from whom to be turned away is to fall: to whom to be turned back is to rise again: in whom to abide is to stand firm. God, from whom to go forth is to die: to whom to return is to revive: in whom to have our dwelling is to live. God, whom no one loses, unless deceived: whom no one seeks, unless stirred up: whom no one finds, unless made pure. God, whom to forsake is one thing with perishing; towards whom to tend is one thing with living: whom to see is one thing with having. God, towards whom faith rouses us, hope lifts us up, with whom love joins us. God, through whom we overcome the enemy, Thee I entreat. God, through whose gift it is that we do not perish utterly. God, by whom we are warned to watch. God, by whom we distinguish good from ill. God, by whom we flee evil and follow good. God, through whom we yield not to calamities. God, through whom we faithfully serve and benignantly govern. God, through whom we learn those things to be another's which aforetime we accounted ours, and those things to be ours which we used to account as belonging to another. God, through whom the baits and enticements of evil things have no power to hold us. God, through whom it is that diminished possessions leave ourselves complete. God, through whom our better good is not subject to a worse. God, through whom death is swallowed up in victory. God, who dost turn us to Thyself. God, who dost strip us of that which is not, and arrayest us in that which is. God, who dost make us worthy to be heard. God, who dost fortify us. God, who leadest us into all truth. God, who speakest to us only good, who neither terrifiest into madness nor sufferest another so to do. God, who callest us back into the way. God, who leadest us to the door of life. God, who causest it to be opened to them that knock. God, who givest us the bread of life. God, through whom we thirst for the draught, which being drunk we never thirst. God, who dost convince the world of sin, of righteousness, and of judgment.

— *Saint Augustine*

God Is Approachable   *February 18*

To think of [God] requires no intellectual technique. The philosophy of the Church is not an esoteric doctrine; it is nothing more formidable than exalted common sense and requires for its understanding only patience and mental simplicity. Indeed, experience shows that scholarship and imaginative brilliance can often be obstacles rather than aids to anything deeper than a verbal appreciation of the *philosophia perennis*. Here, as in another context, the things hidden from the wise and prudent are revealed to babes.

From out of the burning bush God spoke His name to Moses. "I am Who am." The ultimate metaphysical import of that formula doubtless escaped the mind of the Hebrews. They would have held it more profitable to show honour to God than to rest content with defining His essence. The task of the chosen people, of those who kept faith with Yahweh, was to serve Him in hope and holy fear until the great day of His coming. They were not called upon to work out a theology. But the day was to come when that also would have to be undertaken. When, in the fulness of time, divine revelation had been perfected, the moment must arrive for the attempt to systematize, and thus embrace more firmly, the knowledge so acquired. And first, what of God Himself, the author of revelation? What name could best distinguish Him from the creatures He had made?

God *is* what He is. So much had been learned from the name He had given to Himself. The Greek philosophers had thought of Him as the Good, the object of all desire; or else as subsisting self-consciousness, knowledge of knowledge. While these conclusions of philosophy were by no means set aside, it was God's own witness to Himself, the notion of Him as subsisting being, which was at length to prevail as the least inadequate statement of what He is.

—*Dom Aelred Graham*

God Shows Himself   *February 19*

Probably you have heard people say: "What is the good of my trying to think about God? He is too great for my thought!" Or again: "As if God would attend to *me!* I am far too small!" They are mistaken. True, our finite intelligence can never know God as He, the Infinite, knows Himself; but we *can* know much about Him, in our human way: and it is quite impossible that God should not know and attend to us, whom He is at this very moment preserving and for each of whom He has His unique un-share-able purpose, and in whom He—everywhere wholly present—lives and works. "He is not asleep, nor gone upon a journey . . . " (2 Kings 18:27).

Still, when it comes to the love of God—whether it be His lovingness or His lovableness—the Christian naturally looks first of all, to find it, in Our Lord. We have no space to recall how He insisted on His Father's love for the smallest of birds; on His own love for the field-flowers; on His way of taking sick people by the hand and helping them up, or never shrinking from the touch of a leper; on the way that little children evidently *wanted* to come to Him—"*Let* them come! Don't stop them!"—or on His habit of "looking round" at those present, sometimes with tenderness, or again with indignation, but needing, so to say, to share His feelings with the others. Thinking of Calvary, we remember at once the Thief crucified beside Him, and His Mother, standing with other women, and St. John, at the foot of the Cross.

— C. C. Martindale

Jesus Does Divine Things *February 20*

St. Luke relates how the people stood staring at [Jesus], and how their leaders were sneering at Him, and the very soldiers mocking Him, and how one of the two thieves, crucified along with Him, joined in the mockery. The other thief, partly, perhaps, genuinely shocked, partly afraid lest God should retaliate and mock the mocker worse, said: "Aren't you even afraid of God, you that are suffering the same penalty?" But when you have opened your heart even a little to what is better, Grace rapidly enters. He made his confession—"And we, indeed, justly; for we are getting back only what our deeds deserve. But this man"—How shall I translate the next words?—"This man hath done nothing amiss" fails to give the exact savour of the Greek, which was not quite slang, but certainly colloquial; what a rough man might have said—"Has done nothing crooked. . . . " No matter. The thief had become conscious of his own guilt, and, of the utter innocence of Jesus whom, but a moment before, he and his companion had treated as in the same class as themselves. "Save thyself *and us.*" Then the full light broke upon him, and he cried: "Jesus—remember me, when thou shalt come in Thy Kingdom"—in all the glory of Thy Messiahship, Lord of heaven and earth. For, indeed, that is how we should read the Greek. Not "*into* Thy kingdom", as though he said: "When *you* enter heaven, do not forget *me!*" But *in* Thy Kingdom, at that mysterious Last Day. And that gives its full sense to Our Lord's reply. There would be no need to wait for that far distant hour. "In solemn truth, I tell thee—*this day* shalt thou be, with Me, in Paradise."

—*C. C. Martindale*

Salvation from Jesus   *February 21*

[Jesus] was born of a human mother; He grew up through boyhood and youth and into adult years as a working-man: He knew what hunger and thirst and weariness were: He had His friends; He knew every note in the scale of human happiness and heartbreak: He knew us from the inside, so to put it: He knew our life—He would not exempt Himself from knowing too our death. But at that time and in that place, the life He would lead and the doctrine that He would preach, were certain to lead up to that bitter hatred for Him on the part of the Pharisees and Sadducees which was in fact responsible for His arrest, His handing over to Pilate, His cruel scourging, crowning with thorns and all manner of mockery and insult, and finally His most dreadful death upon a cross. Yet He did not consider His work to have been consummated till He should have reached the end common to all men, that is, death, and, in His own case, that terrible death of crucifixion. "Having loved His own who were in the world, He loved them to the *uttermost*" (Jn 8:1). We can put it thus: The Eternal Son of God, having refused to exempt Himself from anything that a full human life lived *then* and *there* would in the natural sequence of events have contained, did not regard His saving work as consummated till He should die—and in fact, be slain.

It is then on the Cross and by the Cross that our salvation is perfected and achieved. It was not, if I may so put it, God who crucified His Son. God did not "kill the child of His own brain"— but it was Sin and Love that crucified Him. It was our Sin, because "He came to His own, and His own received Him not" (Jn 1:11): we rejected Him; He was "despised and rejected by men" (Is 53:3). It was His love, because whatever men did to Him, He would not be deterred from doing His saving work, no, not though it involved His being nailed to a cross as though He were a felon. Yet, since the will of the Son is that too of the Father, God willed what His co-eternal Son chose, decreed that it should be so, *sent* Him into the world to save us, affixing that salvation to that Death which thus became an act of perfect free obedience.

— *Vincent McNabb*

God's Spokesman

The important thing is not what Our Blessed Lord says or does, but what He *is.* His sayings and doings are as nothing in comparison with His being. Grant only that He is a man and His sayings are as the sayings of one man in the market-place to another; His doings are but the doings of a man appointed as ourselves to the quiet of the tomb.

Grant that He is man and God, and at once His sayings and doings are withdrawn from the trammels of time and the short-comings of our humanity. His words are not mere sayings; they are the Truth. His deeds become something more than events; they are justice, mercy, redemption. The Church calls them mysteries. We do not speak of the fact of His birth. It is the Mystery of the Nativity.

If He is merely the Son of Mary, then what He said and did are literature and history. But if He is the Son of God, then what He said and did are Religion.

His sayings and doings put on an infinite value.

Now what happens to His sayings and doings happens to His

Mother. If the Son of Mary is also the Son of God, Mary has a position of superhuman importance.

— Vincent McNabb

How It Started

In the quiet monotony of the simple life of a young Jewish girl, occupied in the household tasks of those days, that is, not only cooking and mending, but also the kneading and baking of bread and the spinning and weaving of wool, a miraculous event had occurred, the one which, more than any other, Mary was to "treasure up in her heart" for a long time. One day when she was alone an angel had appeared to her. A Jewish child, brought up on the Bible, knew that these supernatural beings often intervened in the lives of men. Nevertheless, she had been extremely excited. The strange presence (a human form, a white bird or simply light?) had paused in front of her and Mary had heard its voice saying to her: "Hail, thou who art full of grace, the Lord is with thee; blessed art thou among women." What could this greeting mean? Then the angel had said: "Mary, do not be afraid: thou hast found favour in the sight of God. And behold, thou shalt conceive in thy womb, and shalt bear a son, and shalt call him Jesus. He shall be great, and men will know him for the Son of the Most High." Stupefied, the young virgin had objected, "How can that be, since I have no knowledge of man?" And the angel's reply had been even more stupefying: "The Holy Spirit will come upon thee, and the power of the Most High will overshadow thee. Thus this holy offspring of thine shall be known for the Son of God" (Lk 1:29–35).

— Henri Daniel-Rops

The Incarnation

The problem was how to be a man like us, without being contaminated as we were, by sin. He could be a man like us by being born of woman. He could be a sinless man, or the new Adam, by being born of a Virgin. By dispensing with the act of generation by which original sin was propagated, He escaped its infection. That is why He was born of a Virgin. The Virgin Birth broke the heritage of sin, as now for the first time since Adam there walked on earth a human nature as God meant it to be.

The Incarnation solved the problem that man ought in justice make satisfaction for his sins, but only God *can.* Out of pure love, therefore, God in Christ identified Himself with humanity that He might make reparation in its behalf. By becoming man, He stood on man's level. Knowing no sin, He "became sin" in order to redeem.

Just as it would be foolish to tell a wife that she need feel no shame because her husband had committed a crime, so it would be foolish to tell Christ, the Incarnate God, that He need feel no shame because He was personally guiltless.

—Archbishop Fulton J. Sheen

Jesus

Love means fellowship, not isolation. Human love takes on the burden of its friends; Divine Love takes on Himself the sins of the world. That is why, though sinless, [Jesus] stood silent before the Judges, for the sins of the world were upon Him; that is why He who was guiltless was baptized, that He might identify Himself with the debt which all men owed. And the payment He made was not an individual payment; it was a payment on behalf of humanity whose very nature He shared.

The old human nature descended from Adam was disordered; He would not take that upon Himself. So the Holy Spirit created a perfectly new human nature in the womb of Mary, a new Adam, a new creature, a new pattern. God would not put a patch of holiness on the old garment of nature. He gave the human race a new start.

—Archbishop Fulton J. Sheen

Born in Bethlehem

The prophet Isaias (8:14) says, "A virgin shall conceive and bear a son, and his name shall be called Emmanuel." And about the same time the prophet Micheas (v. 3), speaking plainly of the Messias, uses the phrase "She that travaileth shall bring forth." Always the woman, never a hint of a male parent—and this among a people to whom the father was everything, who would not have bothered to mention the women in their own genealogical trees.

But what has all this to do with Mary's feeling that her child must be born in Bethlehem? In the verse before the one from Micheas just quoted, Mary would have read: "And thou, Bethlehem Ephrata, art a little one among the clans of Juda: out of thee shall he come forth unto me that is to be the ruler in Israel: and his going forth is from the beginning, from the days of eternity." A little later when King Herod asks Jerusalem's learned men where Christ should be born, Matthew tells us that they said in Bethlehem of Juda, and quoted Micheas.

When the decree of Caesar Augustus sent Joseph to Bethlehem, how could Mary have stayed behind? Augustus was not as the pagans thought a god, but Mary and Joseph must have seen the hand of God in the decree which ensured that the Son of David should be born in David's city.

But where in David's city was he to be born? Bethlehem was a village, with perhaps a thousand inhabitants. The census had crammed it with David's descendants, an uncle or two of Joseph's perhaps, countless cousins—first cousins, twentieth cousins, thirtieth cousins; for there were a thousand years and thirty generations between David and Joseph. The birth of a baby calls for privacy. Where was privacy to be had, when every available inch of space was taken?

St. Luke does not tell us exactly where they found it. But when the child was born, he was laid in a manger. And mangers are in stables.

—*Archbishop Fulton J. Sheen*

A Child Is Born

[The] child [was] born in a stable, like a tramp, with literally nowhere to lay his head right from the start of his life, and this child is the one conceived by the Holy Spirit, the child of whom it was predicted that he would be Master of all, the omnipotent Lord. The Christian paradox is already there at the very beginning of the existence of him who was to take it to the world like a challenge. "When I am weakest, then I am strongest of all", says St Paul, echoing his Master. The child of the manger was to be stronger than any human power.

It was only fitting that celestial voices should make this known at the very moment when the child was born. For angels too were mysteriously associated with the whole story. An angel spoke to the shepherds on the hills, announcing news that the child wrapped in swaddling-clothes in the manger was the Lord, the Saviour. . . .

However, the child escaped this "massacre of the Innocents". Once again the angel of the Lord intervened and Joseph had time to take his wife and child away. The Apocrypha have invented all kinds of details about this "Flight into Egypt", and the Fathers of the Church have emphasized its symbolical meaning. It was from Egypt that God brought back his son when the danger was over, just as it was out of Egypt that he had led his people. Jesus must have been between eight and eighteen months old when the death of Herod allowed his parents to return to their own country.

—*Henri Daniel-Rops*

Nazareth

The years flowed quietly by in Nazareth. The shadow of the cross grew more distinct over the home of the carpenter and His mother. Finally, the days of preparation were finished. One day He set out in earnest about His Father's business; Mary's farewell would be said uncomplainingly but the sword would not cut less deep into her heart for all her willing silence. The years had been long and packed tight with joy since Gabriel had come to the child Mary of Nazareth. Now her arms were emptier than her home. The thirty years of Nazareth were over; but their passing did not change the response of the virgin: "behold the handmaid of the Lord; be it done unto me according to thy word."

— Walter Farrell

John the Baptist

[John the Baptist] was certainly what the word "prophet" might lead one to expect. "He wore," say St Mark and St Matthew, "a garment of camel's hair, and a leather girdle about his loins." This is almost word for word the scriptural description of the prophet Elias: "A shaggy fellow, with a skin girt about his loins" (2 Kings 1:8). As for his food, that too was in the tradition of the great solitaries of the spirit, of hermits and ascetics: wild honey and locusts. The rule of the Essene monks expressly included grilled locusts in the bill of fare, and the Bedouins still eat them either crushed up as a seasoning or preserved in honey or vinegar. He had lived like this, so it was said, for years in the valley of the Jordan and the surrounding hills, retiring into the desert in the intervals when he was not taking the word of God to the crowds. If all this did not add up to a prophet, what did?

— Henri Daniel-Rops

John Preaches

Repentance was the first great theme of John's preaching. "Yield the acceptable fruit of repentance", fast, pray, ask pardon of God: John was certainly a lineal descendant of Isaias, of Jeremias, of all the fearless men who had heroically reminded Israel of her obligations. As the monks of the Dead Sea put it: "God, with his truth, will cleanse the works of every man and purify him by the Spirit".

John's tone was by no means gentle. "Who was it that taught you, brood of vipers, to flee from the vengeance that draws near? Come, then, yield the acceptable fruit of repentance; do not presume to say in your hearts, We have Abraham for our father; I tell you, God has power to raise up children to Abraham out of these very stones." But to men of good will who came to him with the sincere wish to do better he gave counsel full of nobility; he advised them to abstain from all violence and any kind of hypocrisy, to share their goods with the needy, and so on. These words were the harbingers of stronger and more precise ones, for John was more than the Baptist: he was the Forerunner.

That in fact was the other great theme of the message delivered by the prophet at the ford. To those who asked him in wonderment, "Who are you? Are you the Messias?" he replied, "No, I am not."

—Henri Daniel-Rops

The Baptism

The Evangelists write . . . that one day, as John stands preaching and baptizing on the Jordan, Jesus suddenly appears and demands baptism. Startled, John replies: "It is I who ought to be baptized by thee, and dost thou come to me?" but Jesus only answers: "Let it be so now, for so it becomes us to fulfill all justice." And John acquiesces.

The heavens open, the dove descends, and the voice is heard: "This is my beloved Son, in whom I am well pleased" (Mt 3:13–17).

Jesus arrives at the Jordan, the profound experience of child-hood and the long process of maturity behind him. He is fully aware of the stupendousness of the task before him and of the powers that rise to meet it from the depths of his being. Yet his first gesture, first words are an expression of deep humility. No claims to special privileges; no: that may be the law for others, but not for me! He goes up to John and asks to be baptized. To demand baptism implies readiness to accept the word of the baptizer, to admit oneself a sinner, to do penance, and to accept willingly all that God sends, however difficult. No wonder John is startled and tries to dissuade him! But Jesus quietly takes his place in line. He refuses to be an exception; voluntarily, he places himself within the law that is valid for all.

This humble descent to the human level was immediately answered by an outpouring from above. Since the fall of man (and the resultant corruption of nature—Rom 8:20–22) a barrier had separated us from the beatific presence of the omnipresent God in his heaven. For a moment this barrier was removed. While Jesus stood there praying, writes Luke, stressing that it was a spiritual event, an infinite encounter took place: the illimitable abundance of the divine Father streamed into the Son's human heart. Event "in the spirit" obviously; yet also an act as real, or more real, than any tangible reality.

—*Romano Guardini*

Son of God   *March 3*

The Holy Spirit lifts man beyond himself in order that he may experience God the Holy One and his love. We [speak] of the mystery of Jesus' existence: he is the actual Son of God, bearer of the living Godhead which streams through him, illuminating every cell of his being; yet he is also true man, like us in all things, sin excepted. In other words, he grows, increases with the years in wisdom and grace, and not only in the eyes of the world, but also in the eyes of God. . . . At this point the mystery deepens: Jesus is the Son of the Father. At all times "I am in the Father and the

Father in me" (Jn 14:11–12). Yet it is also said that he "comes" from the Father and will return to the Father, and what is still more baffling, upon the cross he cries out in an agony of forsakenness (Mt 27:46).

Jesus' every act is governed by the Father; hence the Spirit (through which the Lord was conceived and made man) is always with him, for it is the bond of love uniting Father and Son.

The power of the Spirit descends upon Jesus. Into the rapture of this encounter, into the divine superabundance of the moment, stream the words of paternal love which Luke records in the form of direct address: "Thou art my beloved Son, in thee I am well pleased."

—Romano Guardini

Temptations   *March 4*

Immediately after the baptism, Our Blessed Lord withdrew into seclusion. The wilderness would be His school, just as it had been the school of Moses and Elias. Retirement is a preparation for action. It would later serve the same purpose for Paul. All human consolation was left behind as "He lodged with the beasts." And for forty days, He ate nothing.

Since the purpose of His coming was to do battle with the forces of evil, His first encounter was not a debate with a human teacher, but a contest with the prince of evil himself.

> And now Jesus was led by the Spirit
> Away into the wilderness,
> To be tempted there by the devil.
>
> Mt 4:1

Temptation was a negative preparation for His ministry, as baptism had been a positive preparation. In His baptism, He had received the Spirit and a confirmation of His mission; in His temptations, He received the strengthening which comes directly from trial and testing. There is a law written across the universe, that no one shall be crowned unless he has first struggled. No halo

77

of merit rests suspended over those who do not fight. Icebergs that float in the cold streams of the north do not command our respectful attention, just for being icebergs; but if they were to float in the warm waters of the Gulf Stream without dissolving, they would command awe and wonderment. They might, if they did it on purpose, be said to have character.

—*Archbishop Fulton J. Sheen*

Public Life

March 5

The sick he healed, every one of them, laying his hands on them. And he cast out many devils. These also he had to order to be silent as he had ordered the one in the synagogue that morning, for they were crying out that he was the Son of God. All hell knew by now that he was the Christ.

He continued his miracle-studded way round Galilee, preaching in the synagogues. He was telling of the Kingdom of Heaven, but not yet of himself as King, still less of the essential part the Kingdom would play in his own work of redeeming the world—a part so essential, indeed, that Redemption and entry into the Kingdom would be inseparable. He must still occupy himself with purifying people's expectations, cleansing these of every trace of personal or national egoism, showing them the Kingdom as essentially other-worldly—*in* this world but not of it, established by repentance, not by the sort of conquest of which they dreamed.

We get the impression that, on this preliminary journey, he travelled alone. Three months or so earlier five disciples had attached themselves to him. But they seem to have gone back to their fishing. Now he would call them definitively, beginning with Andrew and Simon Peter, John and his brother James. We should study their calling closely. It was the first stage in the actual building of the Kingdom of which he had been preaching, the Kingdom "built on the foundation of the Apostles" (Eph 2:20), the Kingdom of which there should be no end.

—*Frank J. Sheed*

Peter

Jesus was standing by the lake. The crowds were thronging round him and pressing hard upon him. He had to clear a space. He adopted the only method that could possibly have worked. He got into a fishing boat—it was Simon Peter's—had it rowed out a little from the land, and preached to the crowds as he sat in the boat. To this day Catholics find pleasure in thinking of Christ's voice sounding from Peter's boat.

He told Peter to row out into the deep and lower the nets again. And now for the first time we hear Peter speak: he must have said a good deal before this, for he was almost too ready a talker; but this is the first utterance of his that the Holy Ghost thought worth recording. "Master," he said, "we have labored all the night, and have taken nothing; but at thy word I will let down the net." All Peter's discipleship was in that answer—"It seems impossible, but if *you* say so—!"

We know what followed—a haul of fish that burst the net. Peter and Andrew called to James and John, their partners, who were in another boat near by, and both boats were loaded with fish to the gunwales, nearly sinking under the weight. What was the exact nature of the miracle? Either Jesus knew that the fish would be there—if so, it was by no natural knowledge that a carpenter would read signs that the fishermen missed; or he willed them to be there.

Peter's reaction is fascinating: "Depart from me, for I am a sinful man, O Lord."

—Frank J. Sheed

The Apostles   *March 7*

[The] Apostles to whom, at his death, Jesus entrusted the fate of his work and of his community were very much as one sees them in the Gospels and subsequently in Acts. Most of them were clearly typed; they ranged from Simon Peter, the eldest, enthusiastic and devoted, prompt to speak and act, capable of sudden

79

failures, but so straightforward, to the young and sensitive John, the Benjamin of the group, an adolescent for whom Jesus showed a particular love, even to the point of letting him lay his head on his breast. In between these two came James the Less, so pious that his knees became quite horny from kneeling, and Thomas, who owes his fame to his critical spirit. There was one misfit in this gallery of saints, Judas Iscariot, probably a Judaean, the mystery of whose life 2,000 years of exegesis have failed to elucidate. When Jesus, in his never-failing foreknowledge, chose Judas, he knew that one day he would be the human instrument of the fate decreed for him by providence.

Jesus did not confine himself to laying definite obligations on his envoys and giving them an austere training. He also endowed them with exceptional graces, as if by leading them to note his omnipotence he wished to strengthen their faith still further. Already those who had witnessed the miracle of the wedding at Cana had "believed in him"; their adhesion to Christ had been influenced by the event. They were to witness other sights at least as surprising.

—*Henri Daniel-Rops*

Small Men   *March 8*

It was a big role for such small men, "simple men, without learning", as they are described in Acts (4:13), the very book which recounts the startling deeds performed by several of [the Apostles]. They all belonged to the same social class. They were neither poor nor rich; they were craftsmen earning an honest living, men whose fortune lay in their boats and nets. There was no intellectual among them, in the sense attached to the word in the Israel of that time; that is, there was no specialist in the Scriptures, no rabbi among them. Christ's power must have been great indeed to make these men participants in the great adventure. So true is it that, for the service of God, high qualities of intellect count less than those of the heart and the soul: will-power, loyalty, courage. The Galileans were well endowed with these.

—*Henri Daniel-Rops*

A Night of Prayer

In the quiet of an evening, Jesus left Capharnaum, walking to the nearby mountain; and there, St. Luke tells us, He passed the night in prayer. His sinless, grace-filled soul needed that converse with its Maker, as every man's soul does; at this moment, particularly, He gave us an example of a strong man advancing to crucial choices and bold truths, but not alone. When the day had dawned, He saw that His disciples had followed Him. Calling them closer, He chose twelve whom He named apostles; men chosen to be with Him and to be given the power to preach, to cast out devils, to heal the sick.

— Walter Farrell

His Charisma
March 9

Jesus' mysterious ability to win over a human being with one word, one look, was to succeed several times—twelve, to be exact—in snatching a man from his normal life and launching him into the great adventure of serving God. No one could evade the call, not even men apparently far from a spiritual vocation, such as Levi the publican, that is, an employee of the treasury or the customs, who was torn from his customhouse table by one phrase from Jesus, an imperious "follow me", to become the future evangelist, St. Matthew (Mt 9:9; Mk 2:14; Lk 5:27).

— Henri Daniel-Rops

His Father's Will

The Lord's entire life proceeds from His Father's will. But it is in this wise that He is truly Himself. He is truly Himself in that He does not do His own will, but the will of His Father, and so fulfills the deepest and most private principle of His being. There is a word for this: Love.

His Father's will is the Father's Love. In His will the Father comes to Jesus in person. His appeals, His orders and commands are a "coming." And in accepting this will, Jesus receives the Father. Addressing this Will and its fulfillment is the generous acceptance of this Love. It is only from this point on that words take on the sense of "must," the "meat"; the oneness of blood, concern for fulfillment, "Not my will but thine"; and the beatific triumph of the words: "The will of my Father I shall do always!"

— Romano Guardini

His Concern for Everyone *March 10*

The divine concern for the least of men, for the obscure, the forgotten, the despised, becomes the dominant note of the days that . . . followed. . . . It almost seems as if these days were a continued, vivid, living response to the Baptist's fiery expectations of crashing judgments and quick, decisive victory by almighty power. By contrast, a thread of tenderness runs through these days, thoughtful of men's weakness, patient of their slowness, forgiving of their sins, alert to the value of the most neglected; yet with no trace of weakness or flabby compromise. He was come, not to judge but to save; and to save not only Israel, but all the world of men.

The tiny villages and obscure localities were reached by the preaching journeys, now become more and more systematic. The seed of organization began to sprout in the Lord's own little band which took on steadily a more permanent form. St. Luke's words allow us to look into the womb of that present to see the embryo of the Church in the process of being born. "He travelled through the cities and towns, preaching and evangelizing the kingdom of God; and the twelve with Him."

— Walter Farrell

Someone Special March 11

People must have felt there was something very special about this Man. Their attention was aroused. They were held fast. They were agitated, upset, deeply stirred. They valued Him, and did Him honor. They also felt irritated, became mistrustful, hostile, grew to hate Him.

All this has great meaning—most of all because none of the positions people took concerning Him originated in the intelligence alone, but all derived from a direct motion of the heart. There was something particular about Him which gripped people, radiating from Him, a force that made itself felt all around Him. This meant that all who saw Him were involved in a special way, passionately aroused to love or hate, to very special love, and very special hate.

Right at the beginning of His mission, after the Sermon on the Mount, we read (Mt 7:28): "Afterwards, when Jesus had finished these sayings, the multitudes found themselves amazed at His teaching. For He taught them, not like their scribes and Pharisees, but like one who had authority." Now the scribes were well-instructed people. They reflected a lot, and worked hard. Their sayings were learned and to the point. But their words were cold and hard, rigid, oppressive. And now here stood One Whose words were warm, full of power. This power derived from what He said, from the depth and the truth of the spoken word—but not from that alone. More than anything, it came from the vitality sounding through His speech, from the vital energy of Him Who spoke. Everything about Him was genuine, strong, straight from the mind and heart. It was candid, rang true, had radiance, contained an effective principle of life. It sent out a call, it wakened, lifted up, cleared the mind, clutched at the heart. And there was warranty behind it, an assurance of salvation.

—Romano Guardini

All Came to Him

The true spirit of a man shows itself in the sort of people who feel drawn to Him.

The children must have loved coming to Him, otherwise their mothers would never have brought them. Nor would He have wanted to see them, all fatigued as He must have been in the late afternoon. Anyone with whom children like to be, understands how to get along with them, knows what to say to them; anyone good with children and animals—for He used to love animals too, it showed in the metaphors He used—is a person with a breath of Paradise hovering over him.

The sick came streaming to Him. It reveals a great deal about a man if the suffering press themselves upon Him because they feel they are welcome to do so. . . . There is something extraordinary, beautiful, frightening about a man upon whom the suffering press themselves. Such a thing will devour him. The relief of suffering is paid for with the stuff of blood and heart.

They kept coming to Jesus, from every corner. From the side streets and hovels. From all sides, this dark, embittered army pressed upon Him. He laid His hands upon them, raised them up, touched them, cleansed them, made them whole.

—*Romano Guardini*

Healing

Christ heals the sick. On the very first pages of the Gospels He appears as the Healer. He had hardly begun His teaching when the sick started coming. They were brought to Him from every quarter. It was as if the masses of the afflicted were always opening up around Him, and closing in on Him. They came by themselves, they were led, they were carried, and He passed through the suffering multitude of people and "a power from God was present, and healed."

. . . Christ went on His way (Mk 10:45ff) and many followed along. A blind man sitting by the roadside, heard the crowd's agitation, asked who He was, and called out: "Jesus, son of David, have pity on me!" They tried to make him be quiet, but he would not allow himself to be intimidated; he called out ever louder until Jesus had the man brought before Him: "What wouldst thou have me do for thee?" "Lord, give me back my sight!" And Jesus said: "Away home with thee; thy faith has brought thee recovery." Right on the spot he was able to see again, and he followed along the way after Him.

— Romano Guardini

Great Love March 14

He was the greatest Lover. In the First Epistle of Saint John we read: "God is Love." This word might have been said by Jesus Himself, and it would still be the same: Jesus is love.

Love proceeded from Him everywhere. We encounter love all about Him. But we want to seek it out in the flaming, radiant center. Love is what He shows toward the delicate blossoming of His Father's creation, when He speaks of the lilies of the field, and how God has clothed them more magnificently than Solomon in all his glory. He shows love toward all things. . . .

. . . Love is what seizes Our Lord when He sees the obscure, abandoned masses of the people, and takes pity on them "because they were like sheep that had no shepherd. . . ." There is something heroic, strong, in this love for people forsaken, in distress. But others too have shown this kind of love in their hearts. If our own times have any claim to be well thought of, it is surely because this love is strongly abroad. It is love again when He receives the sick; when He lets that great sea of misery wash up to Him; when He lifts up, strengthens, heals. Love, when He can say: "Come to me all you who are weary and heavily burdened and I will give you rest." Oh, this tremendous Lover and the might and majesty of His heart taking up arms against the massive world-force of sorrow, magnificently sure of His inexhaustible power to comfort, to strengthen, to bless!

— Romano Guardini

"And seeing the crowds, he went up the mountain. And opening his mouth he taught them, saying, . . . " What follows is known as the Sermon on the Mount. It is reported by two Evangelists: by Luke in the sixth, by Matthew in the fifth, sixth, and seventh chapters of his Gospel. The pith of the message, which made a profound impression upon all who heard it, is the same in both. In Luke, clearly sketched, it stands alone, that remarkable annunciation on the mountainside that begins with the Beatitudes and ends with the comparison of the two men, one of whom builds his house on solid rock, the other on rubble. Matthew uses the Sermon to introduce a long row of Jesus' teachings imparted on different occasions, though probably from the same period of his life, since the same joyful plenitude underlies both.

Both accounts of the Beatitudes proper begin with the word "Blessed." In Luke there are four Beatitudes: "Blessed are you poor, for yours is the kingdom of God. Blessed are you who hunger now, for you shall be satisfied. Blessed are you who weep now, for you shall laugh. Blessed shall you be when men hate you, and when they shut you out, and reproach you, and reject your name as evil, because of the Son of Man."

But after the words: "Rejoice on that day and exult, for behold your reward is great in heaven. For in the selfsame manner their fathers used to treat the prophets," come the four adverse prophecies: "But woe to you rich! for you are now having your comfort. Woe to you who are filled! for you shall hunger. Woe to you who laugh now! for you shall mourn and weep. Woe to you when all men speak well of you! In the selfsame manner their fathers used to treat the prophets."

—Romano Guardini

The Storm   *March 16*

Very soon after the Sermon on the Mount, we find him raising a
young man from death to life, because he was moved with mercy
towards his mother, a widow of Naim, a small place some eight
miles from Nazareth (Lk 7:11–17). Some six months later he raised
to life the daughter of Jairus. . . .

He was crossing the Lake of Galilee, dead tired, asleep in the
boat. A gale of hurricane force blew down, as gales still do, from
the mountains around, and the apostles were convinced that the
ship would sink. Since the storm itself did not wake Our Lord,
they finally woke him themselves. The words they used come
down to us through the centuries with all their humanity still
warm in them: *"Don't you care* if we all drown?" (Mk 4:38).

He says, with something that sounds rather like the impatience
we tend to feel ourselves when we are awakened from deep sleep:
"Where is your faith?" Then—having first rebuked the Twelve for
want of trust—he rebuked the wind and said to the sea, "Peace, be
still." And it was still.

—Frank J. Sheed

Much Love   *March 17*

Simon . . . invited Jesus to a meal in his house (Lk 7:36–50). This
one treated his guest with a strict correctness but nothing beyond—
no water for his feet or oil for his head, no kiss of greeting. As
they sat at table, "a woman that was in the city, a sinner," entered
the room carrying an alabaster box of ointment and "began to
wash his feet, with tears, and wiped them with the hairs of her
head, and kissed his feet, and anointed his feet with the ointment."

Simon and the others assumed that a prophet of God would
have known that the woman was a sinner and have drawn away
from contact with her: therefore the carpenter had proved himself
no prophet. It is not easy to follow the detail of Jesus' answer,
beginning with the question about the two debtors forgiven by
their creditor. His mind darts on a path of its own, by rhythm of

its own, back and forth between love causing forgiveness, and forgiveness causing love. Nineteen hundred years afterwards we do not find it easy to understand all that he is saying. Simon and his friends would not have found it any easier. But though the detail may have mystified them, the main point was clear.

"Many sins are forgiven her, because she has loved much."

— *Frank J. Sheed*

Poverty

March 18

And as he was going forth on his journey, a certain man running up fell upon his knees before him, and asked him, "Good Master, what shall I do to gain eternal life?" But Jesus said to him, "Why dost thou call me good? No one is good but only God. Thou knowest the commandments: *Thou shalt not kill. Thou shalt not steal. Thou shalt not bear false witness. Thou shalt not defraud. Honor thy father and mother.*" And he answered and said, "Master, all these I have kept ever since I was a child." And Jesus, looking upon him, loved him, and said to him, "One thing is lacking to thee; go, sell whatever thou hast, and give to the poor, and thou shalt have treasure in heaven; and come, follow me." But his face fell at the saying, and he went away sad, for he had great possessions.

And Jesus looking round, said to his disciples, "With what difficulty will they who have riches enter the kingdom of God!" But the disciples were amazed at his word. But Jesus again addressed them, saying, "Children, with what difficulty will they who trust in riches enter the kingdom of God! It is easier for a camel to pass through the eye of a needle, than for a rich man to enter the kingdom of God." But they were astonished the more, saying among themselves, "Who then can be saved?" And looking upon them, Jesus said, "With men it is impossible, but not with God; for all things are possible with God" (Mk 10:17–27).

— *Saint Matthew*

Saint Joseph March 19

Now the origin of Christ was in this wise. When Mary his mother had been betrothed to Joseph, she was found, before they came together, to be with child by the Holy Spirit. But Joseph her husband, being a just man, and not wishing to expose her to reproach, was minded to put her away privately. But while he thought on these things, behold, an angel of the Lord appeared to him in a dream, saying, "Do not be afraid, Joseph, son of David, to take to thee Mary thy wife, for that which is begotten in her is of the Holy Spirit. And she shall bring forth a son, and thou shalt call his name Jesus; for he shall save his people from their sins." Now all this came to pass that there might be fulfilled what was spoken by the Lord through the prophet, saying,

> "Behold, the virgin shall be with child,
> and shall bring forth a son;
> and they shall call his name Emmanuel";

which is, interpreted, "God with us." So Joseph, arising from sleep, did as the angel of the Lord had commanded him, and took unto him his wife. And he did not know her till she had brought forth her firstborn son. And he called his name Jesus.

— Saint Matthew

The Pharisees March 20

Jesus' mission in Judaea soon provoked a reaction. It was no longer in a remote region that he was preaching his paradoxical message, among people who had the reputation for being not very well informed in matters of religion and doctrinally somewhat unsound. In Jerusalem and the surrounding district a large number of people prided themselves on knowing the Law thoroughly and obeying it in every detail. A nonconformist was bound to arouse discussions and retorts.

The Fourth Gospel, which is particularly precise about the

events of this period, shows very clearly how the opposition to Jesus crystallized, grew and finally ended in the murderous decision to get rid of him. The process began with discussions about him between those who were attracted by him and those who remained mistrustful. "Some of the multitude, who had heard him, said, Beyond doubt, this is the prophet. Others said, This is the Christ; and others again, Is the Christ, then, to come from Galilee? Has not the scripture told us that Christ is to come from the family of David, and from the village of Bethlehem, where David lived?" (Jn 7:40-3).

The leaders of the Jewish community were on the alert; some people were surprised that they let the prophet speak freely; had they recognized him as the Messias? (Jn 7:26). They had to act, but how?

—Henri Daniel-Rops

He Forgives Sins   *March 21*

The opposition and hatred of the Pharisees, Scribes, and temple leaders against Our Lord grew from the inside out, as it does in most human hearts. First, they hated Him in their own hearts; second, they expressed their hatred to His disciples; then, they manifested their hatred openly to the people; and finally, the hatred centered on Christ Himself.

The evil dispositions of their own hearts were manifested when a man sick of the palsy was brought to Our Lord at Capharnaum. Instead of immediately working the miracle, Our Lord forgave his sins. Since sickness, death, and evil were the effects of sin, though not necessarily personal sin in any individual, He went first to the root of the disease, namely sin, and pardoned it:

Son, thy sins are forgiven (Mk 2:6).

Instead of considering the miracle as evidence of the One Who worked it, His enemies:

Reasoned in their own minds.
Why does He speak so?
He is talking blasphemously.
Who can forgive sins,
But God, and God only?

Mk 2:7

They did not mistake the implications that Christ was acting as God.

—*Archbishop Fulton J. Sheen*

Teacher   *March 22*

Great teachers give instructions to their disciples, but has any teacher ever made his death the pattern of theirs? This is impossible, because no earthly teacher could foresee the manner of his death nor was death ever the reason why he came to teach. Socrates, in all his wisdom, never told the young philosophers of Athens to drink hemlock juice, because he would die by it. But Our Lord did make His Cross the basis of His first instruction to His Apostles. It is because this fact is so often missed, and for the moment was missed by the Apostles themselves, that the true vision of the Christ is beclouded. Even when He acted as a Teacher, He made the Cross to cast its shadow over His Apostles. The sufferings they would endure would be identical to what He would endure. He had been called the Lamb of God Who would be sacrificed for the sins of the world.

—*Archbishop Fulton J. Sheen*

Forgiveness

The next to the last request of the [Our Father] runs: "And forgive us our debts as we forgive our debtors." Mark elaborates on the thought: "And when you stand up to pray, forgive whatever you have against anyone, that your Father in heaven may also forgive you your offences" (11:25). And Matthew adds directly to the words of the prayer: "For if you forgive men their offences, your heavenly Father will also forgive you your offences. But if you do not forgive men, neither will your Father forgive you your offences" (Mt 6:14-15). Thus God's forgiveness of our sins depends upon our forgiveness or refusal to forgive others for the injustices they have committed against us.

—*Romano Guardini*

As a Child   *March 23*

"At that hour the disciples came to Jesus, saying, 'Who then is greatest in the kingdom of heaven?' And Jesus called a little child to him, set him in their midst, and said, 'Amen I say to you, unless you turn and become like little children, you will not enter into the kingdom of heaven. Whoever, therefore, humbles himself as this little child, he is the greatest in the kingdom of heaven.' "

Here we catch a glimpse of the daily life that was lived around Jesus, with its human and all too human frailties. We also see how spontaneously, on the spur of the moment as it were, those teachings sprang into being which were to become valid for all times. The disciples are jealous of each other, anxious to secure their positions in the coming kingdom, which for them, though divine, is still inconceivable without the trappings of human rank and glory. St. Mark brings this out even more sharply: "And they came to Capharnaum. When he was at home, he asked them, 'What were you arguing about on the way?' But they kept silence, for on the way they had discussed with one another which of them was the greatest. And sitting down, he called the Twelve and said to them, 'If any man wishes to be first, he shall be last of all, and servant of all' " (see Mk 9:33-37). . . .

After Jesus has spoken of fraternal, mutual correction, the text continues: "Then Peter came up to him and said, 'Lord, how often shall my brother sin against me, and I forgive him? Up to seven times?' Jesus said to him, 'I do not say to thee seven times, but seventy times seven'" (Mt 18:21–22). Forgiveness should be no occasion, but our habitual attitude towards others. To drive this fundamental point home, Jesus illustrates his teaching with the story of the king who audits his accounts. Finding an enormous deficit in the books of one of his administrators, he commands that his property, family and person be placed under custody until the debt is paid. The man begs for mercy, and his master, who is magnanimous, cancels the debt. But the administrator has hardly left the room when he encounters a colleague who owes him an incomparably smaller sum. He seizes him, and deaf to excuse or plea, drags him to the debtors' court—in those days notorious for its harshness. The king learns what has happened, and angered by the man's heartlessness submits him to the same fate he has inflicted upon his debtor. "So also my heavenly Father will do to you, if you do not each forgive your brothers from your hearts" (Mt 18:35).

—*Romano Guardini*

His Deeds   *March 24*

Jesus was speaking in the house of one of his friends at Capharnaum. A delegation of scribes and doctors of the law was there too, questioning him and hearing his replies, but reserving their opinion. Outside a crowd had gathered and, just as today at Lourdes, stretcherbearers brought the paralyzed and helpless in the hope of a miracle. Four of these, realizing that they would never succeed in approaching the healer, had the idea of climbing, with their burden, up the exterior staircase which ran up to the roof, an arrangement which can be seen to this day in many houses in the area. Oriental roofs are mainly composed of a light daub on a foundation of compressed vegetable material and they offer little resistance to anything, even to a heavy rain. It was easy for the stretcher-bearers to make a hole in the roof covering and let down their burden like a package into the very room where Jesus was. Yet this indiscreet solicitation did not annoy him; he saw only the faith of which it was the evidence. "Son, take courage, thy sins are forgiven," he said. There is no doubt that he directed this phrase specifically to the Pharisees. They leapt to their feet in horror. What was it that this man had said? It was blasphemy. God alone had power to remit sin. But Jesus, who could read their hearts, had used the phrase deliberately to let them know who he was even if they refused to understand. It was no more difficult for the living God to cure the twisted body than to forgive sin. "Rise up, take thy bed with thee, and go home," he said to the palsied man.

... As he passed by the customs office, Jesus directed to one of the men working there the same luminous gaze that he had bent on Nathanael and Levi-Matthew arose immediately and followed him. This was a pretty scandal for the orthodox, and it was aggravated by the rumor that the prophet even permitted the new disciple to eat at his table, doubtless with others of the same stripe.

—Henri Daniel-Rops

Restoring Life   *March 25*

St. Luke's eighth chapter tells how Jesus once shipped across the lake, and immediately upon landing was surrounded by a large crowd. A ruler of the synagogue, Jairus by name, pushes his way through the crowd to Jesus and desperately begs him to rescue his dying child, a little girl of twelve. Moved, Jesus accompanies the man to his home. On the way they are stopped by the density of the crowd, and the woman with the issue of blood touches Jesus' garment and is healed. Soon after, a messenger arrives and announces to the father: "Thy daughter is dead; do not trouble him." The parents had placed everything on this one last hope, and now it too is gone. But Jesus turns to the man: "Do not be afraid; only have faith and she shall be saved." They arrive at the house, where they are met by the uproar which is the typical Oriental accompaniment of death. Jesus speaks the mysterious word: "Do not weep; she is asleep, not dead." Understandably, the crowds laugh. Jesus sends them away, and taking only the father and mother and his three most trusted disciples with him (those who are to witness his Transfiguration and to remain with him on the Mount of Olives) he goes up to the bed of the child. Taking its hands in his own he says: "Girl, arise!" and she opens her eyes, rises, and evinces such vitality that the Lord, very likely with a smile, instructs the parents to give her something to eat, as she is doubtless hungry (Lk 8:40–56).

The scene suggests another already reported by St. Luke. Once in his wanderings, Jesus neared the city of Naim. Just as he was about to enter its gates, the body of a young man, the only son of a widow, was carried through them. The woman's grief touched the Lord and he said: "Do not weep" and he laid his hand on the stretcher. The bearers stood still, and Jesus commanded the dead one: " 'Young man, I say to thee, arise.' And he who was dead, sat up, and began to speak. And he gave him to his mother" (Lk 7:11–17).

—Romano Guardini

March 26

Joy

Joy, which was the small publicity of the pagan, is the gigantic secret of the Christian. And as I close this chaotic volume I open again the strange small book from which all Christianity came; and I am again haunted by a kind of confirmation. The tremendous figure which fills the Gospels towers in this respect, as in every other, above all the thinkers who ever thought themselves tall. His pathos was natural, almost casual. The Stoics, ancient and modern, were proud of concealing their tears. He never concealed His tears; He showed them plainly on His open face at any daily sight, such as the far sight of His native city. Yet He concealed something. Solemn supermen and imperial diplomatists are proud of restraining their anger. He never restrained His anger. He flung furniture down the front steps of the Temple, and asked men how they expected to escape the damnation of Hell. Yet He restrained something. I say it with reverence; there was in that shattering personality a thread that must be called shyness. . . .

There was something that He hid from all men when He went

up a mountain to pray. There was something that He covered constantly by abrupt silence or impetuous isolation. There was some one thing that was too great for God to show us when He walked upon our earth; and I have sometimes fancied that it was His mirth.

—*G. K. Chesterton*

Opposition *March 27*

Tension increased from week to week, and all the evidence suggests that Jesus made no effort to prevent it from increasing. It even looks as if he made a special point of snapping his fingers at the formalism and legalism of the Jews at Jerusalem. When he restored a blind man's sight, he performed the miracle on the Sabbath and performed it with a piece of thaumaturgy—the application of mud to the eyelids—which was certainly forbidden by the jurisprudence of the doctors of the Law (Jn 9:1–7). When some doctors were angry and protested, they received a sharp lesson from Jesus about the existence of other blindnesses besides that of the flesh (Jn 9:13–41). A similar incident is reported by St Luke (13:10–17) in connection with a woman knotted with rheumatism whom Jesus put on her feet, again on the Sabbath.

There were many other points in Jesus' teaching which must have caused discontent and anger. On many questions he adopted an attitude contrary not only to the traditional teaching but even, so it seemed, to the Mosaic Law itself. For example, in the matter of marriage, where divorce was permitted so long as certain guarantees about the lot of the woman repudiated were given, Jesus proclaimed that "no man was to separate what God had joined together" (Mt 19:3; Mk 2:12; Lk 16:18). Was this, then, what he meant, people asked, when he spoke of "fulfilling the Law"?

—*Henri Daniel-Rops*

Detestation

It was ordained that everything about Jesus' message should offend the susceptibilities of the traditionalists. For centuries Judaea had considered itself the bulwark of the proudest Israelite nationalism and the most jealous religious fidelity; the two things were in fact identical. How curiously insistent Jesus was in suggesting that the Chosen People would not have sole right of entry to the Kingdom of Heaven! Why did he speak so often of these prodigal sons, of these lost sheep who had as much right to the Master's love as faithful believers? Why did he depict Samaritans, who were so detestable to an Israelite, in morally nobler situations than practising Jews? Did the only leper who showed gratitude and the only charitable traveller in the parable have to be Samaritans? Jesus' words were sometimes even positively insulting to Jewish ears: "You will have to die with your sins upon you; you belong to earth, I to heaven" (Jn 8:21–5). In other words, you can understand nothing.

It was hardly surprising that discussions grew frequent and heated; that he was accused of being a mere magician, an agent of the devil (Jn 8:49).

— Henri Daniel-Rops

They Ask a Sign

After Matthew has reported the evil clash between Christ and the Pharisees in which Christ accuses them of blasphemy against the Holy Spirit, he goes on to say that several Jews come to Christ and ask for a sign—not just any demonstration of supernatural power, but the great, specifically Messianic sign expected by the chosen people as the fulfillment of the promised kingdom.

"But he answered and said to them, 'An evil and adulterous generation demands a sign, and no sign shall be given it but the sign of Jonas the prophet. For even as Jonas was in the belly of the fish three days and three nights, so will the Son of Man be three days and three nights in the heart of the earth. The men of

Nineveh will rise up in the judgment with this generation and will condemn it; for they repented at the preaching of Jonas, and behold, a greater than Jonas is here' " (Mt 12:39–41). Already the shadow of possible rejection and death; the identical demand and answer appear in chapter sixteen. Again Christ's enemies have demanded a sign, but he only replies: " 'When it is evening you say, "The weather will be fair, for the sky is red." And in the morning you say, "It will be stormy today, for the sky is red and lowering." You know then how to read the face of the sky, but cannot read the signs of the times! An evil and adulterous generation demands a sign, and no sign shall be given it but the sign of Jonas.' And he left them and went away" (Mt 16:2–4).

—*Romano Guardini*

The End Is Near   *March 30*

Jesus' position in the world being what it is, and his relations to people developing as they do, the possibility of his destruction gradually swells to what is practically a necessity. It is that "must" which he himself often implies, for example in speaking of the baptism with which he is to be baptized "and how distressed I am until it is accomplished!" (Lk 12:50). What does it mean? One might suppose it to be that type of necessity which arises when the consequences of word and deed become so manifold that everything is crowded into one set direction. In this way catastrophe can become inevitable. However, Christ does not behave like a person about whose head storm-clouds are gathering. Such a person would change his course, or flee, or with a desperate act of the will prepare to go down with all flags flying. Nothing of the kind in Jesus' conduct. He could flee easily, but does not dream of doing so. There is not a word that suggests a change in tactics in order to win over the populace; also not a trace of desperation. Imperturbably he proceeds along the road he has taken. He sees his mission through to the end without a single diminution, consenting to his doom and thus transmitting to it the immeasurable, God-willed purpose of his coming: fulfillment of the act of salvation.

In Matthew sixteen we read that Jesus began to prepare his disciples for the end in Jerusalem, for his death and Resurrection; again in chapter seventeen: " 'The Son of Man is to be betrayed into the hands of men, and they will kill him; and on the third day he will rise again.' And they were exceedingly sorry" (17:21–22). And finally: "And as Jesus was going up to Jerusalem, he took the twelve disciples aside by themselves, and said to them, 'Behold, we are going up to Jerusalem, and the Son of Man will be betrayed to the chief priests and the Scribes; and they will condemn him to death, and will deliver him to the Gentiles to be mocked and scourged and crucified; and on the third day he will rise again' " (20:17–19).

— Romano Guardini

His Friend Dies   *March 31*

Most surprising is the peculiar freedom we find in Jesus' attitude towards death. Not the freedom of the hero who considers death's victory the simple reversal of greatness; also not the freedom of the sage, who has perceived what is lost in death and what remains, and firmly stands his ground. Here is something else. Essentially Jesus knows himself independent of death because death has no claim on him. No part of him is "stung" by mortality; perfect fruit, he is sound to the core.

Because he is entirely alive Jesus dominates death. Death's superior, he voluntarily submits to it, he who has been sent into the world to change death's very essence in the eyes of God.

The freedom Jesus takes with death is most obvious in the raising of the three dead. We see it when he restores the son to the widow of Naim, effortlessly calling the youth back to life as he passes through the city gates (Lk 7:11–17). And when the Lord returns his little daughter to Jairus with such delicate, lovely ease — "the girl is asleep, not dead" — he seems to be playing with death. The terrible one obeys his almost bantering word, and withdraws as lightly as slumber from a child's lids at the waking hand of a mother. [There is] the tremendous event that John describes in his eleventh chapter: the resurrection of Lazarus.

He was Jesus' friend, brother of the sisters Mary and Martha. One day a message comes from them: "Lord, behold, he whom thou lovest is sick." But Jesus only remarks: "This sickness is not unto death, but for the glory of God . . . " and he remains where he is another two days, allowing Lazarus to die. Then he proceeds on his way with the words: "Lazarus, our friend, sleeps. But I go that I may wake him from sleep." (Again death and sleep paired in one breath, and certainly not poetically. Jesus' words are not those of a poet but of a commander.) The disciples misunderstand. "Lord, if he sleeps, he will be safe." Then Jesus says plainly: "Lazarus is dead; and I rejoice on your account that I was not there, that you may believe. But let us go to him."

—*Romano Guardini*

"I Am the Resurrection" *April 1*

What must there have been in his look that made Thomas say impulsively to the others: "Let us also go, that we may die with him." They arrive at Bethany, to find Lazarus already in the tomb. In Jesus we sense a constantly rising excitement. Martha hears of his arrival and greets him with the mild reproach:

"Lord, if thou hadst been here my brother would not have died."

"Thy brother shall rise."

"I know that he will rise at the resurrection, on the last day."

"I am the resurrection and the life; he who believes in me, even if he die, shall live; and whoever lives and believes in me, shall never die." The words span heaven and earth: "I am the resurrection and the life," I and no other. Everything depends on our accomplishing within ourselves this "I am." If only Jesus' vitality were in us, we should not know death. But that that vital quality which in Jesus is not only indestructible, but intrinsic and creative, has been destroyed in us. Hence we die. Our death is not "tacked on" to life, it is the direct outcome of the kind of life we live. In our dying a condition already present in our living asserts itself: a condition—as we see by contrast with Jesus, the full measure of man—which should not exist. Mortality has no foothold in Jesus. For this reason, although he offered himself up in the Eucharist and died the death on the cross, he exists only as "life": (for us, who are mortal, as "the Resurrection"). Thus the human being linked in faith to Christ possesses a life that will outlive death and that already here on earth reaches into eternity. It is as Christ himself once expressed it: "Amen, amen, I say to you, he who hears my word, and believes him who sent me, has life everlasting, and does not come to judgment, but has passed from death to life" (Jn 5:24).

But to return to Bethany: "Dost thou believe this?" Christ asks Martha. Martha does not understand (how could she before the descent of the Holy Spirit?) but she trusts him: "Yes, Lord, I believe that thou art the Christ, the Son of God, who hast come into the world."

—Romano Guardini

Washing Their Feet   *April 2*

In the report on Jesus' last reunion with his disciples we find the description of a strange incident that has seldom failed to make a deep impression on the Christian consciousness: ". . . Jesus, knowing that the Father had given all things to his hands, and that he had come forth from God and was going to God, rose from the supper and laid aside his garments, and taking a towel girded himself. Then he poured water into the basin and began to wash the feet of the disciples, and to dry them with the towel with which he was girded.

"He came, then, to Simon Peter. And Peter said to him, 'Lord, dost thou wash my feet?' Jesus answered and said to him, 'What I do thou knowest not now; but thou shalt know hereafter.' Peter said to him, 'Thou shalt never wash my feet!' Jesus answered him, 'If I do not wash thee, thou shalt have no part with me.' Peter said to him, 'Lord, not my feet only, but also my hands and my head!' Jesus said to him, 'He who has bathed needs only to wash, and he is clean all over. And you are clean, but not all.' For he knew who it was that would betray him. This is why he said, 'You are not all clean.'

"Now after he had washed their feet and put on his garments, when he had reclined again, he said to them, 'Do you know what I have done to you? You call me Master and Lord, and you say well, for so I am. If, therefore, I the Lord and Master have washed your feet, you also ought to wash the feet of one another' " (Jn 13:3-14).

—Romano Guardini

We Live in Him *April 3*

The gift of the Eucharist and Our Lord's death are in the deepest sense one and the same mystery.

The love that drove Him to die for us was the same love that made Him give us Himself as nourishment. It was not enough to be giving us gifts, words, instructions; He gave us Himself as well. Perhaps we must seek out Woman, the loving-mother, to find someone who understands this kind of longing: to be giving not some *thing*, but rather oneself—to give oneself, with all one's being. Not only the spirit, not only one's fidelity, but body and soul, flesh and blood, everything—this is indeed the ultimate love, to want to feed others with the very substance of one's own self. And for that Our Lord went to His death, so He might rise again in the resurrection, in that condition wherein He desired to give Himself to all mankind for evermore.

And now He who died for us lives again, within us.

—Romano Guardini

In His farewell we read (Jn 15:1): "I am the true vine, and it is my Father who tends it. The branch that yields no fruit in me, he cuts away; the branch that does yield fruit, he trims clean, so that it may yield more fruit. You, through the message I have preached to you, are clean already; you have only to live on in me, and I will live on in you. The branch that does not live on in the vine can yield no fruit of itself; no more can you, if you do not live on in me. I am the vine, you are its branches; if a man lives on in me, and I in him, then he will yield abundant fruit; separated from me, you have no power to do anything."

He has gone into us, and works within us, and we live in Him and by Him, just as the vine's branch bears the leaf and fruit from out of the living interdependency of its entire growth. Saint Paul placed this mystery at the foundation of all Christian being.

He says in Romans 6:3ff: "You know well enough that we who were taken up into Christ by baptism have been taken up, all of us, into his death. In our baptism, we have been buried with him, died like him, that so, just as Christ was raised up by his Father's power from the dead, we too might live and move in a new kind of existence. We have to be closely fitted into the pattern of his resurrection, as we have been into the pattern of his death; we have to be sure of this, that our former nature has been crucified with him, and the living power of our guilt annihilated, so that we are the slaves of guilt no longer. Guilt makes no more claim on a man who is dead. And if we have died with Christ, we have faith to believe that we shall share his life. We know that Christ, now he has risen from the dead, cannot die any more; death has no more power over him.

— Romano Guardini

Gethsemane was the hour in which Jesus' human heart and mind experienced the ultimate odium of the sin he was to bear as his own before the judging and avenging countenance of God; hour in which he felt the fury of the Father against sin *per se* as directed against himself, its porter, and therefore suffered the unspeakable agony of "abandonment" by holy God. We are humanizing again. Perhaps it would be better to be silent. But with God's help, possibly that hour in the garden will not be quite lost on us. There Jesus accepted the Father's will and surrendered his own. "His" will was not revolt against God, that would have been sin; it was simply the repulsion of a supremely pure and vital being against the role of scapegoat for the evil of a whole world; revolt against being the one, through no fault of his own but as the price of self-sacrificing love, on whom all God's anger must fall. To accept this was the meaning of his words, " . . . yet not what I will, but what thou willst."

There the real struggle took place. All that came afterwards was the realization of that hour, the actual execution of what had already been excruciatingly anticipated by heart and spirit. And in what solitude! So tremendous that we sense the fundamental guiltlessness of the disciples. In the face of such infinite suffering, their little capacity for compassion must have rebounded like the heart of a small child when the grown-ups are engulfed in some shattering experience: it turns aside, begins to play, or simply falls asleep. The fact that there is no alternative shows how hopeless Christ's isolation is. No one has ever seen existence as Jesus saw it; neither before nor after. In that hour when his human heart lifted the world from its vapors of deception, he beheld it as otherwise only God beholds it—in all its hideous nakedness. What happened was truth realized in charity. And we are given the standpoint from which we too can see through and reject deception. For that is the meaning of salvation: seeing the world as Christ saw it and experiencing his repulsion of sin.

—Romano Guardini

Judas arrived, showing the way to a large crowd—Temple police, servants from the chief priests and the scribes and the elders (Mk 14:43) and Roman soldiers as well (Jn 18:12), with a senior officer in charge of them. There is significance in their presence. Christ's enemies had not dared to arrest him in daylight for fear of the crowds: even less would they have dared to execute him, whether or not they had the right, for fear of those same crowds. They wanted him dead, but somehow they had to get the Occupying Power to kill him. That, one imagines, is why, along with their own people, they had a band of Roman soldiers go there for the arrest. The mere hint that there might be a riot would have got them the soldiers.

Judas told those with him that the man he should kiss was the one they should seize. The word he used for "kiss" applied to the somewhat sketchy embrace normal where the kiss is equivalent to a handshake. But the kiss he actually gave the Lord he was betraying was (as Mark and Matthew tell us) the kiss of warmest devotion: and one marvels at the nerve of the man who so soon after would be driven by remorse to hang himself.

Jesus' response may startle us: "Friend, what have you come for?" It was not so long before that he had said of this same Judas, "I have chosen you twelve, and one of you is a devil." All through the Public Ministry we have noticed in him a terseness which can rise to fierceness: his speech is seldom observably gentle, and never when he speaks to men hardened in evil. From now on we shall hear that tone in him no more. The words to Judas are a reminder that he has entered into his victim-condition, he goes to the slaughter lamb-like: there is no rage in him, no judging even. He is wholly judged.

—Frank J. Sheed

Blasphemy

[At the trial, Jesus] repeated almost word for word what he had said to the High Priest: "The Son of God? Yes, I am." To which the Council replied, in a voice that one might have hoped would have been less unanimous, "The case is over! What need have we of witnesses? We have heard the blasphemy with our own ears!" Blasphemy was the greatest of all crimes, the one which in any circumstances deserved death.

—Henri Daniel-Rops

Before Pilate   *April 7*

Jesus is silent. Also to the procurator's question as to what he has to say to the charges, and Pilate "wondered exceedingly" (Mt 27:14). This is certainly anything but the usual behavior of defendants, excited, verbose, pathetic, insistent—who try anything and everything to save their lives. This man is silent. So Pilate takes him inside, where he can question him privately: "Art thou the king of the Jews?" Jesus replies with a strange counter-question: "Dost thou say this of thyself, or have others told thee of me?" (The accusers, in other words, who charge me with revolt against Caesar.) If you are only questioning me formally, as part of the trial, I have nothing to say. But perhaps you are asking because something in you desires to know. That something I will answer. But Pilate only replies haughtily: "Am I a Jew?" What is your Messiah to me? "Thy own people and the chief priests have delivered thee to me. What hast thou done?"

Nevertheless, Jesus sees that there are depths to this Roman, and he proclaims himself: He is King, yes, but his kingdom is "not of this world." If it were, "my followers would have fought that I might not be delivered to the Jews. But, as it is, my kingdom is not here."

"Art thou then a king?"

"Thou sayest it; I am a king. This is why I was born, and why I have come into the world, to bear witness to the truth." Now

Pilate thinks he knows where he is: the man is obviously one of those wandering philosophers who deny the earthly realm in an attempt to establish an ideal realm of truth—a harmless utopian, to put it in modern speech. For the idea that what the stranger says might be actually true, in the trusting and passionate sense of the word, he has only the skeptical shrug of the cultivated of his day: "What is truth?"

Yet his judiciary eye sees clearly, so he goes outside and announces to the Jews: "I find no guilt in him" (Jn 18:33–38).

But the accusals grow only louder: "He is stirring up the people, teaching throughout all Judea, and beginning from Galilee even to this place" (Lk 23:5). At the word Galilee, Pilate sees a way out. As a Galilean, the accused is under the jurisdiction of Herod, who at the moment happens to be in Jerusalem. By sending the defendant to Herod for judgment, he would simultaneously flatter the nominal sovereign and rid himself of the unpleasant affair. And this Pilate does, but the accusers go along with Jesus.

—*Romano Guardini*

Herod Delighted   *April 8*

Herod is delighted. He has heard much about Jesus and is eager to meet him. The tetrarch is interested in the religious and marvelous (as evinced by his strange friendship with John the Baptist—interest, however, which did not prevent him from beheading the last of the prophets when manoeuvred into an embarrassing predicament). Now he hopes to experience something extraordinary—possibly even a miracle! So he plies question on question, while the representatives of the supreme council stand by violently accusing. But Jesus never says a word. All of them, Sanhedrin, Rome's Procurator, Herod "the Fox" and the rest, can terrorize and murder as they will. They are only slaves (their violence proof enough), at best fallen slaves of God. After Herod has questioned a while in vain, his interest turns to mockery. He and his whole court make sport of this Messiah so obviously impotent, and garbing him in a jester's royal cloak, they send him, a living caricature of his claims, back to Pilate.

"And Herod and Pilate became friends that very day; whereas previously they had been at enmity with each other." The Evangelist states the fact calmly, stripping the human heart bare (Lk 23:12).

—*Romano Guardini*

The Mob *April 9*

Pilate leads the accused outside and seats himself in the judge's seat. One last time, with an uncertainty that is impotent against the fanatical will of the accusers, he tries to save Jesus: "Behold your king."

But they sense their victory and only clamor: "Away with him! Away with him! Crucify him!"

Pilate: (we cannot help sympathizing with this weak man, bullied, against his better judgment, to injustice) "Shall I crucify your king?"

"We have no king but Caesar" (Jn 19:4–15).

Pilate gives up. After the symbolical, oh so paltry gesture of the hand-washing, he makes the ridiculous announcement: "I am innocent of the blood of this just man; see to it yourselves."

To this, the gruesome answer of the mob: "His blood be on us and on our children."

Pilate releases Bar-abbas and surrenders Jesus to their will.

It is frightening to witness this hate-torn world suddenly united for one brief hour, against Jesus. And what does he do? Every trial is in reality a struggle—but not this one. Jesus refuses to fight. He proves nothing. He denies nothing. He attacks nothing. Instead, he stands by and lets events run their course—more, at the proper moment, he says precisely what is necessary for his conviction. His words and attitude have nothing to do with the logic or demands of a defence. Their source lies elsewhere. The accused makes no attempt to hinder whatever is to come; but his silence is neither that of weakness nor of desperation. It is divine reality;

full, holy consciousness of the approaching "hour"; perfect readiness. His silence brings into being what is to be.

—*Romano Guardini*

The Savior

He had ministered to men's miseries both of body and soul: cured all manner of sickness, driven out devils, forgiven sins. He had insisted on the supremacy of God over man, had come to the defense of reason in law, had made good truth's threat to unfounded claims of eminence. Through it all, divine power had been exercised in an almost reckless extravagance to confirm the truth of all that had been done and said. For this, He must die. The shock of God's presence among men does not come from His demands on them so much as His kindness to them and His mighty resistance to man's unkindness to men. It is from the love of God that men flee, for there is no answer to its uncounting generosity, but a proportionately reckless dedication that shrinks all other goods to pygmy proportions.

From this time on, the shadow of death hovered over the head of Jesus. No man believes against his will, and the enemies of Christ had no will to believe. He was a light moving through the blackness of their unbelief, but even this divine light did not dissipate the darkness. It was evident, even as early as this, that His work of saving the men of all ages would be carried on by other hands than His; for His days were numbered and His work had no limits. The welcome of men was the death of God.

—*Walter Farrell*

Peter

When Jesus emerged into the courtyard of the Palace, an incident had just occurred which puts the finishing touch to his isolation and abandonment. Peter, who had followed him at a distance, had entered the courtyard of the High Priest, on the watch for news. As it was a cold night he had gone up to the brazier lit by the guards. A maidservant had recognized him, pointed him out and denounced him. Peter, terrified, had sworn that he did not belong to the Galilean's band, that he did not know the individual, that he had no acquaintance with him. He had just sworn for the third time when Jesus appeared, looked at him—and the cock crew. All Peter could do was flee into the night, weeping.

Jesus remained alone, more alone than ever. The servants and soldiery had him at their mercy. They decided to see what he was capable of, this prophet, this magician, this sorcerer, this self-styled Messias. They played a very amusing game; they blindfolded him, struck him hard, and asked amid laughter, "Come on, Messias, guess who struck you! A prophet should be able to guess where the blows came from!" The scene was a painful one; prisons in all ages have witnessed similar, and worse, ones. Jesus replied to all these insults with silence. To follow Christ, says the Epistle to the Hebrews, one must bear "the ignominy he bore" (13:13). And one must also share his heroic acceptance.

—*Henri Daniel-Rops*

Christ on the Cross *April 12*

The plunge from God towards the void which man in his revolt had begun (chute in which the creature can only despair or break) Christ undertook in love. Knowingly, voluntarily, he experienced it with all the sensitiveness of his divinely human heart. The greater the victim, the more terrible the blow that fells him. No one ever died as Jesus died, who was life itself. No one was ever punished for sin as he was, the Sinless One. No one ever experienced the plunge down the vacuum of evil as did God's Son—even to the excruciating agony behind the words: "My God, my God, why hast thou forsaken me?" (Mt 27:46). Jesus was really destroyed. Cut off in the flower of his age; his work stifled just when it should have taken root; his friends scattered, his honor broken. He no longer had anything, was anything: "a worm and not a man." In inconceivable pain "he descended into hell," realm in which evil reigns, and not only as the victorious breaker of its chains. This came later; first he had to touch the nadir of a personally experienced agony such as no man has ever dreamed. There the endlessly Beloved One of the eternal Father brushed the bottom of the pit. He penetrated to the absolute nothingness from which the *"re-creatio"* of those already created (but falling from the source of true life towards that nothingness) was to emerge: the new heaven and new earth.

Christ on the cross! Inconceivable what he went through as he hung there. In the degree that we are Christian and have learned to love the Lord, we begin to sense something of that mystery of utter helplessness, hopelessness. This then the end of all effort and struggle! Everything, without reserve—body, heart and spirit given over to the illimitable flame of omnipresent agony, to the terrible judgment of assumed world-sin that none can alleviate and whose horror only death can end. Such the depths from which omnipotent love calls new creation into being.

—*Romano Guardini*

The Redemption   *April 13*

Our Blessed Lord, though He was sinless, nevertheless willed "to be made sin for us." As a strong magnet attracts to itself iron filings, so He by an act of His Will drew unto Himself all the sins of the world that have ever been committed, sins of Jews and Gentiles, sins too awful to be mentioned, sins too terrible to be named. He permitted them all to be thrust into His Hands, as if He Himself had committed them, and the very thought of them was so terrible that, one night in the Garden, His Blood poured out from His Body in a crimson sweat. The cup was bitter, but since the Father willed it, He would drink it to its very dregs.

By coming into a world of sin, He, the Sinless One, brought the whole weight of its sin upon His Person. As doctors, who are free from disease, will sometimes accept the possibility of contagion in their eagerness to cure their patients of a disease, so He, though sinless, freely accepted the cumulative weight of human transgression that He might atone for the very punishment which our sins deserved. It was faintly like a rich man who makes himself responsible for the debts of a bankrupt, that he might start business all over again, except with Our Lord the cost was greater, namely, His life. Being God He became man that He might lay down His Life for us who were not His friends, but His enemies.

Imagine a golden chalice which has been consecrated for Divine worship and used on the altar at Mass. Suppose this chalice is stolen, mingled with alloys and beaten down to a cigarette case. Later on, it is recovered. Before the gold of that chalice can be restored to the altar, it must first of all be subjected to purging fires to burn away the dross.

—Archbishop Fulton J. Sheen

Surprising Event   *April 14*

[The] terrible defeat [of Jesus] had plunged [the Apostles] into a mixture of despair, apathy and fear. While the last act of the tragedy was being enacted, they were so afraid of being arrested as accomplices of the condemned man that instead of being present on Golgotha at the foot of the cross on which their Master was dying they had all—with one exception—gone to earth in the poor quarters of the city, barricading themselves inside a few friendly houses.

Yet a mysterious answer had been given to this mortal anguish and to the still more mortal doubt about the truth of the message which they had received. On the third day after the drama—the Sunday of the Passover—some women belonging to their group had gone up to the spot where the condemned man had been buried and had brought back a shattering piece of news; they had found the tomb empty and a luminous charisma had revealed to them that the man who had died on the cross had conquered death and risen again. Then, no doubt, curious phrases which they had heard on his lips in days gone by acquired a prophetic meaning. They recalled that he had told them that he was to conquer death after apparently yielding to it. But the very conditions in which for forty days this new existence went on had left these men in a state of mind in which joy, hope, anxiety and doubt all had a share. It was this strange second life which had just come to an end with a still more surprising event.

In the tradition established by those who were going to be the guardians and heralds of the Message, this surprising event was to have considerable importance. It was to be affirmed in the oldest version of the Apostles' Creed, which was a summary of their faith. In the writings of the first witnesses, this "ascension into heaven", this "taking up into glory" would be regarded as one of the surest signs of the divinity of him who had enjoyed it (Eph 4:8–10; Heb 4:14; 1 Tim 3:16; 1 Pet 3:22). For the moment, however, "the Ascension" did not suffice to dissolve all doubts.

—*Henri Daniel-Rops*

He Stood in Their Midst   *April 15*

A very beautiful portion of St. John's Gospel takes us to the midst of that mystery-charged time between the Lord's resurrection and His quitting the world. At that moment, the disciples must have felt they were both in and out of this central fact of history; they must have had to ask themselves over and over again whether or not what they saw before their eyes was really and truly happening; and yet these events were impressing themselves upon them more intensely than reality. It was a time when their innermost being was disengaging from the associations and obligations of the dying world of the Old Testament, and turning towards a new order of things whose direction they could not yet understand.

It was a strange life they led, frightened and at the same time full of boundless hope. Soon they were to be in the room together; soon by the sea; soon they would be walking on the streets—and time and again they would encounter this mysterious Figure, suddenly, as if out of another world; the Figure speaks to them, instructs them, plays upon them with the exhalation of its power.

So at one point they were seated in a room together (Jn

20:26ff), the doors bolted for fear of the Jews. It was still only a few days since the Lord had been put to death. Unrest was abroad. It had in fact received a fresh impetus from the strange news that had come from the grave. And there Jesus stood in the room right in their midst, and wished them peace.

"Peace be upon you." These words make us reflect. Jesus had indeed said the very opposite: "I come not to bring peace, but a sword." And both are true. Whosoever comes to Jesus receives His peace—"that peace that the world cannot give." The peace that consists of the believer's certainty that God exists; God lives. God is He Himself, the one and only; and He loves me, and nothing can tear me from His love.

—*Romano Guardini*

The Doubting Thomas   *April 16*

"There was one of the twelve, Thomas, who is also called Didymus, who was not with them when Jesus came. And when the other disciples told him, We have seen the Lord, he said to them, Until I have seen the mark of the nails on his hands, until I have put my finger into the mark of the nails, and put my hand into his side, you will never make me believe."

Thomas appears to have been a realist—reserved, cool, perhaps a little obstinate.

The days went by, and the disciples went on living under this considerable tension.

Another week, and they were together again in the house, and this time Thomas was with them. The same thing repeated itself. Jesus passed through closed doors, stepped into their midst, and spoke: "Peace be upon you!" Then He called the man who was struggling against faith: "Let me have thy finger; see, here are my hands. Let me have thy hand; put it into my side. Cease thy doubting, and believe!" At this point Thomas was overwhelmed. The truth of it all came home to him: this Man standing before him, so moving, arousing such deep feelings within him, this Man so full of mystery, so different from all other men—He is the very same One they used to be together with, Who was put to death a short time ago. And Thomas surrendered: "Thou art my Lord and my God!" Thomas believed.

Then we come upon the strange words: "And Jesus said to him, Thou hast learned to believe, Thomas, because thou hast seen me. Blessed are those who have not seen, and yet have learned to believe!"

Such words as these are really extraordinary!

—*Romano Guardini*

They Prayed   *April 17*

In a splendid passage Lacordaire has depicted these men "alone before the world, which holds none of their beliefs, which indeed is totally ignorant of them, and which they must convert to their faith from the foot of the cross on which their Master perished. Was there ever such a moment for men? And who were these men? Craftsmen, fishermen...." Their doubts, even their fears, seem only too natural. The task imposed on them would have made even apparently better prepared men seek to evade it.

Their faith was not in question and their hearts were "filled with joy". They could repeat to each other, as a sign and promise, what one of them was to write later: "No man has ever gone up into heaven except him who has come down from heaven" (Jn 3:13). That was a spiritual guarantee which, coming after others, after the Resurrection, could not be denied by anyone. But for this faith to communicate itself, for their courage to rise to the point of making them take the risk of proclaiming themselves the witnesses of him who was crucified on Golgotha—a mortal risk expressly foretold by their Master (Jn 21:18)—and for them to obey the supreme order which he had given them to "go out all over the world and preach the gospel" (Mt 28:16; Mk 16:15–18; Acts 1:3; 1 Cor 15:9), they needed more than human strength.

For ten days, gathered in the upper room—the very room in which they had celebrated the Last Supper with Jesus—of a house in the upper city which had become the dwelling of the first disciples, who had been joined by Mary, the Mother of Jesus, and the other holy women, they prayed and meditated. Those who had truly loved Jesus joined them there. The group was still quite a small one; perhaps about a hundred and twenty (Acts 1:12, 26).

—*Henri Daniel-Rops*

The Breath of the Spirit   *April 18*

It was the tenth day after the Ascension. In accordance with tradition Israel was celebrating the feast of Pentecost, the anniversary of the dictation of the Law to Moses by Yahweh. The devoted little community was gathered together in the upper room. It was then that the answer came: "All at once a sound came from heaven like that of a strong wind blowing, and filled the whole house where they were sitting. There appeared to them what seemed to be tongues of fire, which parted and came to rest on each of them; and they were all filled with the Holy Spirit" (Acts 2:2–4).

There was no doubt in the mind of any of them. The breath of the Spirit which had just passed over them provoked a tide of memories. The Master had foretold to them: "I will send him to you. He will come, and it will be for him to prove the world wrong.... It will be for him, the truth-giving Spirit, when he comes, to guide you into all truth" (Jn 16:7–13). He had also added: "When the truth-giving Spirit, who proceeds from the Father, has come to befriend you . . . he will bear witness of what I was; and you too are to be my witnesses, you who from the first have been in my company" (Jn 15:26).

—*Henri Daniel-Rops*

"Now Jesus, having come into the district of Caesarea Philippi, began to ask his disciples, saying, 'Who do men say the Son of Man is?'" He is told the various opinions in circulation, then asks who the disciples think he is, and Peter gives his historic answer, "Thou art the Christ, the Son of the living God." Jesus calls him blessed and entrusts to him the keys of the kingdom, names him the rock of his Church, against which "the gates of hell" shall not prevail. We know the passage almost by heart, still there remains one point that we should try to see more clearly.

Here for the first time Jesus declares himself openly and unmistakably the Messiah, and simultaneously he speaks with equal definiteness of his coming death. This hour is also the decisive hour of the Church. From now on three facts belong together: Jesus the Messiah, his death and his Church. Before that hour the Church did not exist, nor did she spring into being later as the result of historical development. Jesus himself founded her in the superabundance of his Messianic power.

The decision regarding the acceptance or rejection of his message has fallen; the Lord is on his way to death. The powers of evil have the upper hand, and the Church will be attacked by them; nevertheless, she will stand, rocklike. The two thoughts belong together, never to be separated.

To the reality of the Church belong other passages which it might be well to mention here, among them Jesus' words about his disciples' mission: "He who hears you, hears me; and he who rejects you, rejects me...." (Lk 10:16). Something more than inspired men capable of inflaming hearts are being sent into the world; they are delegates equipped with full powers, for they bear their high office with them. They are already "Church."

—*Romano Guardini*

Another time Jesus speaks of man's duty toward an erring brother. First one should tactfully speak to him alone. If he refuses to listen, one should approach him with one or two others, that the necessary warning gain weight. If he still remains refractory "appeal to the Church" (*Ecclesia* — the word is still something halfway between church and congregation) and means at least a body with authority. Then Christ continues, "but if he refuse to hear even the Church, let him be to thee as the heathen and the publican" (Mt 18:15–17).

At the Last Supper Jesus instigates the holy mystery of the Eucharist already promised in Capharnaum (Jn 6). It is sacrifice and sacrament in one, mystery of the new community, heart of the new Church's new covenant. Its consummation is her vital heart-beat. (See Mt 26:26–28, Acts 2:46.)

After the Resurrection, the Lord's memorable questioning of Peter on the shore; three times he asks him: Simon, son of John, lovest thou me? And three times, shamefully recalling his treachery, Peter replies: "Yes, Lord, thou knowest that I love thee." And each time he is commanded: "Feed my lambs," "Feed my lambs," "Feed my sheep" (Jn 21:15–16). That too is Church. Once Jesus had said to Peter: You are the rock; then: I have prayed for you, that your faith remain firm; when it is established, confirm your brothers (Lk 22:32). Now he says: Be the shepherd of lambs and sheep, of the whole world, which embraces both the weak and the strong. Church again, founded on the unity of its fundament; constituted with one head and one leader. "Conceived" by the words spoken at Caesarea Philippi, the Church was not born until Pentecost, when the Holy Spirit fused the individual believers in Christ to a single, determined body with a consciousness of its own, fully aware that it lived in Christ and Christ in it: the Corpus Christi. And immediately he whom the Lord has appointed its rock and its shepherd rises and speaks. His words are the first of the new-born Church (I Cor; Acts 2:14).

—*Romano Guardini*

When we define the Church as essentially the Kingdom of God and the Body of Christ, it follows as her first particular attribute that she is supernatural and heavenly. The Church is ordinated towards the invisible, spiritual and eternal. Of this we have spoken already. But the Church is not only invisible. Because she is the Kingdom of God, she is no haphazard collection of individuals, but an ordered system of regularly subordinated parts. And because the Church is the Body of Christ, she is essentially an organism, with its members purposively interrelated, and a visible organism. That is her second particular attribute. The advocates of a purely spiritual religion, both in ancient and in modern Christianity, have maintained that the Spirit of Christ which works in the Church is in it as a sort of freely suspended force, as a saving power that invisibly penetrates only into this or that person. But that is not so. On the contrary, Christ the Lord, as the Head of His members, never works on the individual believer in dissociation from His Body, but always in and through it.

That is to say that the supernatural redemptive might of Jesus, as it reveals itself in the Church, is not tied to a single person, so far as he is a person, but only so far as he is a divinely-appointed organ of the community. The Spirit of Jesus is introduced into our earthly life, not through the medium of individuals endowed with special charismatical gifts, but through the ministry of an ordered hierarchy, which being appointed by Jesus to be the structural basis of the community, creates, supports and develops it.

—Karl Adam

The Many as One   *April 22*

The Church possesses the Spirit of Christ, not as a many of single individuals, nor as a sum of spiritual personalities, but as the compact, ordered unity of the faithful, as a community that transcends the individual personalities and expresses itself in a sacred hierarchy. This organised unity, this community, as germinally given with the Head, Christ, and depending upon His institution, is a fundamental datum of Christianity, not a thing created by the voluntary or forced association of the faithful, not a mere secondary and derivative thing depending on the good pleasure of Christians, but a thing which, in the divine plan of salvation, is in its essence antecedent to any Christian personality and is to that extent a supra-personal thing, a comprehensive unity, which does not presuppose Christian personalities, but itself creates and produces them. The Church did not spring into being when Peter and Paul, James and John, grasped the mystery of Jesus, His God-man being, and on the basis of their common faith formed a fellowship which was called after Him. No, the Church, though certainly achieving full historical actuality only with the association of Christian believers, was already in existence, fundamentally and in germ, and in that sense is a divine creation. For she is the unity of redeemed humanity, a unity made possible by the Incarnation of the Son of God; she is the kosmos of men, mankind as a whole, the many as one.

—*Karl Adam*

The Body of Christ

Now you are the body of Christ, member for member. And God indeed has placed some in the Church, first apostles, secondly prophets, thirdly teachers; after that miracles, then gifts of healing, services of help, power of administration, and the speaking of various tongues. Are all apostles? Are all prophets? Are all teachers? Are all workers of miracles? Do all have the gift of healing? Do all speak with tongues? Do all interpret? Yet strive after the greater gifts.

—*Saint Paul*

The Church Is Christ

Christ the Lord is the real self of the Church. The Church is the body permeated through and through by the redemptive might of Jesus. So intimate is this union of Christ with the Church, so inseparable, natural and essential, that St. Paul in his Epistles to the Colossians and Ephesians explicitly calls Christ the Head of the body. As the Head of the body Christ makes the organism of the Church whole and complete. And Christ and the Church can no more be regarded separately than can a head and its body (Col 1:18; 2:19; Eph 4:15ff).

This conviction that the Church is permeated by Christ, and of necessity organically united with Him, is a fundamental point of Christian teaching. From Origen to Augustine and Pseudo-Dionysius and thence to Thomas Aquinas, and thence on to our own unforgettable Möhler, this conviction stands in the centre of the Church's doctrine. Her teachers delight to repeat in ever new forms those expressions of Augustine wherein he celebrates the mystical oneness of Christ and the Church: the two are one, one body, one flesh, one and the same person, one Christ, the whole Christ.

—Karl Adam

Christ Is the Church

April 24

Christ and the Church, this their intimate oneness, receive no profounder or plainer expression than in the figure of a marriage of Christ and the Church which St. Paul, inspired by the language of several of the prophets (Osee i–iii; Jer. 2:2; Is. 54:5) is the first to employ (II Cor 11:2). According to St. Paul the Church is the Bride of Christ, for whom He gave Himself. And with a like train of thought the Seer of the Apocalypse celebrates the "marriage of the Lamb," and sings of His "bride" that hath prepared herself (19:7–8). Later mystical theology wove out of these scriptural thoughts its wondrously sweet bridal mysticism, in which Christ is the lord, the Church His bride, and the two in closest union generate the children of life.

This supernatural being of the Church expresses itself chiefly in her most primary creations, in dogma, morals and worship.

—Msgr. Ronald Knox

The Church Is Visible

To prove that the Church is, and is meant to be, visibly one, is pretty easy going. You've only to read St Paul's epistles to be struck by the enormous importance which he attaches to the unity of the Church. It's quite true that he will talk about the church at Corinth, say, and the church at Thessalonica, but never with the smallest suggestion that they are two separate entities. No, it's just like talking about the air at Brighton and the air at Blackpool; the Church, for St Paul, is the atmosphere in which a Christian moves and has his being; even when some half-dozen slaves in some rich person's household had been converted to Christianity, St Paul used to speak of the Church in So-and-so's household. And heavens, how he is always going on and on at those early Christians, even then, about unity; telling them to be built up into one another, to grow up into a single body, and so on. For St Paul, the Church is at once something wholly united, and something wholly unique. The Bride of Christ, how could there be more than one Bride of Christ? The building of which Christ is the corner-stone; what more compact idea could you get of Christian fellowship? The Body of which Christ is the Head; how could there be more than one such Body, or how, outside the unity of that Body, can a man have a right to think of himself as united to Christ?

—Msgr. Ronald Knox

Christ Is in the Church

And so I find the living Christ by means of the living Church. That is as true to-day as it was on the first day. My faith in Christ is given me basically and preparatorily by the living apostolic word, perfectly and fulfillingly by the living Pentecostal Spirit. Like the apostles, the Church in her living teaching sets before me the image of the Lord, as the Bible luminously portrays Him, and as she has borne Him still more lovingly and radiantly for centuries in her heart. In a full and true sense she can say that she herself has seen this Jesus, that she stood beneath His Cross, and that she heard His Easter greeting: Peace be to you. Therefore she brings me into the closest historical relation to Jesus. She eliminates time from His picture, and she puts me in religious contact with Him. She can point out that the message of Jesus is not only recorded in lifeless parchment, but is embedded in world history by imperishable signs and wonders, that it is confirmed by a Life and Death of unsurpassable purity and innocence and by a Resurrection of dazzling glory, that it has been sealed by the life-blood of thousands and has given countless multitudes of her sons and daughters a new heart and a new conscience. She can assert further that no other religion has ever approached even distantly the moral and religious sublimity of Christianity. And she can maintain that the radiance of this divinity flashes forth and is externally manifested to-day also in noble saintly figures, that it attests itself in graces that appear ever and again with new brilliance, and in miraculous gifts.

—Karl Adam

Divine Life in the Church

Since her apostolic word proclaims and attests this and much else, the Church can make credible to me the supernatural mystery of Jesus. Her preaching prepares the way for my faith in Jesus. Her testimony becomes in that measure a motive of credibility, as the School expresses it, but is not yet a true motive of faith. It gives

123

me human faith, a certitude which is not as yet absolute, which is still frail.

But to living word is added the Spirit, the inspiration of the one divine Spirit in the communion of the faithful. The Holy Spirit alone gives our will the power and our understanding the light that we may be able to pass from the mere judgment of credibility to the unconditional affirmation of the mysteries of the faith, that is to true divine faith, and so come to the experience of Pentecost. The more closely the Catholic then gets into touch with his Church, nor merely externally, but internally, with her prayer and sacrifice, with her word and sacrament, the more sensitive and attentive will he be to the inspiration of the divine Spirit in the community, the more vitally will he grasp the divine life that flows through the organism of the Church. For "in proportion as a man loves the Church, so has he the Holy Spirit", says St. Augustine.

—*Karl Adam*

A Haven for Saints and Sinners   *April 28*

You may object that St Paul perhaps wasn't thinking of what we mean by the Church; he was thinking of the invisible Church, as it has sometimes been called—not a society of people distinguishable here and now by possessing a common faith and a common organization, but simply an ideal concept, the sum total of those souls whose names will, at last, be found written in the book of life. Only, you see, that won't do, because our Lord himself doesn't think of the Church in that way. The kingdom of heaven (which was his name for it) is like a mixed crop, part of it wheat, part of it cockle, only to be separated at the final judgment; it is like a net cast into the sea, which brings up fish for the dinner-table and fish which are of no use to anybody, not to be separated till the net is brought in to land. The Church, then, as Christ himself envisaged it is a visible Church, rogues and honest men mixed; not all members of the Church are bound for heaven by any means.

And if you look round, to-day, for a visible Church which is visibly one, there is hardly any competition, is there? I mean, Christians who belong to other denominations don't even claim, as a rule, that their denomination is *the* Church. Church unity is something which existed in the early ages, which will, it is to be hoped, come into existence again later on; it doesn't exist here and now. Anybody who has reached the point of looking round to find a single, visible fellowship of human beings which claims to be the one Church of Christ, has got to become a Catholic or give up his search in despair.

—Msgr. Ronald Knox

Jesus Teaches   *April 29*

Nicodemus comes to Jesus, and he is rather frightened. Here is a soul that is timid. Timidity in men, when it does exist, is much more distressing than in women. Men's tears are most unnerving things.

Nicodemus comes to Jesus by night. Without Jesus it is night, and we know, as soon as we get into His company, that before it was only night. No matter how bright outside the sunshine, it was really like night without Jesus.

How often we approach God timidly, wondering what He is going to steal from us, what He will take out of the very meagre store of joy we hold so closely. If we just thought of God as one whose chief aim was to rob us of our joys, we would not see that His presence is the light of day.

Nicodemus takes his courage into his hands and knocks at the door of truth. How much courage is demanded by that knock!

I am not sure that he begins the conversation in the right way. He begins by telling Jesus what he knows. "I know that Thou art a teacher from God." He was right, of course. Our Lord was that, and more. As soon as that Teacher begins to teach, Nicodemus doesn't learn. I think he is a most depressing figure. If we didn't know that after the death of Our Lord he found faith, he would be almost more depressing than the rich young man, who was so saddened because he got an answer to his question. Sometimes nothing so depresses us as an answer to prayer! We ask to do God's will—and He sends us cancer! Nicodemus is the only one of these two whose subsequent career is told. It is as if Our Lord says, "Father Vincent, you mustn't be too depressed about it. You could find yourself, like Nicodemus did."

He doesn't seem prepared to be taught. When Jesus Christ begins to teach him the fundamental things, his reason begins to be active—in the wrong way.

—Vincent McNabb

Nicodemus   *April 30*

Our dear Lord says, "Unless a man be born again, he cannot see the Kingdom of God." Well, of course, Our Blessed Lord is speaking of the soul. We have to take the words we use from the body and apply them to our mind and soul. Our Lord says something quite simple, "Unless you are converted" (turned). There is some higher life to which we must turn. And all the time this poor man's reason is off in the wrong direction, thinking about being born in the bodily sense. He thinks it is a strange sort of teaching. He is very much distressed by the idea of being born. Our dear Lord is saying, "You can't see unless you are born into a higher life, by My grace." God's first grace is to enable us to see what we can do, where we can go. We have to correspond to that first grace. People say, "I've done my best," but perhaps that is only pride. Very often when we say, "I've done my best," it seems to suggest that God hasn't done His best. Somebody hasn't done his best—and that is God. There are only two of us in the perfection of the soul. We say we have done our best, and we seem to be saying to God, "I wish You would do Your best for me." God is very useful for accepting all the blame. God is really at His best when things are at their worst. Can we truthfully say that we here below are all doing our best? That is a saying that should never be on our lips.

We can't even see unless we have accepted God's grace and have done all in our power to reach the higher thing. When we get higher we see more.

Our dear Lord doesn't pay any attention to poor Nicodemus's attempt at reasoning. He just goes on, and adds something. There are no mere repetitions in St. John's Gospel. If you examine closely anything that seems like a repetition, you will find there is a growth in idea. He has just added something that is vital.

This time, something seems to be repeated, "Unless a man be born again," but there is something added, "of water and the Holy Ghost." That is the sacramental system of God's visible Church.

— *Vincent McNabb*

Month of Mary   *May 1*

The problem which chiefly worries us in the world of our day, the problem of these terrible divisions which tear at human unity and destroy the possibility of peace, will be met in the Age of Mary by an understanding of the universal queenship of Our Lady, the Blessed Mother of the Universal Redeemer and Reconciler of all nations, all tribes, all classes, and all peoples.

From the ancient evil of the flesh our modern times have acquired as their besetting worry the contemporary cult of the human body, the quest of physical strength for its own sake, the admiration, indeed the adoration, of mere sensual beauty. Our times are plagued by literal heresies which arise from the cult of the physical and the love of the body: heresies on the political level like the heresy of Nazism with its pagan cult of blood; heresies on the esthetic level like the worship of the human form, the pagan cult of beauty; heresies on the scientific or pseudoscientific level like the health cults, the perverse religions of health which are contemporary expressions of the pagan cult of mere physical strength. In such an age the Church offers Mary assumed into heaven, body and soul integrated for all eternity, as a reminder of the true sanctity of the body, of the true dignity and the true beauty of human flesh as the spouse of the spirit, the servant of the soul, and the instrument of God, a means to the doing of the work of God.

Finally, from the devil in our modern age there comes the specific temptation of our times. The devil speaks to each generation in the terms most likely to seduce it. To one generation the devil speaks in terms of glory, to another in terms of conquest, to all in terms of pride. What is the principal approach which Satan makes in order to tempt our modern generation of Christian believers, and, specifically, of Catholics?

Our generation is too cynical to be seduced by promises of glory and magnificent victories. Wherefore I venture the opinion that the devil speaks to us in terms of worry. He tempts us with the spirit of defeatism and discouragement in the face of the titanic political, military, economic, social, and other worries of our day.

And so Mary, prefigured of old as the Woman who would crush the head of the serpent and cheat Satan of his victory, in our modern times must also help powerfully to correct the universal discouragement of the good, the sense of defeatism in believers, the plague of worry in the hearts of those who love God. In order to rouse our flagging spirits in a generation where Satan attempts to seduce believers by defeatism, discouragement, and worry, the Church offers us Mary of the *Magnificat*.

— *Cardinal John Wright*

The Perfect Christian   *May 2*

God spoke to the Devil and said: "I will establish a feud between thee and the woman, between thy offspring and hers; she is to crush thy head, while thou dost lie in wait at her heels." (Gen 3:15.) God was saying that, if it was by a woman that man fell, it would be through a woman that God would be revenged. Whoever His Mother would be, she would certainly be blessed among women, and because God Himself chose her, He would see to it that all generations would call her blessed.

When God willed to become Man, He had to decide on the time of His coming, the country in which He would be born, the city in which He would be raised, the people, the race, the political and economic systems which would surround Him, the language He would speak, and the psychological attitudes with which He would come in contact as the Lord of History and the Saviour of the World.

All these details would depend entirely on one factor: the woman who would be His Mother. To choose a mother is to choose a social position, a language, a city, an environment, a crisis, and a destiny.

His Mother was not like ours, whom we accepted as something historically fixed, which we could not change; He was born of a Mother whom He chose before He was born. It is the only instance in history where both the Son willed the Mother, and the Mother willed the Son. And this is what the Creed means when it says, "born of the Virgin Mary." She was called by God as Aaron was, and Our Lord was born not just of her flesh, but by her consent.

Before taking unto Himself a human nature, He consulted with *the Woman,* to ask her if she would give Him *a man.* The Manhood of Jesus was not stolen from humanity, as Prometheus stole fire from heaven; it was given as a gift.

The first man, Adam, was made from the slime of the earth. The first woman was made from a man in an ecstasy. The new Adam, Christ, comes from the new Eve, Mary, in an ecstasy of prayer and love of God and the fullness of freedom.

—*Archbishop Fulton J. Sheen*

The Mother   *May 3*

Anyone who would understand the nature of a tree, should examine the earth that encloses its roots, the soil from which its sap climbs into branch, blossom, and fruit. Similarly to understand the person of Jesus Christ, one would do well to look to the soil that brought him forth: Mary, his mother.

We are told that she was of royal descent. Every individual is, in himself, unique. His inherited or environmental traits are relevant only up to a certain point; they do not reach into the essence of his being, where he stands stripped and alone before himself and God. Here Why and Wherefore cease to exist: neither "Jew nor Greek," "slave nor freeman" (Gal 3:27–28). Nevertheless, the ultimate greatness of every man, woman, and child, even the simplest, depends on the nobility of his nature, and this is due largely to his descent.

Mary's response to the message of the angel was queenly. In that moment she was confronted with something of unprecedented magnitude, something that exacted a trust in God reaching into a darkness far beyond human comprehension. And she gave her answer simply, utterly unconscious of the greatness of her act. A large measure of that greatness was certainly the heritage of her blood.

From that instant until her death, Mary's destiny was shaped by that of her child. This is soon evident in the grief that steps between herself and her betrothed; in the journey to Bethlehem; the birth in danger and poverty; the sudden break from the protection of her home and the flight to a strange country with all the rigors of exile—until at last she is permitted to return to Nazareth.

—*Romano Guardini*

Mary Is Holy $\qquad$ *May 4*

God alone can claim the attribute of holiness. Hence we say in the Hymn, *"Tu solus sanctus,"* "Thou only art holy". By holiness we mean the absence of whatever sullies, dims, and degrades a rational nature; all that is most opposite and contrary to sin and guilt.

We say that God alone is *holy,* though in truth *all* His high attributes are possessed by Him in that fulness, that it may be truly said that He alone has them. Thus, as to goodness, our Lord said to the young man, "None is good but God alone". He too alone is Power, He alone is Wisdom, He alone is Providence, Love, Mercy, Justice, Truth. This is true; but holiness is singled out as His special prerogative, because it marks more than His other attributes, not only His superiority over all His creatures, but emphatically His separation from them. Hence we read in the Book of Job, "Can man be justified compared with God, or he that is born of a woman appear clean? Behold, even the moon doth not shine, and the stars are not pure, in His sight." "Behold, among His saints none is unchangeable, and the heavens are not pure in His sight."

This we must receive and understand in the first place; but secondly we know too, that, in His mercy, He has communicated in various measures His great attributes to His rational creatures, and, first of all, as being most necessary, holiness. Thus Adam, from the time of his creation, was gifted, over and above his nature as man, with the grace of God, to unite him to God, and to make him holy. Grace is therefore called holy grace; and, as being holy, it is the connecting principle between God and man. Adam in Paradise might have had knowledge, and skill, and many virtues; but these gifts did not unite him to his Creator. It was holiness that united him, for it is said by St Paul, "Without holiness no man shall see God".

And so again, when man fell and lost this holy grace, he had various gifts still adhering to him; he might be, in a certain measure, true, merciful, loving, and just; but these virtues did not unite him to God. What he needed was holiness; and therefore the first act of God's goodness to us in the Gospel is to take us out of our *un*holy state by means of the sacrament of Baptism, and by the grace then given us to re-open the communications, so long closed, between the soul and heaven.

We see then the force of our Lady's title, when we call her "*Holy* Mary". When God would prepare a human mother for His Son, this was why He began by giving her an immaculate conception.

—*Cardinal John Henry Newman*

Cause of Our Joy

[Mary is the Cause of] Our Joy. It is not only because she brought into the world the Christ who opens up to us the treasures of grace but also because in her human nature she exemplified what grace accomplishes. She is the Cause of Our Joy and therefore in troubled times she inspires us to optimism rather than leaves us in pessimism.

The great ages of faith were joyful and gay, golden and bright blue like the paintings of Fra Angelico because they so readily turned their attention from what human nature is at its worst to what human nature is at its highest and best, as in the immaculately conceived Mother of Christ. So I bid you also do in these days so discouraged, so pessimistic. Lift up your eyes to Mary. Meditate frequently on the doctrines that Holy Church, in such timely and providential fashion, has put before our eyes in these modern days. Think of the Immaculate Conception and the Assumption of the Blessed Mother in terms of what these tell us concerning our own nature, the destiny of our race, and our own spiritual dignity.

Meditating on these mysteries, you will be stirred by nostalgic memories of what we humans were when the world was young and we walked in the Garden of God before our fall in Adam. Then you will be strengthened and encouraged in the hope of what we yet may be, certainly in heaven but in some degree on earth, when we have prayed in Our Mother, Our Queen, but also our sister in humanity, and thus have become worthy of the promises of Christ.

— *Cardinal John Wright*

Mary

For our salvation you said Yes, for us you spoke your *Fiat;* as a woman of our race you accepted and bore in your womb and in your love him in whose Name alone there is salvation in heaven or on earth. Your Yes of consent ever remained, was never revoked, even when the course of the life and death of your Son fully revealed who it was that you had conceived: the Lamb of God, taking on himself the sins of the world; the Son of Man, nailed to the Cross by our sinful race's hatred of God, and thrown, him the Light of the world, into the darkness of death, the lot that was ours. In you, holy Virgin, who stood under the Cross of the Redeemer (the real tree of the knowledge of good and evil, the real tree of life), as the second Eve and mother of all the living, it was redeemed humanity, the Church, that stood under the Cross and received the fruit of redemption and eternal salvation.

Here, virgin and mother, a congregation of the redeemed and the baptized has now gathered together. Here, then, where the communion of all the saints is visible and tangible, in this community, we ask you for your intercession. For the communion of saints includes those on earth and those who have attained their end and perfection, and in it none lives to himself alone. You do not do so either, then. You pray for all who are linked with you in this community as redeemed brothers and sisters.

—Karl Rahner

The Virgin   *May 7*

Holy Virgin, truly mother of the eternal Word who has come into our flesh and our life, Lady who conceived in faith and in your blessed womb the salvation of us all, and so are the mother of all the redeemed, you who live ever in God's life, near to us still, because those united to God are nearest to us.

With the thankfulness of the redeemed, we praise the eternal mercy of God that redeemed you. When your existence began, sanctifying grace already was yours, and that irrevocable grace was with you always. You walked the way of all the children of this earth, the narrow paths which seem to wander so aimlessly through this life of time, commonplace, sorrowful roads, until death. But they were God's ways, the path of faith and unconditional consent: "Be it done unto me according to thy word." And in a moment that never passes, but remains valid for all eternity, your voice became the voice of all mankind, and your Yes was the

Amen of all creation to God's irrevocable decree. You conceived in faith and in your womb him who is at once God and man, creator and creature, changeless unalterable blessedness, and an earthly life marked out for bitter death, Jesus Christ our Lord.

—*Karl Rahner*

Age of Mary   *May 8*

Modern times have been described as the Age of Mary. What does this phrase mean?

I suppose that it means, first of all, that the age in which we live is an age in which we Christians have grown in our understanding of the place of Mary in the life of the Church, in the work of the redemption, and in the divine scheme of things. It is now one hundred years since Pope Pius IX began the modern development of our understanding concerning the Blessed Mother by defining the dogma of her Immaculate Conception. It is but four years since our Holy Father Pope Pius XII defined the dogma of her Assumption into heaven. In between these two polar points of doctrine concerning Mary, a whole world of new understanding of the truth with respect to her and of new appreciation of her privileges has come into being.

Accordingly, we refer to modern times as the Age of Mary because it is in modern times that our Holy Mother the Church has brought us to a more mature understanding of her doctrine concerning the Blessed Mother of Christ.

Then, too, the Age of Mary is properly attributed to our times because of the mighty growth of devotion to the Blessed Mother of Christ in the modern world, a growth in loving piety.

—*Cardinal John Wright*

Mary's Charity

Our most lovable and never-sufficiently-loved Lady and Mistress, the glorious Virgin, had no sooner given her consent to the words of the angel Gabriel than the mystery of the Incarnation was accomplished in her. Upon hearing from the same holy Gabriel that her kinswoman Elizabeth had in her old age conceived a son [Lk 1:36], she desired, being her relative, to go to see her, so that she might wait upon her and be a comfort to her during her pregnancy, for she knew that such was the divine will. And, says the Evangelist St. Luke, she immediately left Nazareth, the little town of Galilee where she lived, to go into Judea to the house of Zechariah. *Abiit in montana:* She went up into the hill country of Juda and set out upon the journey, though it was long and difficult; for, as many authors remark, the town where Elizabeth dwelt is 27 leagues distant from Nazareth; others say a little less, but in any case it was a rough enough road for this weak and delicate Virgin, because it was mountainous.

Thus, aware of a divine inspiration, she started out. She was not drawn by any curiosity to see if what the angel had told her was really true, for she had not the least doubt about it, but rather she was quite certain that things were exactly as he had declared.

— Saint Francis De Sales

The Visitation

It was an unheard-of wonder that St. Elizabeth, who had never had any children, and who was barren, should have in her old age conceived. Or else, say they, it may be that she had some doubt with regard to what the angel had announced to her—which is not true, and St. Luke condemns and refutes them by the words which he writes in his first chapter: that St. Elizabeth, seeing the Virgin enter, exclaimed: Blest is she who trusted that the Lord's word to her would be fulfilled. [Lk 1:45]. It was not therefore curiosity nor any doubt as to the pregnancy of St. Elizabeth which made her undertake this journey, but rather many desirable motives, of which I will mention a few.

She went in order to see that great wonder, or that great grace, which God had worked on behalf of this good old and barren woman, that she should conceive a son in spite of her barrenness, for she knew well that in the Old Law it was a subject of reproach to be childless; but because this good woman was old, she also went that she might be of service to her during this time of her pregnancy, and offer her all the help she possibly could. Secondly, it was in order to tell her of the exalted mystery of the Incarnation which had been worked in her; for Our Lady was not unaware that her kinswoman Elizabeth was a just person [Lk 1:6], very good, and God-fearing. She also knew that she ardently desired the coming of the Messiah, promised in the Law for the Redemption of the world.

— Saint Francis De Sales

Devotion to Mary   *May 11*

I have no intention of attempting a sketch of the history of devotion to Mary—such an effort would require a long book. How much would have to be included, how many names and titles would have to be cited! There are, first of all, those sublimely prayerful and wondrous hymns which rose up like the best fruits of the soul in the Middle Ages: the *Ave Maris Stella,* the *Regina Coeli,* the *Alma Redemptoris Mater,* the *Salve Regina* so dear to Godefroy de Bouillon's Crusaders, and dear to Saint Bernard as well. There is also the angelical salutation, the *Ave Maria,* whose history is linked to the development of devotion to Our Lady. Pages of meditations, ceaselessly repeated through the ages, recount the grace and virtues of Mary, and the words in which they do so are the words of Saint Anselm, Saint Bernard, Saint Albert the Great, Saint Thomas Aquinas, Saint Bonaventure, Blessed Henry Suso, Saint Francis de Sales, Cardinal de Bérulle, M. Olier, and the great Jacques-Bénigne Bossuet, as well as of a host of others. In the roll of poets who have sung her glory, poets from Ruteboeuf to Péguy, we find names of varying degrees of fame, among them Arnoul Gréban and Pierre Gringoire, Dante, Camoëns, and Corneille. The great Marian devotion, the Rosary, began obscurely in the eleventh century and was later systematically developed by Saint Dominic.

—Henri Daniel-Rops

Be Like Mary

May 12

Our dear Lady wrapped Him up in swaddling-clothes. The original Greek means "swathed Him," clad Him. That means our actions should be clad with the supernatural garment of Charity, which keeps Life in them. Our Lady clothed Him; and our actions, too, should be clothed in the Love of God, done for the Love of God and from the desire of doing His Holy and Adorable Will. The most important of all unions with the Beloved is identity of will. We remember the man who was expelled from the Feast. He did not have on the garment of Charity.

There is another point that is also very important. Our Lady laid Him in His little manger—a place of protection. Our actions are not safe except when they are in their proper place. Don't think this is just advice to lay folk. I don't know that there is any person who should be so careful to fly the occasions of sin as a priest. It is no good his preaching these things to you if he is not preaching much more intimately to himself. Perhaps Our dear Lord is saying: "Yes, Father Vincent, I hope you are taking it all to yourself. Don't you preach to those people as if you are all right." If there is anyone in the whole world should be most careful, it is the priest who carries such treasures in an earthen vessel, and who has to be in the world and yet not of it. Please don't think I am suggesting this for you alone.

—Vincent McNabb

Her Humility

Many of the tragedies of the mind and will not made up are really tragedies of not getting the proper circumstances. It is exceedingly difficult. Being in the religious life is not an occasion of sin, but it might be the occasion of my wasting my time in this, that or the other. Certain circumstances of our own doing and our own choice make it more difficult for us to do the right thing. It is always difficult. There is no reason why we should make it harder.

We have to take very great care to lay our first-born in the manger. Only there shall we find hard things made as easy as can be. They are never easy—exhilarating sometimes, but never easy. It is always folly to make them more difficult.

Well then, we can just speak to Our Lady about her Little One, her First-born, and about her perfection, "How are you so perfect?" She would reply: "Go away, child. I'm not perfect. What do I know about perfection? Go and ask my Son about it." Her reply would be one of the most perfect humility. She would know all about it in the concrete, but she might not be able really to express it. I expect there would be tears in her eyes and in her voice, as she began to sing the "Magnificat." I hope one day we shall be able to sing it, too. Even now we may just cry out with Our Lady: "He hath done great things to me, in regarding the humility of His servant."

—Vincent McNabb

Our Mother

The coming of Christ through Mary was God putting Himself under an obligation to God. The Incarnation put us into relations with God the Son and Father. And at the same time it put the human race into the same charmed circle of relations. That is the reason why, one day on the mountain-top, Jesus taught us to say "Our Father" and another day, on another sad mountain-top, His dying lips taught us to say "Our Mother."

Mother's love is boundless. No matter how much God blesses

her with offspring, she loves each as all and all as each. Friends' love often fades. It is for the day and when the day passes the friendship passes with it. Mother's love never changes, nor grows old, nor passes away. Whilst she lives, it lives.

—*Vincent McNabb*

Woman of Sorrow

Mary was also a Woman of Sorrow, To love God immediately and uniquely makes a woman hated. The day she brought her Babe, her Divine Love, to the Temple, the old priest Simeon told her that a sword her soul would pierce. The hour the Roman sergeant ran the spear into the Heart of Christ, he pierced two hearts with one blow—the heart of the God-man for Whom Mary gave up the knowledge of pleasure, and the heart of Mary, who gave her beauty to God and not to man.

—*Archbishop Fulton J. Sheen*

Mary's Suffering   *May 15*

There may be something unreal in picturing Our Blessed Lady in throes of grief with Our Blessed Lord on her lap. We have nothing to go upon in the Gospels. Only once does her name appear in the account of the Crucifixion, in the words, "Now there *stood* by the Cross of Jesus His Mother." (John 19:25.) Sorrow had been so faithful a companion of her life that she knew well how to meet it and ride its storms. It is consciousness of pain that is the greatest pain. Every paroxysm of grief that distracts the soul from the source of its pain is an anodyne. Our Blessed Lord drank, or more truly sipped, the chalice to the dregs by the unruffled vividness with which He allowed each spring of anguish to play upon Him. He bore His cross not merely patiently but calmly. It was only at the last moment, when His heart was breaking, that He cried out "with a loud voice." Those who saw

Our Blessed Lady standing at the foot of the cross might have taken her calmness for the daze of sudden shock or for the unresponsiveness of a dull heart to great mental anguish. But her apparent indifference was in a manner the ecstasy of suffering in which her soul, at issue with a great sorrow, allowed it the unruffled, undistracted sovereignty of her sensitive nature.

— Vincent McNabb

Beneath the Cross   *May 16*

Ecce Mater Tua. "And He gave him to His Mother." This sounds like a prelude to the sweetest words ever uttered on Calvary. For how else could He give a son to His mother but by saying, "Woman, behold thy son?" (John 19:26).

The Catholic tradition on the meaning of these words gives us a fair idea of Our Blessed Lady's place in Tradition. From the first times, I believe, these words were taken to mean that Our Divine Lord on the Cross had two thoughts in His poor suffering mind. He was a son; thus He thought of His Mother. He was a Saviour, and He thought of sinners. The longing to see His Mother's grief stayed made Him give her St. John as her son; now He Himself was leaving her. The longing to comfort His shepherdless flock made Him give His own Mother to be their Mother. You may deny this tradition and say it is untrue; but you cannot deny that for hundreds of years it was held to be true; and you have a hard task before you to prove that your opinion of the nineteenth century is truer than the constant opinion of the second and third centuries.

— Vincent McNabb

Sin, in all its forms, is the deliberate eviction of Love from the soul. Sin is the enforced absence of Divinity. Hell is that absence of God made permanent by a last act of the will. God does not do anything to the soul to punish it; the soul produces hell out of its very self. If we excluded air from the lungs as we exclude love from the soul, the lungs could not blame God because we got red in the face or fainted, or our lungs collapsed. What the absence of air is to the lungs, that the absence of love in the soul is to the soul. On this earth want of love makes people red; in the next life want of love makes a red hell.

The great problem is now how to save these two groups, those who have taken the Gift and forgotten the Giver, and those who have rejected both Gift and Giver.

The answer is to be found in the attention that a mother would give to her little son with the stomach-ache. It is not in the nature of a mother to abandon those children who hurt themselves by their own folly. Immediately, she manifests what might be called "the mutual relation between contraries," for example, the rich helping the poor, the healthy nursing the sick, the learned instructing the ignorant, and the sinless helping the sinful. There is something about motherhood which is synonymous with the maximum of clemency, and which prevents us from being conquered in advance through despair and remorse by giving us hope in the midst of sins. It is the nature of a human mother to be the intercessor for the child before the justice of the father, pleading for her little one, asking that the child be dismissed, or saying that he is not understood, or that he should be given another chance, or that, in the future, he will improve. A mother's heart is always full of pity for the erring and the sinner and the fallen. No child ever offended a father without offending a mother, but the father concentrates more on the crime, the mother on the person.

—*Archbishop Fulton J. Sheen*

As a physical mother watches over an ailing child, so does Mary watch over her erring children. The one word never associated with her is Justice. She is only its mirror. As the Mother of the Judge, she can influence His Justice; as Mother of Mercy, she can obtain mercy. Twice in history, kings of power promised half their kingdom to a woman: once when a woman solicited a king by her vice; once when a woman inspired a king by her virtue. King Herod, seeing his stepdaughter Salome dance, and being less intoxicated by the wine than by the lasciviousness of her as a whirling dervish, said: "Ask me whatever you will and I will give it to thee, even though it be half of my kingdom." Salome consulted with her mother, Herodias, who, recalling that John the Baptist had condemned her divorce and remarriage, said to her daughter: "Ask for the head of John the Baptist—on a dish." Thus John lost his head. But it is always better to lose one's head in John's way than in Herod's!

The other king was Assuerus, who had made the dust of the land run red with the blood of the Jews. Esther, the beautiful Jewish maid, fasted before petitioning him to have mercy on her people; the fasting made her more lovely than before. The cruel tyrant, as cruel as Herod, seeing the loveliness of the woman said: "Ask me whatever you desire and I will give it to you though it be half my Kingdom." Unlike Salome, she asked not for death but for life, and her people were spared. Woman is by nature the temptress. But she can tempt not only toward evil like Salome, but to goodness as did Esther.

—Archbishop Fulton J. Sheen

Our Intercessor *May 19*

Through the centuries the Church Fathers have said that Our Lord keeps for Himself half His regency, which is the Kingdom of Justice, but the other half He gives away to His Mother, and this is the Kingdom of Mercy. At the Marriage Feast of Cana, Our Lord said that the hour of His Passion was not yet at hand—the hour when Justice would be fulfilled. But His Blessed Mother begged Him not to wait, but to be merciful to those who were in need, and to supply their wants by changing water into wine. Three years later, when not the water was changed into wine, but the wine into blood, He fulfilled all Justice, but surrendered half His Kingdom by giving to us that which no one else could give, namely, His Mother: "Behold thy Mother." Whatever mothers do for sons, that His Mother would do, and more.

Throughout all history the Blessed Mother has been the link between two contraries: the eternal punishment of hell for sinners and the universal unlimited Redemption of Her Divine Son. These extremes cannot be reconciled except by mercy. Not that Mary pardons—for she cannot—but she intercedes as a mother does in the face of the justice of the father. Without Justice, mercy would be indifference to wrong: without mercy, Justice would be vindictive. Mothers obtain pardon and forgiveness for their sons without ever giving them the feeling of "being let off." Justice makes the wrongdoer see the injustice in the violation of a law; mercy makes him see it in the sufferings and misery he caused those who love him deeply.

—*Archbishop Fulton J. Sheen*

Mary Will Assist Us   *May 20*

An evil man who is let off will probably commit the same sin again, but there is no son saved from punishment by his mother's tears who did not resolve never to sin again. Thus, mercy in a mother is never separated from a sense of justice. The blow may not fall, but the effect is the same as if it had.

What mysterious power is it that a mother has over a son that, when he confesses his guilt, she strives to minimize it, even when it shocks her heart at the perversity of the revelation? The impure are rarely tolerant of the pure, but only the pure can understand the impure. The more saintly the soul of a confessor, the less he dwells on the gravity of the offense, and the more on the love of the offender. Goodness always lifts the burden of conscience, and it never throws a stone to add to its weight. There are many sheaves in the field which the priests and sisters and the faithful are unable to gather in. It is Mary's role to follow these reapers to gather the sinners in. As Nathaniel Hawthorne said: "I have always envied the Catholics that sweet, sacred, Virgin Mother who stands between them and the Deity, intercepting somewhat His awful splendor, but permitting His love to stream on the worshipper more intelligibly to human comprehension through the medium of a woman's tenderness."

Mary will assist us if we but call upon her. There is not a single unhappy soul or sinner in the world who calls upon Mary who is left without mercy.

—Archbishop Fulton J. Sheen

Mother of Christ   *May 21*

Each of the titles of Mary has its own special meaning and drift, and may be made the subject of a distinct meditation. She is invoked by us as the *Mother of Christ.* What is the force of thus addressing her? It is to bring before us that she it is who from the first was prophesied of, and associated with the hopes and prayers of all holy men, of all true worshippers of God, of all who "looked for the redemption of Israel" in every age before that redemption came.

Our Lord was called the Christ, or the Messias, by the Jewish prophets and the Jewish people. The two words Christ and Messias mean the same. They mean in English the "Anointed". In the old time there were three great ministries or offices by means of which God spoke to His chosen people, the Israelites, or, as they were afterwards called, the Jews, *viz.,* that of Priest, that of King, and that of Prophet. Those who were chosen by God for one or other of these offices were solemnly anointed with oil—oil signifying the grace of God, which was given to them for the due performance of their high duties. But our Lord was all three, a Priest, a Prophet, and a King—a Priest, because He offered Him-

144

self as a sacrifice for our sins; a Prophet, because He revealed to us the Holy Law of God; and a King, because He rules over us. Thus He is the one true Christ.

—Cardinal John Henry Newman

Mother of the Messiah   *May 22*

It was in expectation of this great Messias that the chosen people, the Jews, or Israelites, or Hebrews (for these are different names for the same people), looked out from age to age. He was to come to set all things right. And next to this great question which occupied their minds, namely, *When* was He to come, was the question, *Who* was to be His Mother? It had been told them from the first, not that He should come from heaven, but that He should be born of a woman. At the time of the fall of Adam, God had said that the *seed* of the *Woman* should bruise the Serpent's head. Who, then, was to be that Woman thus significantly pointed out to the fallen race of Adam? At the end of many centuries, it was further revealed to the Jews that the great Messias, or Christ, the seed of the Woman, should be born of their race, and of one particular tribe of the twelve tribes into which that race was divided. From that time every woman of that tribe hoped to have the great privilege of herself being the Mother of the Messias, or Christ; for it stood to reason, since He was so great, the Mother must be great, and good, and blessed too. Hence it was, among other reasons, that they thought so highly of the marriage state, because, not knowing the mystery of the miraculous conception of the Christ when He was actually to come, they thought that the marriage rite was the ordinance necessary for His coming.

—Cardinal John Henry Newman

We Need Mary *May 23*

The worries of our generation which spring from the center and move about into the spirit of the world are worries due to the aggressive and fratricidal divisions which plague mankind. We have inherited all the old vertical divisions of the human race: the divisions of race, nations, languages, and empires. All these old vertical divisions which pit man against man and brother against brother, these are with us still because of the spirit of the world. To these vertical divisions, as if to complicate them, there have been added new horizontal divisions which now cut across nations, language groups, and empires to set class against class within the same nation, child against parent within the same family, generation against generation within the same community, liberal versus conservative within the same party.

And so, in an age which finds the world plagued by horizontal and vertical divisions which pit us against one another, the Church offers us the image of Mary.

— Cardinal John Wright

Our Mother *May 24*

Ours is the Age of Mary because the worries of our generation are such as invite her sweet mercies and such as call for the healing influence of the truths which the Holy Catholic Church preaches concerning the Mother of Christ. It is always dangerous to speak of the evils of the hour as if they were something entirely new and hitherto unheard of. They are not. The things which discourage us, the things which sicken us, are all of them as old as sin, as old as treason, as old as death, as old as defeat, as old as sickness, as old as war. These are, of course, the very things which worry us. These are the evils of the hour, and they are the oldest worries in the world.

They are the evils which from time immemorial the spirits of truth and virtue have associated with the three-fold source of all sin and all grief. The worries of our modern age are as old as the world; they are as old as the flesh; they are as old as the devil. We pay the evils of the world too great tribute when we pretend that they are new and strong and fresh. They are not! They are merely new manifestations, at the most new forms, of these old unholy three—the world, the flesh, and the devil. They take new emphases. They appear in changing and sometimes novel forms, but it is to these three, the world, the flesh, and the devil, in the modern guises of their old temptations, that the doctrine of Holy Mother Church concerning the Blessed Mother of Christ brings timely and powerful counteraction.

—Cardinal John Wright

Queen of Our Country   *May 25*

The petition for the designation of the Immaculate Conception as the patroness of the United States was made eight years before the solemn definition of the dogma in her regard has always been a further joy to Catholic Americans. One cannot doubt that it has also been a source of special graces to the United States and, one ventures to say, to the hierarchy which officially took the action by which this happy choice was made in 1846. It is surely not too much to suggest that the Blessed Mother must have exercised a providential patronage over the proceedings of the Plenary Council itself and, as a result, over the myriad aspects of Catholic American life subsequently influenced by it.

—Cardinal John Wright

Blessed Mary

All generations have called her blessed. The Angel began the salutation; he said, "Hail, thou that art highly favoured; the Lord is with thee; blessed art thou among women." Again he said, "Fear not, Mary, for thou hast found favour with God; and, behold, thou shalt conceive in thy womb, and bring forth a Son, and shalt call His name Jesus. He shall be great, and shall be called the Son of the Highest." Her cousin Elizabeth was the next to greet her with her appropriate title. Though she was filled with the Holy Ghost at the time she spake, yet, far from thinking herself by such a gift equalled to Mary, she was thereby moved to use the lowlier and more reverent language. "She spake out with a loud voice, and said, *Blessed art thou* among women, and blessed is the fruit of thy womb. And whence is this to me, that the mother of my Lord should come to me?" ... Then she repeated, "Blessed is she that believed; for there shall be a performance of those things which were told her from the Lord." Then it was that Mary gave utterance to her feelings in the Hymn which is the Magnificat.

— *Cardinal John Henry Newman*

Our Patroness

May 26

The intercessory power of the servants of Christ who have triumphed through His grace is great before the throne of God. How much greater is the power of her who is not only a servant of God but the mother of His incarnate Son? Christ gave His Mother to all Christians on Calvary. The universal Catholic people have taken Mary to themselves by their creed and their cult, but Catholic Americans have made her their especial patroness by the deliberate and formal action of the special representatives of her Son in His Church in the United States.

The ties that bind us to the Immaculate Mother are therefore many and strong. The needs of the Church and of the members of Christ's Mystical Body in the United States are many and urgent. There is no one who can intercede for us with Christ more effectively than His Mother. The consequences of her patronage for us cannot be exaggerated and should not be minimized. Catholic Americans are Mary's devotees by the added title of her election as our principal patroness.

— *Cardinal John Wright*

Mother of the Church

The Blessed Virgin Mary is the Mother of the Church and therefore the example, as well as the guide and inspiration, of everyone who, in and through the Church, seeks to be the servant of God and man and the obedient agent of the promptings of the Holy Spirit.

The Holy Spirit, as Pope Leo XIII reminded us, is the soul of the Church: All the activity and service of the members of the Church, beginning with the supreme participation of the Blessed Mother in the work of the Church, is vivified by the Holy Spirit as the body, in all its activities, is vivified by its soul. The Holy Spirit is the Paraclete, Advocate, and Comforter which Christ Himself sent to be our consolation in the sorrowful mysteries of life, our source of moderation in the joyful mysteries of life, our added principle of exaltation in the glorious mysteries of life.

So He was for the Blessed Mother; so also He is for the least of us; so also He is for the rest of the Church, even for those who are its *unconscious* but *conscientious* members.

Wherever there is *faith* there is the example of Mary, because she lived by faith as the Scriptures remind us. . . .

If, then, piety is the virtue which binds us to the sources of all life, to God, to our parents, to the Church, to Christ, certainly Christian piety binds us, in grateful love, to Mary—or our acceptance of Christ and of the mystery of our kinship with Him is imperfect, partial, and unfulfilled.

—Cardinal John Wright

Magnificat

The Seed of the woman, announced to guilty Eve, after long delay, was at length appearing upon earth, and was to be born of [Mary]. In her the destinies of the world were to be reversed, and the serpent's head bruised. On her was bestowed the greatest honour ever put upon any individual of our fallen race. God was taking upon Him her flesh, and humbling Himself to be called her offspring;—such is the deep mystery! She of course would feel her own inexpressible unworthiness; and again, her humble lot, her ignorance, her weakness in the eyes of the world. And she had moreover, we may well suppose, that purity and innocence of heart, that bright vision of faith, that confiding trust in her God, which raised all these feelings to an intensity which we, ordinary mortals, cannot understand. *We* cannot understand them; we repeat her hymn day after day,—yet consider for an instant in how different a mode *we* say it from that in which she at first uttered it. *We* even hurry it over, and do not think of the meaning of those words which came from the most highly favoured, awfully gifted of the children of men. "My soul doth magnify the Lord, and my spirit hath rejoiced in God my Saviour. For He hath regarded the low estate of His hand-maiden: for, behold, from henceforth all generations shall call me blessed. For He that is mighty hath done to me great things; and holy is His name. And His mercy is on them that fear Him from generation to generation."

— Cardinal John Henry Newman

Mary Is Chosen   *May 29*

Now in the sixth month the angel Gabriel was sent from God to a town of Galilee called Nazareth, to a virgin betrothed to a man named Joseph, of the house of David, and the virgin's name was Mary. And when the angel had come to her, he said, "Hail, full of grace, the Lord is with thee. Blessed art thou among women." When she had seen him she was troubled at his word, and kept pondering what manner of greeting this might be.

And the angel said to her, "Do not be afraid, Mary, for thou hast found grace with God. And behold, thou shalt conceive in thy womb and shalt bring forth a son; and thou shalt call his name Jesus. He shall be great, and shall be called the Son of the Most High; and the Lord God will give him the throne of David his father, and he shall be king over the house of Jacob forever; and of his kingdom there shall be no end."

But Mary said to the angel, "How shall this happen, since I do not know man?"

And the angel answered and said to her, "The Holy Spirit shall come upon thee and the power of the Most High shall overshadow thee; and therefore the Holy One to be born shall be called the Son of God. And behold, Elizabeth thy kinswoman also has conceived a son in her old age, and she who was called barren is now in her sixth month; for nothing shall be impossible with God."

— Saint Luke

The Kindness of Mary   *May 30*

Now in those days Mary arose and went with haste into the hill country, to a town of Juda. And she entered the house of Zachary and saluted Elizabeth. And it came to pass, when Elizabeth heard the greeting of Mary, that the babe in her womb leapt. And Elizabeth was filled with the Holy Spirit, and cried out with a loud voice, saying, "Blessed art thou among women and blessed is the fruit of thy womb! And how have I deserved that the mother of my Lord should come to me? For behold, the moment that the sound of thy greeting came to my ears, the babe in my womb leapt for joy. And blessed is she who has believed, because the things promised her by the Lord shall be accomplished."

And Mary said,

> "My soul magnifies the Lord,
>   and my spirit rejoices in God my Savior;
> Because he has regarded the lowliness of
>   his handmaid;
>   for, behold, henceforth all generations shall
>   call me blessed;
> Because he who is mighty has done great things
>   for me,
>   and holy is his name;
> And for generation upon generation is his mercy,
>   to those who fear him.

He has shown might with his arm,
    he has scattered the proud in the conceit of
      their heart.
He has put down the mighty from their thrones,
    and has exalted the lowly.
He has filled the hungry with good things,
    and the rich he has sent away empty.
He has given help to Israel, his servant,
    mindful of his mercy—
Even as he spoke to our fathers—
    to Abraham and to his posterity forever."

And Mary remained with her about three months and returned
to her own house.

—Saint Luke

Blessed Virgin *May 31*

Let us consider in what respects the Virgin Mary is Blessed; a title
first given her by the Angel, and next by the Church in all ages
since to this day.

I observe, that in her the curse pronounced on Eve was changed
to a blessing. Eve was doomed to bear children in sorrow; but
now this very dispensation, in which the token of Divine anger
was conveyed, was made the means by which salvation came into
the world. Christ might have descended from heaven, as He went
back, and as He will come again. He might have taken on Himself
a body from the ground, as Adam was given; or been formed, like
Eve, in some other divinely-devised way. But, far from this, God
sent forth His Son (as St. Paul says), "made of a woman." For it has
been His gracious purpose to turn *all* that is ours from evil to
good. Had He so pleased, He might have found, when we sinned,
other beings to do Him service, casting us into hell; but He
purposed to save and to change *us*. And in like manner all that
belongs to us, our reason, our affections, our pursuits, our relations in life, He needs nothing put aside in His disciples, but all

sanctified. Therefore, instead of sending His Son from heaven, He sent Him forth as the Son of Mary, to show that all our sorrow and all our corruption can be blessed and changed by Him. The very punishment of the fall, the very taint of birth-sin, admits of a cure by the coming of Christ.

— *Cardinal John Henry Newman*

The Church Sanctifies Her Members   *June 1*

We must consider the . . . holiness of the Church. Here we are in a somewhat more embarrassing position when we start arguing with our friends outside the Church; they're so apt to expect rather too much, aren't they? The usual explanation the books give . . . is that "holiness" in the Church is proved partly by the continuance of miracles within her fold, and partly by the existence of the religious orders, with their special cult of perfection. The Church (we are told) has her ups and downs, her bad patches here and there, but we've still got Lourdes and we've still got Carmel. I've no quarrel with that explanation, but I think you can put the thing rather more simply in this way — Christians of any other denomination, if they describe that denomination as "holy" at all (which they very seldom do), are referring in fact to the individual holiness of its members. Whereas when we talk about the Holy Catholic Church we aren't thinking, precisely, of the holiness of its members. We think of the Church as sanctifying its members, rather than being sanctified by its members. Sanctity — what a hard thing it is to define! There is a kind of *bouquet* of mystery about Catholic ceremonial, there is a kind of familiarity about the attitude of Catholics towards death and what lies beyond death, there is a patient acceptance of little oddnesses and inconveniences about the practice of religion, which you don't find outside the Church itself.

— *Msgr. Ronald Knox*

The author of the *Imitation of Christ* says: "I had rather feel compunction than know how to define it." It is his own emphatic and strenuous way of saying that a full and perfect following of Christ is less a matter of theology than of ascetics. Life in the meaning of the scholastics was essentially motion arising within a soul and coming to rest outside its starting-point. Christian life was action rather than contemplation, warfare rather than peace.

I have been called upon to write on that most ascetic of all subjects, prayer. I should be doing myself and you an ill turn if at the end you knew whatever concerned prayer, yet did not know or know better how to pray. The words I shall address to you would be vain babbling if they charged and overcharged your mind and failed to stimulate your will. I had rather you knew how to pray than that you knew the definition of prayer. Yet because of him who writes and you who read it will not be within our power to keep ourselves altogether away from that philosophical appeal to principles which is the essence of theology. One who has been brought up on theology can hardly banish it from his thoughts and words. Nor if he could would he feel called upon to do so in speaking to what might be called the undergraduates of life. For we are looking forward to you becoming in God's day the lay-folk of thought and action who are to champion God's interests. No seeming humility will divorce you from your responsibilities. If you are to be men and women of work and worth, you must be men and women of principle, that is, you must not merely act upon principles, but you must know the principles upon which you act.

Now the appeal to the principles of our acts leads some men to occupy themselves with thoughts rather than deeds, with philosophy rather than with ethics, with theology rather than with ascetics; and all this to the utter emptying of the true content of a following of Jesus Christ.

— *Vincent McNabb*

Here, in one phrase of Our Lord, is the essential prayer of the soul, "Lord, be merciful to me, a sinner."

You and I can say that we sin seven times a day, not necessarily with a sin that is grievous, but at least a sin. Its guilt can be wiped away by any act of charity or act inspired by charity. Then humility utters the second prayer and beseeches God for mercy; and, of course, we are less anxious to obtain mercy from God than God is to give it to us. We poor strayed sheep never seek to return to God as earnestly as He seeks to find us when we have strayed. "God, be merciful to me, a sinner."

This then is one of the essential parables, with a great lesson for us to learn. I have suggested that in many of these parables God is teaching us that new thing not to be found in the Old Book, the *how* to grow nearer to Him. Here it is described in one story — that of the soul's approach to God by prayer. This is one way in which our prayer can fulfil His own command and be something that we can do always.

The very work of our hands can be a prayer; indeed I have ventured to suggest that our first duty lies in our work, and that work done as the will of God is our first prayer. I think that, if you and I carry into our work this conviction that we are sinners and need God's mercy, our very work can be the prayer of prayers. How very different would be our relations with our neighbour if we realized we were sinners and needed not God's justice, but God's mercy. These thoughts are not just for the hours we spend within the walls of a church, before the Blessed Sacrament, but something we have to take out into the world. This spirit must go through all our actions and then our actions will be right with our neighbour.

— *Vincent McNabb*

How wonderfully reassuring are Our Lord's words, "He returned to his own home, justified." There is no mention of the Pharisee going back to his own home. It seems as if our dear Lord has spoken deliberately of home in one case and withheld all mention of it in the other;—because I think the poor sinner through pride is a homeless being; he doesn't own his soul; he is only a lodger in it.

But Our Lord says of the humble soul, conscious almost more of its sin against God than of God Himself, that he went back to his own house; and now his house is his home in a way it had never been before, because God is now a guest of that soul; and when God is a guest in the soul, that soul is at home with itself.

The Publican went back justified, raised up to the supernatural, lifted beyond earth. In his contrition, he felt himself less than the earth, sinful; in his humility he was raised above man, companion of the very angels who now have full sight of the face of God.

I think it will be easy for us to take into our thoughts this inimitable story Our Lord has told. "I hope, dear Lord, You have told it to me about myself. I hope I am not being the Pharisee. I fear that I may be. I do not know if I am the Publican. At least I desire to be. I know that if I confess my sins, I shall be his brother. He has not sinned more than I. Shall I have his humility? Is my confession of sin merely lip-humility, or is it humility of heart? I know not. Thou who alone readest the heart can tell each heart what is in it, for in these great matters of humility every heart is hidden from itself.

"I do not ask to know if I am justified; but oh, dear Lord, I wish to go down justified into my own home. Come Thou into my heart that Thou mayest there be at home and I at home with Thee."

—Vincent McNabb

The style of the prayer of Jesus is revealed in the prayers to which we have just alluded and, with the most unimpeachable authenticity, in the *Pater*. We find nothing sentimental in it, no bombast, no rhetoric. With God also, our word must be "Yes? Yes. No? No" (Mt 5:37). We must not be forever repeating the same old thing, as the pagans do (cf. Mt 6:17). The prayer of Jesus is simple and manly, direct, sure, filled with nobility and grandeur. It translates in perfect fashion the filial attitude, made up of submission and love, confidence and fearlessness, of which Jesus is the very revelation.

Scripture is not very specific about the concrete aspects, external and perceptible, of the prayer of Jesus. He raised His eyes to heaven (cf. Mk 7:34; Jn 11:41; 17:1). During His agony, He prayed on His knees (Lk 22:41) and even prostrated with His face to the ground (Mt 26:39). He prayed with loud cries and tears (cf. Heb 5:7). Outside of these particular instances, Scripture says nothing about the bodily attitudes Jesus preferred while praying. Did He stand up? Did He bend His knees, as in Christian practice? This is not made clear.

The prayer of Jesus embraces the two great themes of all prayer: simple praise and petition. The *Pater* itself is thus apportioned. It sums up all the prayer of Jesus, all Christian prayer, and we understand why the Christian authors who wanted to write a treatise on prayer simply commented on the Our Father. This apportionment into two parts evidently corresponds to the double and unique commandment of love of God and of our neighbor, and also to the two tables of the Law which are summed up and consummated in this love.

We have heard Jesus giving thanks (Mt 11:25; Lk 10:21; Jn 11:41; and note 12 above). Jesus loved His Father so much and adhered to His will with so much filial love that He experienced, in the Holy Spirit, great thrills of joy in seeing the Father's design of salvation being realized, a design which was to lead to glory, not by the way of exaltation and power, but by the way of abasement and weakness. It cannot be questioned that this prayer of loving and joyous adherence to the will of the Father was coextensive with the whole earthly life of Jesus.

— Yves Congar

The Necessity of Prayer   *June 6*

Our prayer will be quite out of place if we are not doing our duty towards others. We should never break off an act of charity to others in order to pray. If our prayer is inconvenient to somebody else we ought to be serving, it is not in the right place. If it is a burden to someone else to whom we have a duty, it will have no cutting edge, it will be of little value. That is often a distinct difficulty among some Catholics. They make it appear that the Church fosters a kind of piety which depends on somebody else working so that we may pray. You see here that Our Lord was busy right up to the time when He went up into a mountain to pray. It is no good starting our prayers until we have fulfilled all our duties.

Well, dear children in Jesus Christ, prayer is absolutely necessary. When we have attained to the use of reason, we cannot be saved without prayer. I need not say, therefore, that there are a great number of ways of praying. Our dear Lord said we should pray always. Everything we are doing should be either a prayer in itself or can be made into a prayer. Any action that is not in itself wrong can be done in union with God and His divine will.

— Vincent McNabb

Accept God's Will   *June 7*

The Apostles saw Our Lord praying and they were so struck that they asked Him to teach them to pray. "John taught his disciples. Would You teach us?" They had really been praying when they asked Him, because that asking was a prayer, though they did not know it.

He answered their request at once. They never thought He

would give them this wonderful prayer, the "Our Father." That prayer instructs us at once that anything can be made into a prayer. We can pray "Thy will be done" about everything that comes into our lives. If at the back of our minds we do not want God's will to be done, then our words are not a prayer. If we try to twist God's will round to our will, it is no use praying "Thy will be done." We are really asking God to come round to our point of view. And yet, in our heart, as we say those words, we really do want to come round to His point of view. I am quite sure that God's Intelligence Department understands exactly what we mean, and even though it seems as if we want our own will, He understands when we pray "Thy will be done" that we are wishing we could accept His will for us. St. Augustine said that even when God refuses the desire of our heart, He never refuses the heart of our desire. That is very beautiful, and it is right. I am sure there is no such thing as unanswered prayer. All prayers are answered. Sometimes the answer doesn't suit, that's all. We think God hasn't answered us, when He has answered us bountifully. We ask Him to make us good, and He tries to make us saints, but we go about grousing and saying that He never answers our prayers!

— *Vincent McNabb*

The Our Father   *June 8*

You will remember that Our Blessed Lord had said to the seventy-two disciples that they should pray to the Lord of the harvest that He send labourers into His vineyard. I can quite imagine that they discussed that matter with each other. Discussions like that are better than mere gossip. No doubt, therefore, they discussed that matter of prayer, and said, "We had better ask Him." I imagine it would be St. Peter. They saw their Master praying and they took that opportunity to put their question to Him. It really was a perfect prayer. No doubt they did not think they were praying. Some persons say, "I don't know how to pray," when they may be praying all day long, their whole attitude one of prayer. St. Peter would have been greatly surprised if I had said to him, "Well, St.

Peter, I am a theologian and that is a most perfect little prayer." It would be most interesting to go through the Gospels and see the number of times Our Lord was asked a question, and how it was answered. I think the "Our Father" was given to us on the spur of the moment and it is one of the great proofs that Our Lord is God. What genius did it take to make it! It is like a blade of grass, made so simply but in such a way that all the geniuses in the world have not discovered all about it.

— Vincent McNabb

Ask Help

Our prayer, then, may well consist, in its substance, in a petition for grace to do God's will in all the duties of our life. There is quite possibly a danger that we may think prayer consists in a number of pious thoughts about Jesus Christ and other holy things, but if all that does not end with a petition for help to supernaturalize all the ordinary duties of our life, our prayer would be merely intellectually satisfying, and of no real value whatever.

Just look at the practical value of the "Our Father." "Give us this day our daily bread," give us grace to go out and do our daily work. May I be a good clerk, or milliner, or whatever it is, "and please give me grace not to be impatient with the children."

There is no grace (grace is the ladder to glory) that comes to us without petition. Hence the necessity for saying the "Our Father." In that prayer we ask explicitly for all the supernatural things we need. That is why the Church has put the "Our Father" solemnly into Holy Mass. It comes into the Divine Office again and again, in every hour, so that when the hours are said aloud there are fourteen or fifteen "Our Fathers" said every day. Why? Because we are asking for things we cannot obtain without our asking, and we must obtain them.

— Vincent McNabb

Heavenly bliss is conditioned by our asking. If we really do ask for these things, all our other petitions are conditioned by them. When we say "Thy will be done," we really mean, this thing is bigger than we know. Give us what Thou art prepared to give. It might be this thing or the other, some temporal help, or a bodily affliction. We are conforming our will implicitly to whatever He sends. We don't know what it is, yet we say "Thy will be done. Let Thy grace come into my soul that I may be able to do Thy will." It is like the word Our Blessed Lady said, *"Fiat,"* "Let it be done," as if the doing were going to come from above—as it does. We cannot believe, or do, without God's strength, and so we pray "Thy will be done."

Hence, when we say the "Our Father," we are meditating on all these things. If we meditate on the scourging, or the crowning with thorns, it would not be much use if it were only that. We must think, too, "To-day I have got to get over my impatience. Yesterday I betrayed You by my impatience or my selfishness. I wouldn't listen. I was very headstrong. And to-day so-and-so is coming and I mustn't lose my temper." I rather think that should be the substance of the beginning of our prayer.

And so I think all this comes out of the extraordinary story about the woman who wanted to be revenged and who went off to the judge who was not afraid of man or of God. She nagged at him. Ah, he yielded merely because she persevered in going on asking.

Dear Lord, perhaps to ask once is not sufficient sign of desire; but we must ask again and again; and our continual knocking on the door that is closed will tell the Doorkeeper that we really want to go in; we feel left out in the darkness, and we really do want to enter. The Doorkeeper opens, not because we have tried His patience, but because He knows that the thing we utter frequently we really do desire, and that we have gone on knocking through the conviction that our desire will at last be fulfilled.

—*Vincent McNabb*

"Thy Will Be Done" *June 11*

All our prayer should be conditioned by the "Our Father." We should never really pray about individual things except by praying "Thy will be done"; because we can never tell what individual thing is going to profit us, or whether it will turn out to be a catastrophe. I have known people who have lost all their money. If you had told them six months before that it was going to happen, they would have nearly died of shock. Later on they blessed God for it. They had become very much happier. They had found their friends. People really don't know at the time how to value what comes to them at the hands of God. The way to take it is to say "Thy will be done." It doesn't make for fatalism. It is still God's holy and adorable will that we should do what we can. I speak feelingly. When I was a child, two doctors said I was going to die. My mother took me off to a third. That was the proper way of interpreting God's will. It was not God's will that St. Joseph should leave Our Lady and the Child in Bethlehem to be killed. No, they must go off to Egypt. I always love to think of how St. Joseph would break the news to Our Lady. "My dear, I have terrible news." "What is that, dear?" "We have got to go into Egypt." "I'll be ready in a minute." They had not much luggage, of course.

— Vincent McNabb

Keep Asking *June 12*

We have this extraordinary story about the woman who wanted vengeance. A woman who wants vengeance is ten times worse than a man; it is so unnatural to women. The corruption of the best is always the worst. When women want vengance there is almost no satisfying them—like the woman who asked for the head of John the Baptist. Herod wouldn't have killed him, but she wanted vengeance. We have to be careful about seeking vengeance, even in slight things. We never know where it may lead us.

Who would have believed that Our Blessed Lord would have

used this parable about—prayer! So many books have been written about prayer! (Some I think ought not to have been written!) How many would begin like this? It was told in this way that people might be jolted into remembering. A placid inland river is quite easy to forget; but a wild seascape is quite impossible to forget.

We ask, how could God tell a story like that? It is introduced to tell us something about prayer. The great essential quality of prayer is asking for something, and going on asking. To go on asking is a little bit difficult. We must ask for the right things, of course. It is not easy to know what is the right thing to ask. The right things are all in the "Our Father," but they are all in general—ultimate right things for eternity. As a rule we are far more concerned with the things of to-day than with eternity. We seem to say, take care of to-day, and eternity will take care of itself. Well, in a sense, to-day is the making of eternity. It is the way in. If we really did take proper care of to-day eternity would be all right, but only on condition that we look on to-day as a preparation for eternity.

—Vincent McNabb

Parables   *June 13*

From a literary standpoint, the parables are frequently wonderful little works. Having first tickled our curiosity, they charm us by their stories, by their features so finely observed and set forth. We get the inkling that there is something in them that we must figure out, some application of them that we must make. Each parable is a challenge: it is not simply a riddle, for it aims at getting the one who hears it into action; it puts him a question; better still, it puts *him* in question.

When the high priests and the pharisees are told the parable of the two sons sent by their father into the vineyard, or the one about the murderous vine-dressers, they are being asked to see themselves in the son with the willing words and the disobedient will, or in the vine-dressers who kill the servants and even the son of the master, so as to preserve their exploitation from interference.

Long since, under the former dispensation, the prophets had put forward similar parables. When David had had Uriah, Bathsheba's lawful husband, put to death, so that he could freely possess her, Nathan told him the tale of the rich man with many flocks and herds, who, to entertain a travelling friend, took the one little lamb, tenderly pampered, of a poor man.... "The man who has done this deserves to die!", David cried out. Nathan replied: "You are the man" (2 Sam 12:1ff.).

—*Yves Congar*

"Teach Us to Pray" *June 14*

St Luke, the special Evangelist of our blessed Lord's priesthood and prayer, relates that on a certain day his divine master "was in a certain place praying," and "when he ceased one of his disciples said to him, 'Lord, teach us to pray'" (Luke 11:1). His little band of followers had come upon him perhaps at daybreak after one of those long night watches that spurred rather than curbed the fervour of his soul. And his prayer seemed in its mysterious and profound self-abasement so far beyond them that the secret of it appeared to them to be something which he alone could teach. Somewhat in the same way we may have found that whereas the many words we have hitherto heard on prayer have left us unmoved, the thought of our blessed Lord's mysterious communion with his heavenly father may move us to make our own that child-like cry of the Apostles, "Lord, teach us to pray." Moreover, such is the difficulty of dealing with the subject of Christ's prayer that unless he who is called upon to speak looked beyond and above himself for light he could but shrink from the task as above his strength. Only under the sure guidance of divine teaching can the preacher there unveil the mysteries and impart the lessons that lie hidden in the communion of the soul of Christ with his heavenly father. In what we are about to say, our own words shall be as few as may be. Our whole aim will be to set down with what order and clearness we can, all that is taught us of our blessed Lord's prayer by the Gospels and by theology, nor shall we overlook anything that should be spoken by confining ourselves almost wholly to St Luke amongst the Evangelists, and to St Thomas amongst the theologians.

The Gospel of St Luke, like the same writer's Acts of the Apostles, opens with scenes that lead the reader straightway into an atmosphere of prayer. With Hellenic grace the Evangelist opens the story of Jesus Christ in the Temple of Jerusalem, where Zachary, a priest, is about to offer incense and prayer. Outside, "the multitude of the people were praying." And God, who loves to yield to a people's prayer, sent down that day the first glad tidings of the herald of the Great King.

— Vincent McNabb

Jesus Prays   *June 15*

To St Luke, . . . we are indebted for the story of the Presentation, when Mary brought her male child to the Temple, and a greater than Zachary offered up his mute child-prayers to his heavenly father. Again, it is the same Evangelist who recalls the yearly paschal pilgrimage to the Holy City, together with what befell the parents of Jesus when he stayed behind in the Temple on his father's business. All these brief descriptions serve St Luke to introduce the priesthood and the sacerdotal prayer of the God made Man.

Now, though the mentions of Christ's prayer are not very numerous, even from the pen of St Luke, it is astonishing how much is conveyed by them. To bring this home to our mind we will arrange what we have to say under certain headings. Thus our blessed Lord used *mental prayer* as the very breath of his human soul. No special mention is made of this form of prayer, probably for the reason that he followed his own command of "praying always." With us, continuity of prayer is insured by our good intention. Even as we cannot explicitly love God in every act of our daily lives, neither can we explicitly pray at all times. It is only from time to time that we can raise our minds to God, thanking him for the moments or hours that have sped, and offering up the moments, hours, or years that still remain to us. Our blessed Lord suffered no interruption to his continuous prayer. His mind always saw the face of his father, and the inward conversation of his soul was of and in Heaven. There were times, no doubt, of special dedication to mental prayer. The long watches of the night were no doubt given over to this exercise. But at all times his soul was raised on high in a region of divine things, where, to use the striking saying of St Augustine, "He took counsel of the eternal ideas."

— Vincent McNabb

Christianity

June 16

Christianity is a mystery of death and life, but it is especially a mystery of life. As you know, death was not included in the Divine plan; it was the sin of man that brought it upon the earth; sin, which is the negation of God, has produced the negation of life, namely, death. If therefore, Christianity requires renunciation, it is in order to immolate that in us which is contrary to life; we must remove the obstacles that are opposed to the free development within us of the Divine life which Christ brings us: He is the great Author of our holiness, without Him we can do nothing. It is therefore not a question of seeking or practising mortification for itself, but primarily in view of facilitating the development of the Divine germ placed within us at Baptism. St. Paul, in telling the neophyte he must "die to sin", does not include in this single formula all the practice of Christianity: he adds that he must still be "alive unto God, in Christ Jesus".

— Abbot Marmion

God is omnipotent and has the right of claiming the obedience of beings that receive their life from Him; . . . God is supreme goodness worthy of being preferred to all that is not Himself; [sin] puts God beneath the creature. *Non serviam:* "I know Thee not, I will not serve Thee," says this soul, repeating the words of Satan on the day of his revolt. Does it say them with the lips? No, at least not always; perhaps it would not like to do so, but it says them in act. Sin is the practical negation of the Divine perfections; it is the practical contempt of God's rights: practically, if such a thing were not rendered impossible by the nature of the Divinity, this soul would work evil to the Infinite Majesty and Goodness; it would destroy God.

And was it not this that happened? When God took to Himself a human form, did not sin slay Him?

I have already said that the Passion of Christ is the most striking revelation of God's love, *Greater love than this no man hath.* Neither is there a deeper revelation of the immense malice of sin. Let us for a few moments contemplate the sufferings that the Incarnate Word endured when the hour came for Him to expiate sin; we can hardly form any conjecture into what an abyss of agony and humiliation sin caused Him to descend.

Christ Jesus is God's own and only Son. In Him His Father is well pleased; all the work of the Father is to glorify Him: *I have both glorified . . . and will glorify again,* for He is full of grace, grace superabounds in Him; He is "a high priest holy and innocent"; though He is like unto us, He, however, knows neither sin nor imperfection. "Which of you," said He to the Jews, "shall convince Me of sin?" "The prince of this world" (that is to say, Satan) " . . . in Me hath not anything." This is so true that it is in vain His most bitter enemies, the Pharisees, searched into His life, examined His doctrine, spied upon all His actions, as hatred knows how to do, and sought to ensnare Him in His speech. They could find no pretext to condemn Him; in order to invent one, they had to have recourse to false witnesses. Jesus is purity itself, the reflection of His Father's infinite perfections, "the brightness of His glory".

—Abbot Marmion

What is demanded of the Christian is to *intervene* in the destiny of the world, winning at great pains and at the risk of a thousand dangers—through science and through social and political action—a power over nature and a power over history, but remaining, whatever he does, more than ever a *subordinate* agent: servant of divine Providence and activator or "free associate" of an evolution he does not direct as a master, and which he also serves, insofar as it develops according to the laws of nature and the laws of history (themselves founded on the dynamism of "natures").

One must understand, moreover, that the Christian can, and must, ask for the coming of the kingdom of God in glory, but is not entitled to ask for—nor to propose as the end of his temporal activity—a definite advent of justice and peace, and of human happiness, as the term of the progress of temporal history: for this progress is not capable of any final term.

—Jacques Maritain

Love

He, who is filled with the love of God, is moved by every aspect of the Word made flesh. At prayer, the sacred image of the Man-God is constantly before his eyes; he sees him at birth, sees him grow to manhood, sees him teach, die, rise from the dead, ascend into heaven.

— Saint Bernard Of Clairvaux

Jesus Tells of Truth   *June 19*

Son: Walk before Me in truth: and seek Me ever in simplicity of thy heart. He that walks before Me in truth; shall be safe from the approach of harm: and the Truth shall set him free from seducers and from the slanders of unjust men. If the Truth have made thee free thou shalt be free indeed: and shalt not heed vain words of men.

Lord it is true. As Thou sayest, so I beseech Thee let it be with me. Let Thy Truth teach me; guard me: and keep me unto salvation at the last. Let it release me from all evil affection and inordinate love: and I shall walk with Thee in great freedom of heart.

I will teach thee saith the Truth what is right: and pleasing in My sight. Think on thy sins with great displeasure and grief: and never hold thyself in honour because of good works. In truth thou art a sinner: assailed and encompassed by many passions. Of thyself thou art ever drifting towards nothingness; quickly falling, quickly conquered: quickly confounded, quickly dissolved. Thou hast nought to boast of; but much reason to scorn thyself: for thou art far weaker than thou canst understand. Therefore let nothing seem great unto thee of all that thou doest. Let nothing seem great, nothing precious and wonderful, nothing worthy of esteem; nothing high, nothing truly praiseworthy and desirable: but that which is eternal. Let the eternal Truth delight thee above all things: and let thy utter unworthiness be a constant grief unto thee. Fear nothing blame nothing flee nothing so anxiously, as thy vices and sins: which ought to discomfort thee more than any losses of earthly things.

Some walk not sincerely in My sight, but led by curiosity and pride wish to know My secrets and understand the high things of God: neglecting themselves and their salvation. These often fall into great temptations and sins through their pride and curiosity when I set myself against them. Fear the judgments of God: dread the wrath of the Almighty. Do not pry into the works of the Most High: but search diligently thine own iniquities what great faults thou hast committed: and how much good thou hast neglected.

— *Thomas à Kempis*

Serving God

We are to serve God. How we do this will depend on each one's personal vocation. God calls us to serve Him in different ways. One factor is common to all of us. Everything human, except sin, has a new significance since God became man. Jesus Christ lived the ordinary life of a carpenter of his day in Nazareth, and by doing so he has made holy all ordinary things and activities. When you work, for example, the Father is reminded of the fact that His divine Son once worked too; when you sit around chatting to friends, the Father remembers that His Son did the same. This may sound just a bit naive on a first reading, but think about it. It is an idea rich in consequences, for it means that whatever we do (except, always, what is sinful) looks different to the Father than it does to us. You have that floor to sweep. Nothing very dramatic in that. God sees more than the sweeping. He sees it as a service of Him, and this because His Son did that kind of thing for thirty years of his life. Almost nothing has been recorded of those years lived by Our Lord in the family at Nazareth. As news value they are of no consequence, but where it truly matters those years are precious indeed. And so it is for all of you. Your daily work is your daily service of God. To make that service a loving one adds to it, both in giving honour to God and in the joy you will experience.

—Cardinal Basil Hume

Love Our Neighbor

The more we get to know God, and the greater our understanding of His love for us becomes, the more easily does our service through ordinary tasks become deeply satisfying. It will not stop work from being burdensome, boring and frustrating at times. The satisfaction comes from it being a loving service of God; in itself the task to be done may be unspeakably dull. Much of our work is.

When we think of our lives in terms of service of God, we

cannot, must not, neglect the second commandment. We have to love our neighbour as ourselves. It is important to be clear about our responsibilities and duties in respect of other people. Our spiritual lives are not ways of being comfortable, of finding peace and joy for ourselves only. Our striving for union with God is a personal and private matter no doubt. But the Gospel command to love other people is very clear. And this does not mean just having a vague sense of goodwill towards people. It involves not only wishing good things for other people, but helping them to obtain them. It will involve action. Would you leave a man to die starving in the street outside your home, while you remain within reading the Bible and praying? That contrast is perhaps expressed too brutally, but it makes a telling point; the first and second commandments are not easily separated. St John puts it clearly enough: "Let us therefore love God, because God first hath loved us. If any man say 'I love God', and hateth his brother whom he seeth, how can he love God whom he seeth not? And this commandment we have from God, that he who loveth God love also his brother" (1 Jn 4:19–21).

— *Cardinal Basil Hume*

Courage   *June 22*

Discretion warns us against wasted effort: but for the coward all effort is wasted effort. Discretion shows us where effort is wasted and when it is obligatory.

Laziness flies from all risk. Discretion flies from useless risk: but urges us on to take the risks that faith and the grace of God demand of us. For when Jesus said the kingdom of heaven was to be won by violence, He meant that it could only be bought at the price of certain risks.

And sooner or later, if we follow Christ we have to risk everything in order to gain everything. We have to gamble on the invisible and risk all that we can see and taste and feel. But we know the risk is worth it, because there is nothing more insecure than the transient world. *For this world as we see it is passing away.* (1 Cor 7:31)

Without courage we can never attain to true simplicity. Cowardice keeps us "double minded"—hesitating between the world and God. In this hesitation, there is no true faith—faith remains an opinion. We are never certain, because we never quite give in to the authority of an invisible God. This hesitation is the death of hope. We never let go of those visible supports which, we well know, must one day surely fail us. And this hesitation makes true prayer impossible—it never quite dares to ask for anything, or if it asks, it is so uncertain of being heard that in the very act of asking it surreptitiously seeks by human prudence, to construct a makeshift answer. (cf. James 1:5–8)

What is the use of praying if at the very moment of prayer, we have so little confidence in God that we are busy planning our own kind of answer to our prayer?

— Thomas Merton

The Way of Jesus   *June 23*

[Jesus] is the Way, the only way by which to come to the Eternal Father: NO MAN *cometh to the Father,* BUT *by Me;* except this foundation pre-established by God, nothing is stable: *For other foundation* NO MAN *can lay, but that which is laid: which is Christ Jesus.* Without this Redeemer and without faith in His merits, there is no salvation, still less holiness: NEITHER *is there salvation in* ANY OTHER. *For there is no other name under heaven given to men, whereby we must be saved.* Christ Jesus is the only Way, the only Truth, the only Life. Who follows not this way goes astray from truth and seeks in vain for life. *He that hath the Son hath life. He that hath not the Son hath not life.*

To live supernaturally is, for us all, to share in the plenitude of Divine life that is in Jesus Christ: *I am come that they may have life... And of His fulness we all have received.* We received our state of adoption through him. We are only children of God in the measure we are conformed to Him Who, alone, is by right the only true Son of the Father, but Who wills to have with Himself a multitude of brethren through sanctifying grace. All the supernatural work considered from God's point of view is summed up in this.

It was in order that we might receive this grace of adoption that Christ came and gave Himself to us: *That we might receive the adoption of sons;* and that He has confided all His treasures and all powers to the Church. He sends and continues to send "the Spirit of Truth", the sanctifying Spirit, to direct her and perfect, by His action in souls, the work of sanctification, until this mystical body comes, at the end of time, to its last perfection. Beatitude itself, the crowning of our supernatural adoption, is nothing less than the inheritance Christ shares with us: *Heirs of God, and joint heirs with Christ.*

—Abbot Marmion

Feast of John the Baptist   *June 24*

Now in the fifteenth year of the reign of Tiberius Caesar, when Pontius Pilate was procurator of Judea, and Herod tetrarch of Galilee, and Philip his brother tetrarch of the district of Iturea and Trachonitis, and Lysanias tetrarch of Abilina, during the high priesthood of Annas and Caiphas, the word of God came to John, the son of Zachary, in the desert. And he went into all the region about the Jordan, preaching a baptism of repentance for the forgiveness of sins, as it is written in the book of the words of Isaias the prophet,

> "The voice of one crying in the desert,
>   'Make ready the way of the Lord,
>   make straight his paths.
> Every valley shall be filled,
>   and every mountain and hill shall be
>   brought low,
> And the crooked shall be made straight,
>   and the rough ways smooth;

and all mankind shall see the salvation
of God.'"

He said therefore to the crowds that went out to be baptized by
him, "Brood of vipers! who has shown you how to flee from the
wrath to come? Bring forth therefore fruits befitting repentance,
and do not begin to say, 'We have Abraham for our father'; for I
say to you that God is able out of these stones to raise up children
to Abraham. For even now the axe is laid at the root of the trees;
every tree, therefore, that is not bringing forth fruit is to be cut
down and thrown into the fire."

And the crowds asked him, saying, "What then are we to do?"
And he answered and said to them, "Let him who has two tunics
share with him who has none; and let him who has food do
likewise."

— Saint Luke

Follow Jesus *June 25*

What could be more touching than this, "They heard John speak
and they followed Jesus." They had been learning from John,
learning to follow. John had set them this lesson of lessons, "I am
the voice of one crying in the wilderness—heralding Another."
When greatness hails still further greatness, it is at its highest. This
is John the Baptist at his greatest, humility at its highest.

"And they followed Jesus"—of course not knowing exactly
whom they were following, or why. They were just following.

The soul is not beginning well until it has the idea of following
somebody. Until it has the sense of being quite unworthy of following, it is not going forward. Unless we feel unworthy of the company of the glorious Leader we are following, we are going back.

It says so simply, "Jesus turning and seeing them." God sees us,
not for the first time, but in a new way, seeing something more in
us that He has now given to the soul. One who was a sinner is
now His son, or daughter. "Son, thy sins are forgiven thee." "Be
of good heart, daughter."

He asks them, "What seek ye?" How wonderful of God to ask a question. Of course every step we take, by God's grace, towards Himself is instantly rewarded by another grace of God. Now He asks them what they are seeking—what is their aim in life. I imagine He gave them the grace of coming close to the right answer, when they put another question, "Rabbi" (Master, a very sweet and tender name for God), "where dwellest Thou?" As the name of no town is given, possibly they were not near any town, but were scattered in tents, like those tents children put up in the London parks in summer time, just a pole with something stretched across, to protect from the heat of the day and the cold radiation of the night. "The Word was made flesh and dwelt among us." Of course, as you know, the Greek word is "to tent with," to set up His little tent with ours.

— *Vincent McNabb*

"Come and See" *June 26*

Many souls are not interested in where Jesus Christ dwells. But there alone is Truth to be found.

Then the words, "Come and see," and they came and saw. It is like St. John's story of the blind man (in the ninth chapter of his Gospel). Our dear Lord told him to go to the pool of Siloe and wash, and the man said "I went. I washed. I see."

"They came and they saw where He dwelt." They came to Love and saw where Love dwelt. Of course it was to no palace that they came, but to something poorer than their own fisher dwellings by the lakeside. The riches of a home are not the walls and roof and furniture, but the One who dwells there. How poor is a home without love! But how rich is the stable and the manger, full of the love of God for you and me—for sinful you and me.

Well, to-night, we listen to Our Lord saying to us "Come and see." And we might say to Him, very humbly, "Where dwellest Thou?" To-night it is very dark all over the land. There are a few stars, but they are very dim and we can't see by them. We cannot see very far ahead into the future. There is no certainty in the world to-day. We cannot see what is coming. Ah! Jesus tells us to come and we shall see. We will see how vain are the merely earthly pursuits of men. All their designs for making a heaven on earth are not worth seeing. If we go to Nazareth we will see not many things—perhaps a vine trailing on the wall, a little hand clutched in love and fear, as the little one is in danger of the dark. But God is dwelling with us, and surely that is enough for human life. We who are inside God's covenanted mercies, we come and we see.

—Vincent McNabb

To God through Christ   *June 27*

To approach Christ in all the attractiveness of His humanity is at the same time to draw near to the God Who "inhabiteth light inaccessible." Though devotion may dwell, human-wise, upon the mysteries which reveal His manhood, we should never forget that it is strictly unorthodox to consider Our Lord's human nature apart from the Godhead with which it is inseparably united. We must pass "by the wounds of His humanity so as to reach the intimacy of the divinity." The same truth is taught us by the Preface for the Mass of Christmas: "so that while we acknowledge Him as God seen by men, we may be drawn by Him to the love of things unseen." It is in this connection that St Thomas makes the following observation: "Matters concerning the Godhead are, in themselves, the strongest incentives to love and consequently to devotion, because God is supremely lovable. Yet such is the weakness of the human mind that it needs a guiding hand, not only to the knowledge, but also to the love of divine things by means of certain sensible objects known to us. Chief among these is the humanity of Christ . . . Wherefore matters relating to Christ's humanity are the chief incentive to devotion, leading us thither as a guiding hand, although devotion itself has for its principal object matters concerning the Godhead."

—Dom Aelred Graham

Be devoted to God and do not fear, for no wounds can come to those who follow Christ. Even if they take away the life of your body, Christ is still with you. When you have found him, know how to live with him so that he may not have to leave you. He is quick to desert those who do not care for him.

Nobody can teach you better than the Church herself how you are to keep Christ with you. As the Scripture says, "Then when I had scarce left them, I found him so tenderly loved; and now that he is mine I will never leave him, never let him go." With what ties Christ is to be held. We hold him not by force, nor by chains, but rather by the bonds of love. He is held by the mind knowing him and the heart loving him. So if you want to hold Christ, seek him constantly and do not fear. It is frequently in pain of the body, amid the very hands of persecutors, that Christ really is found. "When I had scarce left them, I found him." In a little while, in a brief moment, when you have escaped the hands of your persecutors, and have not given in to the ways of the world, Christ will meet you and will not allow you to be tempted further.

One who seeks Christ and finds him can say with the Scripture writer, "I will never leave him, never let him go till I have brought him into my mother's house, this room that saw my birth." What is this room except the inner secret of your own person? Keep this inner room clean, so that when it is pure, unstained by sin, your spiritual home may stand as a priestly temple with the Holy Spirit dwelling in it. One who seeks and entreats Christ is never abandoned, but visited by him frequently, for he stays always with us.

— Saint Ambrose

Depend on Jesus   *June 29*

God cannot reject us when we thus rely on the power of His Son; for the Son treats with Him as equal with equal. When we thus acknowledge that of ourselves we are weak and . . . that we can do nothing, *Without Me you can do nothing,* but that we hope for everything from Christ, all that we need in order to live by the Divine Life, *I can do all things in Him who strengtheneth me,* we acknowledge that this Son is everything for us, that He has been established as our Chief and High Priest. That is, says St. John, to render very acceptable homage to the Father "Who loves the Son", Who wills that everything should come to us through the Son because He has given Him all power of life for souls. The soul that has not this *absolute* confidence in Jesus does not fully acknowledge Him for what He is—the beloved Son of the Father, and hence does not render to the Father that honour which He absolutely requires: *For the Father loveth the Son, ... that all men may honour the Son, as they honour the Father. He who honoureth not the Son, honoureth not the Father Who sent Him.*

In the same way, when we approach the Sacrament of Penance, let us have great faith in the divine efficacy of the Blood of Jesus. It is this Blood which in this sacrament cleanses our souls from their sins, purifies them, renews their strength, and restores their beauty.

—Abbot Marmion

We Will Be Raised Up   *June 30*

But we carry this treasure in vessels of clay, to show that the abundance of the power is God's and not ours. In all things we suffer tribulation, but we are not distressed; we are sore pressed, but we are not destitute; we endure persecution, but we are not forsaken; we are cast down, but we do not perish; always bearing about in our body the dying of Jesus, so that the life also of Jesus may be made manifest in our bodily frame. For we the living are constantly being handed over to death for Jesus' sake, that the life also of Jesus may be made manifest in our mortal flesh. Thus death is at work in us, but life in you. But since we have the same spirit of faith, as shown in that which is written—"I believed, and so I spoke"—we also believed, wherefore we also speak. For we know that he who raised up Jesus will raise up us also with Jesus, and will place us with you. For all things are for your sakes, so that the grace which abounds through the many may cause thanksgiving to abound, to the glory of God.

Wherefore we do not lose heart. On the contrary, even though our outer man is decaying, yet our inner man is being renewed day by day. For our present light affliction, which is for the moment, prepares for us an eternal weight of glory that is beyond all measure.

—*Saint Paul*

Religious Authority   *July 1*

The sages, it is often said, can see no answer to the riddle of religion. But the trouble with our sages is not that they cannot see the answer; it is that they cannot even see the riddle. They are like children so stupid as to notice nothing paradoxical in the playful assertion that a door is not a door. The modern latitudinarians speak, for instance, about authority in religion not only as if there were no reason in it, but as if there had never been any reason for it. Apart from seeing its philosophical basis, they cannot even see its historical cause. Religious authority has often, doubtless, been oppressive or unreasonable; just as every legal system (and especially our present one) has been callous and full of a cruel apathy. It is rational to attack the police; nay, it is glorious. But the modern critics of religious authority are like men who should attack the police without ever having heard of burglars. For there is a great and possible peril to the human mind: a peril as practical as burglary. Against it religious authority was reared, rightly or wrongly, as a barrier. And against it something certainly must be reared as a barrier, if our race is to avoid ruin.

—*G. K. Chesterton*

Reason and Faith July 2

That peril is that the human intellect is free to destroy itself. Just as one generation could prevent the very existence of the next generation, by all entering a monastery or jumping into the sea, so one set of thinkers can in some degree prevent further thinking by teaching the next generation that there is no validity in any human thought. It is idle to talk always of the alternative of reason and faith. Reason is itself a matter of faith. It is an act of faith to assert that our thoughts have any relation to reality at all. If you are merely a sceptic, you must sooner or later ask yourself the question, "Why should *anything* go right; even observation and deduction? Why should not good logic be as misleading as bad logic? They are both movements in the brain of a bewildered ape?" The young sceptic says, "I have a right to think for myself." But the old sceptic, the complete sceptic, says, "I have no right to think for myself. I have no right to think at all."

There is a thought that stops thought. That is the only thought that ought to be stopped. That is the ultimate evil against which all religious authority was aimed. It only appears at the end of decadent ages like our own.

—G. K. Chesterton

Moral Duty July 3

In reality the life and death of Jesus are tokens not of God's justice but of His friendship and loving kindness. Even the attribute of divine mercy, with its faint suggestion of patronage and aloofness, is withheld from our eyes in order that we may perceive more clearly what it means to be beloved of God. Equality is the keynote of the Incarnation; for by it we are no longer, or not only, the King's servants, we are also His friends. To this we shall return; it is mentioned here by way of emphasizing the gratuitousness of grace. Without a realization of this we can understand neither the significance of the supernatural life nor the innate potentialities of the human nature which that life elevates and perfects.

A word must now be said about man's activities viewed in their moral aspect. This is in fact the ultimate point of view, the final court of appeal. By the moral goodness or badness of our actions do we have status as men, by them shall we be judged in eternity if not also in time. As we shall attempt to show later, religion and the love of God are above the plane of the moral virtues—it is better to have charity than to be merely prudent—but, far from excluding them, they derive from those virtues almost all their constancy and operative force. It is notorious that religion can make an emotional and intellectual appeal while leaving the moral character practically untouched. A liturgical revival, for example, is not necessarily a sign of a renewal of religious spirit nor an interest in Catholic philosophy a proof of the divine predilection; even a taste for "mysticism" and the refinements of spirituality is compatible with lapses from obvious duty which are curiously unimpressive. Only when we have laid firm hold of the infused virtues of prudence, justice, fortitude and temperance may we safely set our course for the stars.

—*Dom Aelred Graham*

Right Conduct   *July 4*

Charity, as well as faith, must die without good works. And good works are themselves the issue of moral character.

Morality, it is useful to recall, is a quality of every human act. Unfortunately the word has come in many contexts to be associated exclusively with a particular department of moral conduct, that of sex; with unhappy results. It is often assumed that once a tolerable standard of sexual purity has been attained nothing further is to be hoped for. There are occasions when one might be pardoned for supposing that all the resources of religion have been placed at our disposal for no other purpose than to provide an armoury against this sort of temptation. Nor does the treatment of the matter in some of the modern manuals of moral theology do much to dispel this impression. Experience no doubt justifies the authors' preoccupation with the subject, but it is surely desirable that the practice were more widespread of treating sexual immorality as an infringement of the virtue of temperance. It is so handled by St. Thomas, who thus gives it its rightful place in the exhaustive outline of Christian ethics which forms the second part of the *Summa Theologica.* In this way we are allowed to view a restricted field of moral activity in its due perspective.

—*Dom Aelred Graham*

We Trust God   *July 5*

Faith is the adherence of our intelligence to the word of another. When an upright, loyal man tells us something, we admit it, we have *faith* in his word; to give one's word is to give one's self.

Supernatural faith is the adherence of our intelligence, not to the word of a man, but to the word of God. God can neither deceive nor be deceived. Faith is the homage rendered to God as the supreme truth and authority. In order that this homage may be worthy of God, we must submit ourselves to the authority of His word, whatever be the difficulties our mind encounters. This Divine word affirms the existence of mysteries beyond our reason; faith can be required from us in things where our senses, our experience seem to tell us the very contrary of what God tells us; but God requires our conviction in the authority of His revelation to be so absolute that if all creation affirmed the contrary we should say to God in spite of everything: "My God, I believe because Thou sayest it."

To believe, says St. Thomas, is to give, under the empire of the will, moved by grace, the assent and adherence of our intelligence to the Divine truth. It is the mind that believes, but the heart is not absent from believing.

—*Abbot Marmion*

I understand that while you were full of temporal troubles you were at peace internally. Now, on the contrary, you are better in health, and temporal matters are going well, whereas you feel "depression and anxiety", together with "bewilderment".

The obvious fact is, that a man of prayer has to bear with equal patience temporal and spiritual difficulties. To bear sickness, pain, poverty, is a simple matter; I mean that it may be very hard, and need great heroism, but it is simple, straightforward and obvious, and therefore easy (in one sense). Just as it is easy to walk twenty miles, but difficult to drive a motor twenty miles, though the former is far more tiring.

So it is less painful (sometimes) to bear spiritual discomfort, but it is much more difficult to do, — or rather, more difficult to know how — because it is not simple, straightforward and obvious. But when once you know how, it is quite simple; just as a chauffeur, who drives daily, does it automatically and unconsciously.

Now the way is this: — accept with simplicity, or (better) take and seize with both hands, whatever feelings God sends you.

How is it possible to be anxious, worried, self-conscious, bewildered, "with simplicity"?

The answer is *"abandon"* — which is a French word (*"une âme abandonnée"* always sounds to me like "an abandoned character").

The point is that all anxiety, worry, etc., has its seat in the lower (not the lowest) part of the soul — in the imagination and emotions, or even in the intellect; but above this (or below it, if you like) is the "apex" or "ground" of the soul, wherein prayer takes place, and union with God. Simplicity consists in keeping the whole soul subject to this ground (*fundus*) or apex; and this sovereign point (or hidden ground — whichever metaphor you like) must be continually united to God's Will.

If the soul turns to prayer, it *feels* the division: there is (1) worry and anxiety and trouble and bewilderment, and there is (2) also an unfelt, yet real, acquiescence in being anxious, troubled and bewildered, and a consciousness that the *real* self is at peace, while the anxiety and worry is unreal. It is like a peaceful lake, whose surface reflects all sorts of changes, because it is calm. If you were not seeking God, you would not feel this spiritual worry and bewilderment. Therefore, the very fact that you do feel it, should help to make you feel at peace.

—Abbot John Chapman

The Christ-Follower *July 7*

Faith is the first virtue Our Lord claims from those who approach Him and it remains the same for us all.

When, before ascending into Heaven, He sends His Apostles to continue His mission throughout the world, it is faith He requires; and in this faith He sums up, as it were, all the Christian life: "Go, teach all nations . . . he that believeth and is baptised, shall be saved: but he that believeth not shall be condemned."

Is faith alone then sufficient? No, the sacraments and the observance of the commandments are necessary too, but a man who does not believe in the Divinity of Jesus Christ is a stranger to His commandments and sacraments. Besides, it is because we believe in the Divinity of Jesus that we observe His precepts and approach the sacraments. Faith then is the basis of all our supernatural life.

God wills that during the stage of our mortal life we should serve Him by faith. His glory requires it to be so. It is the homage He expects from us and the probation we have to pass through before arriving at the eternal goal. One day we shall see God unveiled; His glory will then consist in communicating Himself fully in all the splendour and brightness of His eternal beatitude. But as long as we are upon earth, it enters into the economy of the Divine Plan that God should be for us a hidden God. Here below, God wills to be known, adored and served by faith;—and the greater, the more ardent and practical this faith is, the more we are pleasing to God.

—Abbot Marmion

Alone with God *July 8*

You must go in the way in which God leads you; it is a very ordinary way, and you will find yourself continually humiliated in it, especially by feeling that you are entirely unsuccessful in prayer. But don't give it up.

Of course you can meditate—anybody can. Only you can do it with a pencil in your hand, or a pipe. It is not prayer, though it is useful, and even necessary. Spiritual reading or study of theology, if made devoutly, is most fruitful meditation.

I think you will find that the more time you can reasonably give to being alone with God, the easier it becomes to enjoy it (I don't mean pleasure, but the feeling that it is worth doing—that you are not simply lazy and wasting time). The test is not whether you feel anything at the time, but whether *afterwards* you feel (quite illogically) better, and more determined to serve God. The one thing you should gain by quiet prayer (just remaining with God, and making a number of aspirations to keep your imagination from wandering) is to feel the rest of the day that you want God's Will and nothing else.

Now, though this induces a certain *passivity in the spiritual life,* on account of which it seems that we make no effort, but God does everything, it ought not to produce passivity in other things. You should be as energetic, or more energetic, in all you do.

—Abbot John Chapman

Love Leads to God *July 9*

Charity, love, achieves the work of bringing us here below nearer to God, whilst we await the possession of Him above: charity completes and perfects faith and hope; it makes us experience a real complacency in God; we prefer God to all things and we try to manifest towards Him this complacency and preference by observing His will. "The companion of faith," says St. Augustine, "is hope; it is necessary because we do not see what we believe; with hope, we are not overcome with faint-heartedness in the waiting; then charity comes and places in our souls the hunger and thirst for God and makes our aspirations soar up to Him." For the Holy Spirit has shed abroad in our hearts the charity whereby we cry to God: Father! Father! It is a supernatural faculty that makes us adhere to God as to the Infinite Goodness we love more than anything besides. *Who shall separate us from the love of Christ?*

. . . From his prison [Paul] wrote to the Philippians: "And this I pray that your charity may more and more abound . . . that you may be sincere and without offence unto the day of Christ, filled with the fruit of justice, through Jesus Christ unto the glory and praise of God." And yet more insistently: "May the Lord . . . confirm your hearts without blame in holiness, before God and our Father, at the coming of Our Lord Jesus Christ with all His Saints . . . brethren, we pray and beseech you in the Lord Jesus; that as you have received from us how you ought to walk and to please God, so also you would walk, that you may abound the more. For you know what precepts I have given to you by the Lord Jesus. For this is the Will of God, your sanctification."

Let us then seek to realize this Will of our Heavenly Father. Our Lord demands that the brightness of our works be such that it leads those who behold it to glorify His Father.

—*Abbot Marmion*

Glory to the Father   *July 10*

Look at Christ Jesus. All His life is consecrated to the glory of His Father Whose will He always accomplishes: *I seek not My own will, but the will of Him that sent Me.* He seeks only that. At the moment of achieving His life here below, He says to His Father that He has fulfilled His mission: "I have glorified thee on the earth." The desire of His Divine Heart is that we too should seek the glory of His Father. And what does that mean for us?

Our Lord tells us: "That we should bear much fruit", that our perfection should not remain mediocre, but that our supernatural life should be intense, *In this is My Father glorified, that you bring forth* VERY MUCH *fruit.* Was it not for this moreover that Jesus came, that He shed His Blood and gave us a share in His infinite merits? He came that the Divine life might abound in us to overflowing: *I am come that they may have life, and may have it* MORE ABUNDANTLY. Like the Samaritan woman to whom He had revealed the greatness of the "Divine Gift" let us ask Him to give us "of the living water"; let us ask Him to teach us, through His Church, to what sources we must go in order to find the abundance of these waters; for they make us produce numerous fruits of life and holiness pleasing to His Father; they quench our thirst unceasingly until the day of eternal life.

The sacraments are the principal sources of the Divine life in us. They act in our souls through their intrinsic efficacy (*ex opere operato*), as the sun produces light and heat; it is only necessary there should be no obstacle within us to oppose their operation. The Eucharist is, of all the sacraments, the one that most augments the Divine life within us, because in it we receive Christ in person, we drink at the very fountainhead of the living waters.

—*Abbot Marmion*

Don't Crowd out God   *July 11*

We can sometimes crowd out God because we are making room for a number of other things. Sometimes people have so many books, they have no time to read them, and none for study. They are entirely occupied with the care of things. It is pathetic, for instance, in this country to see how a certain group of people overbuilt themselves. They built tremendous country residences, and had so many things to see to they were very soon impoverished, just looking after a number of things. If you do that, it is very difficult to have any room for God. What an array of things are to be seen in any great town a week before Christmas!—some cheap (at least low-priced), quite a number of things that are new and novel, so that people who hadn't any money to buy the things felt a great deal of pleasure in going round and looking at them. That is a subject of meditation. Interests like that can crowd out God. I wonder how much of the very essence of Christmas was recognised in the spilth of things? I was quite astonished, passing by one of the great centres just before Christmas, to see hundreds and hundreds of electric lights twinkling, opening and shutting their eyes in a kind of twinkling. And of course the number of things inside was very much greater than the number of things outside. I wondered how many people were thinking of the little stable at Bethlehem, with possibly one little lamp, possibly none; and how many were realising that was the most important thing for their mind to rest upon. We couldn't face God really if He were crowded out by things.

Perhaps God has been crowded out of our soul by persons. That is more human, more excusable, and sometimes more noble — when God is just crowded out of our life by our soul's having no room in it for more than a few persons, possibly only room for one; and there is no room for anyone else, even in our thoughts. Sometimes a life is dominated by another person, and there is hardly the possibility of consecutive thought on any other subject. Another person reigns as well as dwells.

— Vincent McNabb

Make Room *July 12*

Let us consider this very simple thing. Strangely enough, by Our dear Lord being denied entrance to the hostelry, or khan, He becomes much more accessible. The stable now that has room for God becomes much more accessible than the inn which has not had room. That little cave is not shuttered and barred and locked against beasts and men. He is with the beasts, and the shepherds come in at midnight. The shepherds wouldn't have been allowed into the khan; they would have disturbed the house. But they could come into this little thing.

The soul that finds room for God is widened, of course. If the soul has denied entrance to God in order to find room for things or persons, it has instantly narrowed itself. Indeed there is not much room for the things, or for the persons! But as soon as there is room for God in our soul, there is room for all those persons who have really a claim on our heart. They can come and go. The shepherds are not challenged—only to a more perfect life. Kings can come and go, and bring gifts, and go off again. The widest thing in the whole world is the stable that has room for God.

Monsignor Benson said that the fifth note of the Church was that it is accessible, get-at-able. I don't know if he borrowed that from St. Thomas Aquinas.

—Vincent McNabb

Greatest Gift   *July 13*

God has made us an immense gift in the Person of His Son Jesus. Christ is a tabernacle wherein are "hidden all the treasures of divine wisdom and knowledge" that He has there stored up for us. Christ Himself, by His Passion and death, merited to communicate them to us, and He is always living, interceding with His Father for us. But we must know the value of this gift and how to use it: *If thou didst know the gift of God!* Christ with the plenitude of His sanctity and the infinite value of His merits and credit is this Gift; but this gift is only useful to us according to the measure of our faith. If our faith is great, intense, profound, and reaching to the height of this gift as far as is possible for a creature, there will be no limit to the divine communications made to our souls by the Sacred Humanity of Jesus. If we have not a boundless esteem for Christ's infinite merits, it is because our faith in the Divinity of Jesus is not intense enough; and those who doubt this divine efficacy do not know what is the Humanity of a God.

We ought often to exercise our faith in the satisfactions and merits acquired by Jesus for our sanctification.

When we pray, let us come before the Eternal Father with an *unshaken confidence* in the merits of His Son. Our Lord has paid all our debt; He has gained all for us, and He unceasingly intercedes with His Father for us: *Ever living to make intercession* FOR US.

—Abbot Marmion

How often I failed in my duty to God, because I was not leaning on the strong pillar of prayer. I passed nearly twenty years on this stormy sea, falling and rising, but rising to no good purpose, seeing that I went and fell again. I may say that it was the most painful life that can be imagined, because I had no sweetness in God and no pleasure in the world.

When I was in the midst of the pleasures of the world, the remembrance of what I owed to God made me sad, and when I was praying to God my worldly affections disturbed me. This is so painful a struggle that I know not how I could have borne it for a month, let alone for so many years. Nevertheless I can trace distinctly the great mercy of our Lord to me, while thus immersed in the world, in that I had still the courage to pray. I say courage, because I know of nothing in the whole world which requires greater courage than plotting treason against the King, knowing that He knows it, and yet never withdrawing from His presence; for, granting that we are always in the presence of God, yet it seems to me that those who pray are in His presence in a very different sense, for they, as it were, see that He is looking upon them, while others may be for days together without even once recollecting that God sees them.

During eight and twenty years of prayer, I spent more than eighteen in that strife and contention which arose out of my attempts to reconcile God and the world. As to the other years, of which I have now to speak, in them the grounds of the warfare, though it was not slight, were changed; but inasmuch as I was—at least, I think so—serving God, and aware of the vanity of the world, all has been pleasant.

The reason, then, of my telling this is that, the mercy of God and my ingratitude, on the one hand, may become known; and, on the other, that men may understand how great is the good which God works in a soul when He gives it a disposition to pray in earnest, though it may not be so well prepared as it ought to be. If that soul perseveres in spite of sins, temptations, and relapses, brought about in a thousand ways by Satan, our Lord will bring it at last—I am certain of it—to the harbour of salvation, as He has brought me myself; for so it seems to me now. May His Majesty grant I may never go back and be lost! He who gives himself to prayer is in possession of a great blessing, of which many saintly and good men have written—I am speaking of mental prayer—glory be to God for it and, if they had not done so, I am not proud enough, though I have but little humility, to presume to discuss it.

I may speak of that which I know by experience; and so, I say, let him never cease from prayer who has once begun it, be his life ever so wicked; for prayer is the way to amend it, and without prayer such amendment will be much more difficult.

—Saint Teresa of Avila

A Heart of Mercy   July 15

Put on therefore, as God's chosen ones, holy and beloved, a heart of mercy, kindness, humility, meekness, patience. Bear with one another and forgive one another, if anyone has a grievance against any other; even as the Lord has forgiven you, so also do you forgive. But above all these things have charity, which is the bond of perfection. And may the peace of Christ reign in your hearts; unto that peace, indeed, you were called in one body. Show yourselves thankful. Let the word of Christ dwell in you abundantly: in all wisdom teach and admonish one another by psalms, hymns and spiritual songs, singing in your hearts to God by his grace. Whatever you do in word or in work, do all in the name of the Lord Jesus, giving thanks to God the Father through him.

—Saint Paul

True Wisdom

Wisdom, however, we speak among those who are mature, yet not a wisdom of this world nor of the rulers of this world, who are passing away. But we speak the wisdom of God, mysterious, hidden, which God foreordained before the world unto our glory, a wisdom which none of the rulers of this world has known; for had they known it, they would never have crucified the Lord of glory. But, as it is written,

> "Eye has not seen nor ear heard,
> Nor has it entered into the heart of man,
> What things God has prepared for those
>   who love him."

— Saint Paul

The End of All   *July 16*

The Christian religion, . . . teaches men these two truths; that there is a God whom men can know, and that there is a corruption in their nature which renders them unworthy of Him. It is equally important to men to know both these points; and it is equally dangerous for man to know God without knowing his own wretchedness, and to know his own wretchedness without knowing the Redeemer who can free him from it. The knowledge of only one of these points gives rise either to the pride of philosophers, who have known God, and not their own wretchedness, or to the despair of atheists, who know their own wretchedness, but not the Redeemer.

And, as it is alike necessary to man to know these two points, so is it alike merciful of God to have made us know them. The Christian religion does this; it is in this that it consists.

Let us herein examine the order of the world, and see if all things do not tend to establish these two chief points of this religion: Jesus Christ is the end of all, and the centre to which all tends. Whoever knows Him knows the reason of everything.

Those who fall into error err only through failure to see one of these two things. We can then have an excellent knowledge of God without that of our own wretchedness, and of our own wretchedness without that of God. But we cannot know Jesus Christ without knowing at the same time both God and our own wretchedness.

— Blaise Pascal

Son: hear My words, words most sweet: surpassing all knowledge of philosophers and wise men of this world. My words are Spirit and Life: not to be weighed by the understanding of man. They are not to be abused for complacent vanity; but heard in silence: and received with all humility and great affection.

And I said. Blessed is the man whom Thou shalt instruct O Lord: and shalt teach out of Thy Law. That Thou mayest give him rest from evil days: and that he be not desolate upon earth.

I taught the Prophets from the beginning saith the Lord and cease not even to this day to speak to all: but many are deaf to My voice and hard. Most men listen to the world more readily than to God; they follow more readily the lust of their flesh: than the good pleasure of God. The world promises things temporal and little and is served with great avidity; I promise things high and eternal: and the hearts of men remain untouched. Who serves and obeys Me in all things so punctually; as the world and its lords are served.

For a slender benefice men will run for miles: for eternal life few will once lift a foot from the ground. The poorest price is deemed worth effort, for a single coin at times there is shameful contention; for a vain matter and a light promise men shrink not from toil by day and night: but alas for an unchangeable good for a priceless reward, for the highest honour and endless glory men grudge even the least fatigue.

Write thou My words in Thy heart and meditate diligently on them: for in time of temptation they will be very needful. What thou understandest not when thou readest: thou shalt know in the day of visitation. In two ways I visit Mine elect: namely with temptation and with consolation. And daily I read two lessons to them; one in reproving their vices: another in exhorting them to the increase of virtues.

He that hath My words and despiseth them: hath One that shall judge him in the last day.

— Thomas à Kempis

A man once told me, with considerable satisfaction, that it was no good his being sorry, because he had committed all the sins committable. I said: "No, you haven't." "Mention one!" he said indignantly. "Suicide," I said. He was so annoyed that he finally laughed, made friends, and ended up a happy man, in very good dispositions, as they say. (I add, in brackets, that one may genuinely trust that suicide is committed when a man is of "unsound mind" in which event it is not a sin: but final despair of God's mercy would, in itself, be sin.) That man knew perfectly well that he had sinned and had not simply committed crimes: in fact, he did not really care so much about his crimes *as such* as about his sins. It was because they were sins against God, and not against the State or Society merely, that he became sorry for them. Yet I once heard the stupefying statement that until we get rid of the "sense of sin" we shall not have begun to be civilised. Well, that is one extreme. Christ teaches that there *is* such a thing as sin—and, what is more, that there are degrees in sin, unlike the other extreme which says that all sins are equal, all being committed against an infinite God, or even, that all human acts are sinful, because man is utterly corrupt. But Our Lord said to Pilate: "He that delivered Me up to thee hath the greater sin" (John 19:11). The Jewish authorities, who had taken the initiative and knew what they were about better than the pagan Pilate did, sinned worse than he did, however unjust his decision to let them crucify our Lord might be. And as for the poor soldiers who hammered the nails in; after all, they were only doing what they were told—someone has to be executioner . . . and our Lord could say: "Father, forgive them, for they do not know what they are doing." "He was saying it—He went on saying it," writes St. Luke (23:34), using the imperfect tense: the agony became more and more intolerable; yet He *went on* praying lovingly for those men.

— *C. C. Martindale*

The Greatest Is Charity

And I point out to you a yet more excellent way. If I should speak with the tongues of men and of angels, but do not have charity, I have become as sounding brass or a tinkling cymbal. And if I have prophecy and know all mysteries and all knowledge, and if I have all faith so as to remove mountains, yet do not have charity, I am nothing. And if I distribute all my goods to feed the poor, and if I deliver my body to be burned, yet do not have charity, it profits me nothing.

Charity is patient, is kind; charity does not envy, is not pretentious, is not puffed up, is not ambitious, is not self-seeking, is not provoked; thinks no evil, does not rejoice over wickedness, but rejoices with the truth; bears with all things, believes all things, hopes all things, endures all things.

Charity never fails, whereas prophecies will disappear, and tongues will cease, and knowledge will be destroyed. For we know in part and we prophesy in part; but when that which is perfect has come, that which is imperfect will be done away with. When I was a child, I spoke as a child, I felt as a child, I thought as a child. Now that I have become a man, I have put away the things of a child. We see now through a mirror in an obscure manner, but then face to face. Now I know in part, but then I shall know even as I have been known. So there abide faith, hope and charity, these three; but the greatest of these is charity.

— Saint Paul

Loving the Lord

Our Blessed Lord was intensely loved, with a concrete sort of love. When St. John told St. Peter that Our Lord was on the shore, Peter simply leapt out of the boat. You don't do that for Omnipotence, the great force that has made the Alps. You might feel inclined to run away from that. A dearly-beloved brother of mine, now gone, went to the Norwegian fjords for a summer holiday. After a time, he felt he could hardly bear them, the mountains were so tremendous. They were nothing like so near and lovable as a little village in England, with its cluster of thatched cottages, with trees against the wall. Those things are very lovable. It is very strange how love is kindled. The highest beings set more store on love than on anything else. It must be one of the greatest trials of sovereigns that they never know exactly when they are loved; so much is official, so much policy. If evil days come upon them, if once being rich they become poor, false friends fade away; and someone who is almost no one, some poor woman from the crowd, will then show her love. Genuine self-sacrificing love is almost overwhelming. No greater compliment can be paid to human nature than to offer that.

Our Lord gives a whole series of parables which, of course, do prove that He is to be loved. But I don't think He is at all concerned to prove that He ought to be loved. He tries to show us that He wants to forgive; He almost suggests that there is nothing to forgive. He wants to describe His attitude towards us. It is a most lovable attitude, bewildering. It almost seems to be setting a premium on sin. We can remember that exquisite story of St. Thomas More. He was so lovable, even when reprimanding his children, that the children used to do naughty things for the joy of being reprimanded.

— *Vincent McNabb*

He Turns to Us

July 21

Out of the Sacred Heart comes this story, to describe what He is, and to show us what is God's attitude towards us poor wretched sinners.

On the Cross, He will continue to say to His Father that we did not know what we did.

Some people have an idea that Our Lord came to show us His Omnipotence. He came to show us that on His side there was no quarrel. If anyone was to be punished, He was to be punished. If any blood was to be shed, it would be His.

So now He just tells the story of the lost sheep. I presume it doesn't require very much imagination for us to think of ourselves as lost sheep; the Shepherd seeking us for years, and we would not go back.

There is, of course, nothing in the Old Testament like this beautiful story. There is one lovely story of God carrying Israel on His shoulders; but there is not that idea of God seeking the sinner. Throughout the Old Testament we will find that God's forgiveness is conditional on our sorrow. When we turn to Him, He will turn to us. That is the God-inspired statement by man. But this beautiful story in the New Testament is the authentic statement of God about Himself. It is overwhelming. We almost ask ourselves, "Is He a God of righteousness?" His attitude to sinners is so amazing, so full of love and mercy that He seems to be condoning evil. This is His own account of His attitude towards us poor sinners when we stray away from Him. It is just an outline, but what an outline! Everything we need is there in outline, to be filled in by our own equivalent humility. This is the humble God who in a few days will kneel down at our feet and wash them. He will approach us as the lowliest servant; and this is the same Jesus Christ who is drawing this lovely story of the lost sheep.

— Vincent McNabb

Temptation   *July 22*

Moreover, St. Paul tells us, "God will not suffer you to be tempted above that which you are able; but will make also with temptation issue, that you may be able to bear it". The great Apostle is himself an example of this. He tells us that lest he should exalt himself on account of his revelations, God placed what he called a thorn in his flesh, a figure of temptation; "there was given me . . . an angel of Satan, to buffet me". "Thrice," he says, "I besought the Lord, that it might depart from me. And He said to me: My grace is sufficient for thee: for power is made perfect in infirmity" — that is to say in making it triumph by God's grace.

197

It is indeed Divine grace that helps us to surmount temptation, but we have to ask for it: *Watch ye* AND PRAY. In the prayer Christ taught us, He makes us beseech our Father in Heaven "lead us not into temptation, but deliver us from evil". Since Jesus has willed to place this prayer upon our lips, let us often repeat it whilst relying on the merits of Our Saviour's Passion.

Nothing is more efficacious against temptation than the remembrance of the Cross of Jesus. What did Christ come to do here below if not "destroy the works of the devil". And how has He destroyed them, how has He "cast out" the devil, as He Himself says, "if not by His death upon the Cross?" During His mortal life, Our Lord cast out devils from the bodies of the possessed; He cast them out also from souls, when He forgave the sins of Magdalen, of the paralytic man and of so many others; but it was above all, as you know, by His blessed Passion that He overthrew the dominion of the devil. At the precise moment when, in bringing about the death of Jesus at the hands of the Jews, the devil hoped to triumph for ever, he himself received the death-blow. For Christ's death destroyed sin, and gave as a right to all who are baptized, the grace of dying to sin.

— Abbot Marmion

Sin Is Rebellion   *July 23*

No one who believes in God, and believes that the human will is in any sense free, will deny the possibility of sin. And certainly the world is full enough of disorder, ugliness, and, we must say, badness, to make us clear that the Plan of God has been and is consistently violated. Before speaking of sin from our chosen point of view—the Love of God—I think I ought briefly to remind you of the Christian doctrine of Sin from that more "authoritarian" point of view—as a rebellion against God's will. Grave sin involves the deliberate rebellion against the will of God in a grave matter. I have to know that the matter *is* grave and gravely forbidden. For example, those African natives who kill their twins honestly think they are right in doing so; they think that twins are the product of witchcraft and infect the tribe. I must be free to act in this way or in that. Thus, if I murder a man in my sleep or blaspheme when drugged, my will is not free.

— C. C. Martindale

Good Works

"Whether you eat or drink, or whatsoever else you do, do all to the glory of God"; and to the Colossians: "All whatsoever you do in word or in work, do all in the name of the Lord Jesus Christ, giving thanks to God the Father by Him."

As you see, it is not only the actions which, of their nature, refer directly to God, such as the "exercises" of piety, assistance at Holy Mass, Communion and the reception of the other sacraments, the spiritual and corporal works of mercy; but also the most commonplace actions, the most ordinary incidents of our daily life, such as taking food, attending to our business or work, fulfilling our social duties, taking rest or recreation; all those actions that occur every day and literally weave, in their monotonous and successive routine, the thread of our entire life, can be transformed, by grace and love, into acts very pleasing to God and rich in merit.

— Abbot Marmion

Full of Courage   July 24

For we know that if the earthly house in which we dwell be destroyed, we have a building from God, a house not made by human hands, eternal in the heavens. And indeed, in this present state we groan, yearning to be clothed over with that dwelling of ours which is from heaven; if indeed we shall be found clothed, and not naked. For we who are in this tent sigh under our burden, because we do not wish to be unclothed, but rather clothed over, that what is mortal may be swallowed up by life. Now he who made us for this very thing is God, who has given us the Spirit as its pledge.

Always full of courage, then, and knowing that while we are in the body we are exiled from the Lord—for we walk by faith and not by sight—we even have the courage to prefer to be exiled from the body and to be at home with the Lord. And therefore we strive, whether in the body or out of it, to be pleasing to him. For all of us must be made manifest before the tribunal of Christ, so that each one may receive what he has won through the body, according to his works, whether good or evil.

—Saint Paul

Use Your Talents

The servant who is given his talents, his coins of spiritual grace, who instead of soundly investing them hides them in the ground, either through lack of enterprise or through greed, will most certainly get into trouble when the Master returns, as Matthew tells us. My own talents are small. But I still have the duty of investing the divine word in the minds of the people. I fear the day when I shall be asked to show the interest accruing. I am even more afraid because the Lord is going to look for effort rather than effect.

—Saint Ambrose

God in Our Thoughts   *July 25*

Well, dear children in Jesus Christ, we must get God into our thoughts, and then our thoughts will become golden. When God is in our thoughts, they have a sort of kingliness.

Again, too, in all our loves and affection, God must come first. He is supreme. No one should be a rival to God in our heart. But our love for others will be a borrowing from the love we give to

God. The moon is not a rival to the sun; all its life is just a borrowing from the sun, a borrowing from the sunlight that will be to-morrow. The love of husband and wife should not be a rival to the love each has for Jesus in the Blessed Sacrament, as if each makes a separate act of the love of God, quite apart from the love each bears the other. Their love of Jesus should make them nearer to each other; nearer to God in the common love they have for Him.

So, dear children in Jesus Christ, we must beseech the grace of having God more and more, first, in our *imagination,* especially in the beginning of our spiritual life. When it is endangered by an unruly, uncurbed imagination, our duty is to rein that in and master it. The Incarnation, with its wonderful series of appeals to our imagination, will be the greatest help.

Again, in our *thoughts,* we should ask God to come and be sovereign of our thoughts. If our thoughts are wrong, our life is wrong.

— *Vincent McNabb*

The Good and the Bad   *July 26*

I neither have used toward the clergy nor toward the temporalty any warm, displeasant word, but have forborne to touch in special either the faults of the one or of the other. But yet have I confessed the thing that truth is: neither part to be faultless. But then, which is the thing that offendeth these blessed brethren, I have not [stated]; furthermore, to say the thing which I take also for very true, that as this realm of England hath had hitherto, God be thanked, as good and as laudable a temporalty, number for number, as hath had any other Christian region, ... so hath it had also, number for number, compared with any realm Christened of no greater quantity, as good and as commendable a clergy, though there have never lacked in any of both the parts plenty of such as have always been [bad]; whose faults have ever been their own, and not to be imputed to the whole body, neither of spiritualty nor temporalty, saving that there have been peradventure on either part, in some such as by their offices ought to look thereto, some lack of the labor and diligence that in the reforming of it should have belonged unto them, which I declare always that I would wish amended, and every man specially labor to mend himself and rather accustom himself to look upon his own faults than upon other men's; and against such as are in either sort found openly evil and [bad] unto the common weal, as thieves, murderers, and heretics, and such other wretches; the whole corpus of the spiritualty and temporalty both, each with other lovingly to accord and agree, and according to the good ancient laws and commendable usages long continued in this noble realm, either part endeavor themselves diligently to repress and keep under those evil and ungracious folk that, like sores, . . . trouble and vex the body; and of all them to cure such as may be cured, and for health of the whole body cut and cast off the incurable, cankered parts therefrom, observed in the doing evermore such order and fashion as may stand and agree with reason and justice, the king's laws of the realm, the Scripture of God, and the laws of Christ's Church, ever keeping love and concord between the two.

— *Saint Thomas More*

Materialism   *July 27*

In an age when totalitarianism has striven, in every way, to devaluate and degrade the human person, we hope it is right to demand a hearing for any and every sane reaction in the favor of man's inalienable solitude and his interior freedom. The murderous din of our materialism cannot be allowed to silence the independent voices which will never cease to speak: whether they be the voices of Christian Saints, or the voices of Oriental sages like Lao-Tse or the Zen Masters, or the voices of men like Thoreau or Martin Buber, or Max Picard. It is all very well to insist that man is a "social animal"—the fact is obvious enough. But that is no justification for making him a mere cog in a totalitarian machine—or in a religious one either, for that matter.

In actual fact, society depends for its existence on the inviolable personal solitude of its members. Society, to merit its name, must be made up not of numbers, or mechanical units, but of persons. To be a person implies responsibility and freedom, and both these imply a certain interior solitude, a sense of personal integrity, a sense of one's own reality and of one's ability to give himself to society — or to refuse that gift.

— Thomas Merton

One Must Listen   *July 28*

When men are merely submerged in a mass of impersonal human beings pushed around by automatic forces, they lose their true humanity, their integrity, their ability to love, their capacity for self-determination. When society is made up of men who know no interior solitude it can no longer be held together by love: and consequently it is held together by a violent and abusive authority. But when men are violently deprived of the solitude and freedom which are their due, the society in which they live becomes putrid, it festers with servility, resentment and hate.

No amount of technological progress will cure the hatred that eats away the vitals of materialistic society like a spiritual cancer. The only cure is, and must always be, spiritual. There is not much use talking to men about God and love if they are not able to listen. The ears with which one hears the message of the Gospel are hidden in man's heart, and these ears do not hear anything unless they are favored with a certain interior solitude and silence.

In other words, since faith is a matter of freedom and self-determination — the free receiving of a freely given gift of grace — man cannot assent to a spiritual message as long as his mind and heart are enslaved by automatism. He will always remain so enslaved as long as he is submerged in a mass of other automatons, without individuality and without their rightful integrity as persons.

— Thomas Merton

Be Generous

Mark this: he who sows sparingly will also reap sparingly, and he who sows bountifully will also reap bountifully. Let each one give according as he has determined in his heart, not grudgingly or from compulsion, for "God loves a cheerful giver." And God is able to make all grace abound in you, so that always having ample means, you may abound in every good work.

—Saint Paul

Pride

Let no one deceive himself. If any one of you thinks himself wise in this world, let him become a fool, that he may come to be wise. For the wisdom of this world is foolishness with God. For it is written, "I will catch the wise in their craftiness." And again, "The Lord knows the thoughts of the wise, that they are empty." Therefore let no one take pride in men.

—Saint Paul

The Gospel

July 30

Now I recall to your minds, brethren, the gospel that I preached to you, which also you received, wherein also you stand, through which also you are being saved, if you hold it fast, as I preached it to you— unless you have believed to no purpose. For I delivered to you first of all, what I also received, that Christ died for our sins according to the Scriptures, and that he was buried, and that he rose again the third day, according to the Scriptures, and that he appeared to Cephas, and after that to the Eleven. Then he was seen by more than five hundred brethren at one time, many of whom are with us still, but some have fallen asleep. After that he was seen by James, then by all the apostles. And last of all, as by one born out of due time, he was seen also by me. For I am the least of the apostles, and am not worthy to be called an apostle, because I persecuted the

Church of God. But by the grace of God I am what I am, and his grace in me has not been fruitless—in fact I have labored more than any of them, yet not I, but the grace of God with me. Whether then it is I or they, so we preach, and so you have believed.

— *Saint Paul*

The Witness   *July 31*

The Catholic position regarding the Church as the one true Witness can be briefly set forth. It is logical at every step and reasonable to the last degree.

If a revelation of God to man has been made, it is a past fact. And a past fact is to be learned from history, or from reason based upon present observed fact.

Do we find in history anything bearing on the one true Witness? The New Testament writings, considered merely as trustworthy historical documents, inform us that in Palestine, nineteen hundred years ago, there presented himself a man claiming to have a divine revelation for men. His intellectual and moral character was, by universal consent, supereminently and uniquely admirable. The deeds he performed, the predictions he made, were not seldom such as could be explained only by referring to a special divine cooperation. He wrought, in brief, miracles of various sorts and uttered prophecies. To these he himself appealed as the seal of his authority.

Better attested than these facts are none in history. In addition he plainly predicted the details of his own death, and foretold to his disciples his glorious resurrection and his public ascension, clearly beheld by many who laid down their lives in testimony of the truth. The historical documents relating all these events were written in the lifetime of the men who themselves had walked with him, and were the witnesses to both his mortal and his risen life.

— *Hilaire Belloc*

Why Did God Make You?   *August 1*

Every man who refuses to worship God is a social climber who
wants to sit on God's throne and thus become hateful and mean
because of a terrible inferiority complex: he knows down deep in
his creature-heart that he is not a Creator, and that he could not be
godless if there were no God. The man who is irreligious is like
the man who is ignorant: both are imperfect, one in relation to his
intellect, the other in relation to his whole being and his happiness.

God made you to be happy. He made you for your happiness,
not His. God would still be perfectly happy if you never existed.
God has no need of your love for His sake for there is nothing in
you, of and by yourself, which makes you lovable to God. Most
of us are fortunate to have even a spark of affection from our
fellow creatures.

God does not love us for the same reason that we love others.
We love others because of need. Our need of love is born of our
poverty. We find in someone else the supply of our lack. But God
does not love us because He needs us. He loves us because He put
some of His love in us. God does not love us because we are
valuable; we are valuable because He loves us.

— *Archbishop Fulton J. Sheen*

Suicidal Mania   *August 2*

To sum up our contention so far, we may say that the most
characteristic current philosophies have not only a touch of mania,
but a touch of suicidal mania. The mere questioner has knocked
his head against the limits of human thought; and cracked it. This
is what makes so futile the warnings of the orthodox and the
boasts of the advanced about the dangerous boyhood of free
thought. What we are looking at is not the boyhood of free
thought; it is the old age and ultimate dissolution of free thought.
It is vain for bishops and pious bigwigs to discuss what dreadful
things will happen if wild scepticism runs its course. It has run its
course. It is vain for eloquent atheists to talk of the great truths

that will be revealed if once we see free thought begin. We have seen it end. It has no more questions to ask; it has questioned itself. You cannot call up any wilder vision than a city in which men ask themselves if they have any selves. You cannot fancy a more sceptical world than that in which men doubt if there is a world.

— *G. K. Chesterton*

To Know Christ *August 3*

To know Christ Jesus: if we do not know him as he lived among us, acted and reacted and suffered among us, we risk not knowing him at all. For we cannot see him at the right hand of the Father as we can see him in Palestine. And we shall end either in constructing our own Christ, image of our own needs or dreams, or in having no Christ but a shadow and a name. Either way the light he might shed is not shed for us—light upon himself, light upon God.

For the kind of ignoring I have in mind cuts off a vast shaft of light into the being of God. The truth "Christ is God" is a statement not only about Christ but about God. Without it, we could still know of God, certainly, but in his own nature only — infinite, omnipotent, creating of nothing, sustaining creation in being. It would be a remote kind of knowledge, for of none of these ways of being or doing have we any personal experience. In Christ Jesus we can see God in our nature, experiencing the things we have experienced, coping with situations we have to cope with. Thereby we know God as the most devout pagan cannot know him.

— *Frank Sheed*

Frail Humans *August 4*

O Sun, my only Love, I am happy to feel myself so small, so frail in Thy sunshine, and I am in peace . . . I know that all the eagles of Thy Celestial Court have pity on me, they guard and defend me,

207

they put to flight the vultures—the demons that fain would devour me. I fear them not, these demons, I am not destined to be their prey, but the prey of the Divine Eagle.

O Eternal Word! O my Saviour! Thou art the Divine Eagle Whom I love—Who lurest me. Thou Who, descending to this land of exile, didst will to suffer and to die, in order to bear away the souls of men and plunge them into the very heart of the Blessed Trinity—Love's Eternal Home! Thou Who, reascending into inaccessible light, dost still remain concealed here in our vale of tears under the snow-white semblance of the Host, and this, to nourish me with Thine own substance! O Jesus! forgive me if I tell Thee that Thy Love reacheth even unto folly. And in face of this folly, what wilt Thou, but that my heart leap up to Thee? How could my trust have any limits?

I know that the Saints have made themselves as fools for Thy sake; being "eagles," they have done great things. I am too little for great things, and my folly it is to hope that Thy Love accepts me as victim; my folly it is to count on the aid of Angels and Saints, in order that I may fly unto Thee with Thine own wings.

—Saint Thérèse of Lisieux

Jesus Loves Us   *August 5*

O my Divine Eagle! For as long a time as Thou willest I shall remain—my eyes fixed upon Thee. I long to be allured by Thy Divine Eyes; I would become Love's prey. I have the hope that Thou wilt one day swoop down upon me, and, bearing me away to the Source of all Love, Thou wilt plunge me at last into that glowing abyss, that I may become for ever its happy Victim.

O Jesus! would that I could tell all *little souls* of Thine ineffable condescension! I feel that if by any possibility Thou couldst find one weaker than my own, Thou wouldst take delight in loading her with still greater favours, provided that she abandoned herself with entire confidence to Thine Infinite Mercy. But, O my Spouse, why these desires of mine to make known the secrets of Thy love? Is it not Thyself alone Who hast taught them to me, and canst

Thou not unveil them to others? Yea, I know it, and this I implore Thee! . . .

I entreat Thee to let Thy divine eyes rest upon a vast number of little souls; I entreat Thee to choose, in this world, a legion of little victims of Thy love.

— Saint Thérèse of Lisieux

Feast of the Transfiguration   *August 6*

Now after six days Jesus took Peter, James and his brother John, and led them up a high mountain by themselves, and was transfigured before them. And his face shone as the sun, and his garments became white as snow. And behold, there appeared to them Moses and Elias talking together with him. Then Peter addressed Jesus, saying, "Lord, it is good for us to be here. If thou wilt, let us set up three tents here, one for thee, one for Moses, and one for Elias." As he was still speaking, behold, a bright cloud overshadowed them, and behold, a voice out of the cloud said, "This is my beloved Son, in whom I am well pleased; hear him." And on hearing it the disciples fell on their faces and were exceedingly afraid. And Jesus came near and touched them, and said to them, "Arise, and do not be afraid." But lifting up their eyes, they saw no one but Jesus only.

And as they were coming down from the mountain, Jesus cautioned them, saying, "Tell the vision to no one, till the Son of Man has risen from the dead." And the disciples asked him, saying, "Why then do the Scribes say that Elias must come first?" But he answered and said, "Elias indeed is to come and will restore all things. But I say to you that Elias has come already, and they did not know him, but did to him whatever they wished. So also shall the Son of Man suffer at their hands." Then the disciples understood that he had spoken to them of John the Baptist.

— Saint Matthew

It is the Christ of the earthly life who is now at the right hand of the Father—that Christ, now risen, in whom we live. And, in any event, our salvation is not all that matters in religion, or even what matters most. That was the mistake of the old-type Bible Christian: he was saved, the rest was mere theology. His fellow Bible Christians might believe that God was three Persons or one only, that Christ was God and man or man only—these were secondary, the sole primary being to accept Christ as one's personal Saviour. It made the self unhealthily central, un-Christianly central. "This is eternal life: to know thee, the one true God, and Jesus Christ, whom thou hast sent" (Jn 17:3).

—Frank Sheed

Love the Unlovely

You want a religion which starts not with how good you are, but with how confused you are. Conscious as you are of being in bondage to perverted desires, selfishness and churlish refusal to help someone in need, you cry out with the poet: "O my offense is rank: it smells to heaven."

You can love the lovable without being religious; you can respect those who respect you without religion; you can pay debts without being religious, but you cannot love those who hate you without being religious; you cannot atone for your guilty conscience without being religious.

Possibly the only reason in the world for loving the unlovely, for forgiving the enemy, is that God is love; and since as such He loves me who am so little deserving of His love, I also ought to love those who hate me.

—Archbishop Fulton J. Sheen

Lord, truly I am Thy servant; I am Thy servant, and the son of Thine handmaid: Thou hast loosed my bonds. I will offer to Thee the sacrifice of thanksgiving. Let my heart and my tongue praise Thee, and let all my bones say, "Lord, who is like unto Thee?" Let them so say, and answer Thou me, and "say unto my soul, I am Thy salvation." Who am I, and what is my nature? How evil have not my deeds been; or if not my deeds, my words; or if not my words, my will? But Thou, O Lord, art good and merciful, and Thy right hand had respect unto the profoundness of my death and removed from the bottom of my heart that abyss of corruption. And this was the result, that I willed not to do what I willed, and willed to do what Thou willest. But where, during all those years, and out of what deep and secret retreat was my free will summoned forth in a moment, whereby I gave my neck to Thy "easy yoke," and my shoulders to Thy "light burden," O Christ Jesus, "my strength and my Redeemer"? How sweet did it suddenly become to me to be without the delights of trifles! And what at one time I feared to lose, it was now a joy to me to put away. For Thou didst cast them away from me, Thou true and highest sweetness. Thou didst cast them away, and instead of them didst enter in Thyself, —sweeter than all pleasure, though not to flesh and blood; brighter than all light, but more veiled than all mysteries; more exalted than all honour, but not to the exalted in their own conceits. Now was my soul free from the gnawing cares of seeking and getting, and of wallowing and exciting the itch of lust. And I babbled unto Thee my brightness, my riches, and my health, the Lord my God.

—Saint Augustine

Christ Comes *August 9*

The former dealings of God with man were official, formal, as if God were a Commander-in-Chief, Commissioner of Charity; Guardian of Public Morals. Hence Heaven was high. Few sighed after it. The Jews seemed to be able to forgo the joys of Paradise in the hope of seeing a new Judea flowing with milk and honey. The very prophets and holy men sighed as they passed away from the present things, as if God, to whom they were finally tending, was of no present comfort to them. All this was a consequence of God's not having made known the Secrets of Heaven, the Life of Love, the Home Life of God.

The coming of Christ changed the common notions of God from good to better. What was said of Him in the Old Testament and what care He took to punish the waywardness of the Jewish people were enough to convince anyone that the God of Armies was a mighty Prince, whose Will was Law and whose Justice was inflexible; whom indeed we leant upon for our daily bread but whose punishing hand fell infallibly and unflinchingly on evildoers. The great beauty of the New Testament is the picture it gives of human affection.

— Vincent McNabb

God Is beyond Words *August 10*

God is ineffable. That is to say, no words are able to describe Him. Human language, for all the richness and subtlety it has acquired through centuries of development, must still wait upon our thought. And our thought in its turn has its limitations; it is generated, to speak somewhat loosely, by the senses and the imagination. In our present mode of existence thought must always bear the signs of its origin; our ideas are expressed in and bounded by imagery. The fusion of idea and image is natural to our way of thinking; only by reflection and a certain effort do we learn to separate them and consider the idea, the concept, in detachment from the particular embodiment of it which forms the object of sense-knowledge; the notion of man, for example, in isolation from the individuals with whom we are acquainted.

. . . Man could not presume to add to or improve upon, but he could at least attempt to search into, the meaning of what God had revealed. He might legitimately strive to realize its implications and demonstrate its bearing upon his every-day life. Such was to be the work of theology. It began at the opening of the Christian era, in the New Testament writings, and has continued in the Church down the centuries. To assist them in their work of explanation the fathers and theologians made use of the philosophers. At first Plato, and later Aristotle, was appealed to in the immense task of expressing in human modes of thought truths that were essentially divine. The Church, in her anxiety to penetrate more deeply into "the Faith once delivered to the saints," has never hesitated to utilize the instruments forged by a purely rational philosophy. Accordingly we should be false to the traditional Christian method, and courting failure in advance, were we to attempt a discussion of our subject without reference to the hard-won philosophical concepts in which a universal religion must necessarily express itself.

—Dom Aelred Graham

Apart from God August 11

A cow can't be very good or very bad; a dog can be both better and worse; a child better and worse still; an ordinary man, still more so; a man of genius, still more so; a superhuman spirit best—or worst—of all.

How did the Dark Power go wrong? Well, the moment you have a self at all, there is a possibility of putting yourself first—wanting to be the centre—wanting to *be* God, in fact. That was the sin of Satan: and that was the sin he taught the human race. Some people think the fall of man had something to do with sex, but that's a mistake. What Satan put into the heads of our remote ancestors was the idea that they could "be like gods"—could set up on their own as if they had created themselves—be their own masters—invent some sort of happiness for themselves outside God, apart from God. And out of that hopeless attempt has come nearly all that we call human history—money, poverty, ambition, war, prostitution, classes, empires, slavery—the long terrible story of man trying to find something other than God which will make him happy.

The reason why it can never succeed is this. God made us: invented us as a man invents an engine. A car is made to run on petrol, and it won't run properly on anything else. Now God designed the human machine to run on Himself. He Himself is the fuel our spirits were designed to burn, or the food our spirits were designed to feed on. There isn't any other. That's why it's just no good asking God to make us happy in our own way without bothering about religion. God can't give us a happiness and peace apart from Himself, because it isn't there. There's no such thing.

—*C. S. Lewis*

Religion Civilizes   *August 12*

"What is the advantage of having a religion, as opposed to having none?" There are all sorts of answers, obviously, that can be given. You can treat it as a mere question of happiness; point out how much fuller life is if you believe that Man has a tangible end to fulfil, and is doing so under the eyes of a benign Task-master — still more if you believe, as our religion teaches and many others teach, that there will be a reward for us, in another world, if the task is well done. You can treat it as a question of intellectual satisfaction: point out that all the riddles which our thought comes up against, as it tries this avenue of speculation or that, become less of a nightmare to us if we believe that there is a supreme Intelligence which knows the answer to them all, even where it is hidden from us. You can treat it as a question of general human well-being: how long would it be before we threw over all the restraints of morality, if we did not believe that there were supernatural sanctions at the back of all our ideas of right and wrong? Oh, to be sure, we all know good atheists. But we all have the feeling about them that they are, as it were, chewing the cud of that Christianity in which their ancestors believed; they are living up to a code which is in fact Christian, although they do not acknowledge it. Construct a godless civilization and you do not have to wait long before you find out whether the children bred in it acquire pretty habits or not. All that is true; that the world would be very much poorer if it had no leaven of religion in it, and that a great many of us, who haven't got good digestions to start with, would find life a [mess].

—*Msgr. Ronald Knox*

For Thousands of Years   *August 13*

But I do think you can say this; that if mankind generally, for thousands of years, has been in the habit of recognizing, and living up to, the presence of an unseen spiritual world, it is likely that this attitude of worship is part of man's natural make-up. He is the only animal that finds it confortable to remain on bent knees. *Dis te minorem quod geris, imperas;* if we are lords of creation, it is only as the vassals of an Overlord higher than ourselves—if it were not so, how could we be so ludicrously incomplete, so undignified, so dissatisfied as we are? Say, if you like, that our habit of addressing worship to Powers whom we think of as reigning above us is an inference, perhaps an unconscious inference, from that feeling of inferiority. Say, if you will, that it is an instinct, which neither has nor demands an explanation, apart from the obvious explanation that a supernatural world really exists, containing Powers that are worthy of worship. What seems evident in either case is that we are built to be a half-way house between the natural and the supernatural; that adoration is a congenital posture with us. If we try to rise above our own level we immediately sink beneath our own level, for we lose our place in creation.

—*Msgr. Ronald Knox*

Men blaspheme what they do not know. The Christian religion consists in two points. It is of equal concern to men to know them, and it is equally dangerous to be ignorant of them. And it is equally of God's mercy that He has given indications of both.

And yet they take occasion to conclude that one of these points does not exist, from that which should have caused them to infer the other. The sages who have said there is only one God have been persecuted, the Jews were hated, and still more the Christians. Thy have seen by the light of nature that if there be a true religion on earth, the course of all things must tend to it as to a centre.

The whole course of things must have for its object the establishment and the greatness of religion. Men must have within them feelings suited to what religion teaches us. And, finally, religion must so be the object and centre to which all things tend, that whoever knows the principles of religion can give an explanation both of the whole nature of man in particular, and of the whole course of the world in general.

And on this ground they take occasion to revile the Christian religion, because they misunderstand it. They imagine that it consists simply in the worship of a God considered as great, powerful, and eternal; which is strictly deism, almost as far removed from the Christian religion as atheism, which is its exact opposite. And thence they conclude that this religion is not true, because they do not see that all things concur to the establishment of this point, that God does not manifest Himself to men with all the evidence which He could show.

But let them conclude what they will against deism, they will conclude nothing against the Christian religion, which properly consists in the mystery of the Redeemer, who, uniting in Himself the two natures, human and divine, has redeemed men from the corruption of sin in order to reconcile them in His divine person to God.

—*Blaise Pascal*

Feast of the Assumption

We must ask Our dear Lady to let us into the secret of her humility. Many of the complications of our souls are due to our failure in humility. Any defects in the best we may do are not God's doing, but ours. Everything in Our dear Lady was good; but she knew that was God's work in her. She was nothing. He had done everything for her, and for Him to work through her who was less than nothing was just a sign of His greatness. It was all His work entirely.

We need that humility of soul, too, in our life; and it must be a humility that authenticates itself by being taught. None learns so easily as he who is humble. Here we have an example of Our Lady willing to learn through the shepherds. Our dear Lady did not grow in Grace, but she grew in knowledge. God used these simple night watchmen to give some further illumination to the mind of Our Blessed Lady. They were as much the Messengers of God as was the Angel Gabriel who came from heaven. They were messengers of God to the mind of Our Lady, and it was part of her perfect humility to recognise that, and to listen to their words as if indeed they were not shepherds speaking to her but messengers of God Himself.

Well, we can be humble only in so far as we, too, are teachable and are willing to learn even from the simplest some lesson for our soul. May Our dear Lady, then, teach us some lesson of her great humility, so that in serving God we may reign over our own souls and catch from the Queen of Angels the peace and the beauty of her deep humility.

— *Vincent McNabb*

Love and Sorrow *August 16*

No one in the world can carry God in his heart without an inner joy, and an outer sorrow; without singing a *Magnificat* to those who share the secret, and without feeling the thrust of a sword from those who want freedom of the flesh without the law. Love and sorrow often go together. In carnal love, the body swallows the soul; in spiritual love, the soul envelopes the body. The sorrow of the first is never to be satisfied; one who wants to drink the ocean of love is unhappy if limited to a mere cup with which to drink. The sorrow of the second love is never being able to do enough for the beloved.

In the human love of marriage, the joys of love are a prepayment for its duties, responsibilities, and, sometimes, its sorrows. Because the crosses lie ahead in human love, there is the Transfiguration beforehand, when the face of love seems to shine as the sun, and the garments are as white as snow. There are those who, like Peter, would wish to capitalize the joys and to make a permanent tabernacle of love on the mountaintops of ecstasy. But there is always the Lord, speaking through the conscience and saying that to capture love in a permanent form one *must* pass through a Calvary. The early transports of love are an advance, an anticipation, of the real transports that are to come when one has mounted to a higher degree of love through the bearing of a Cross.

—Archbishop Fulton J. Sheen

Foolish Reformers

August 17

In the matter of reforming things, as distinct from deforming them, there is one plain and simple principle; a principle which will probably be called a paradox. There exists in such a case a certain institution or law; let us say, for the sake of simplicity, a fence or gate erected across a road. The more modern type of reformer goes gaily up to it and says, "I don't see the use of this; let us clear it away." To which the more intelligent type of reformer will do well to answer: "If you don't see the use of it, I certainly won't let you clear it away. Go away and think. Then, when you can come back and tell me that you *do* see the use of it, I may allow you to destroy it."

This paradox rests on the most elementary common sense. The gate or fence did not grow there. It was not set up by somnambulists who built it in their sleep. It is highly improbable that it was put there by escaped lunatics who were for some reason loose in the street. Some person had some reason for thinking it would be a good thing for somebody. And until we know what the reason was, we really cannot judge whether the reason was reasonable. It is extremely probable that we have overlooked some whole aspect of the question, if something set up by human beings like ourselves seems to be entirely meaningless and mysterious. There are reformers who get over this difficulty by assuming that all their fathers were fools; but if that be so, we can only say that folly appears to be a hereditary disease.

— G. K. Chesterton

Logic *August 18*

When we say that we doubt the intellectual improvement produced by . . . Rationalism and the modern world, there generally arises a very confused controversy, which is a sort of tangle of terminology. But, broadly speaking, the difference between us and our critics is this. They mean by growth an increase of the tangle; whereas we mean by thought a disentangling of the tangle. Even a short and simple length of straight and untangled wire is worth more to us than whole forests of mere entanglement. That there are more topics talked about, or more terms used, or more people using them, or more books and other authorities cited—all this is nothing to us if people misuse the terms, misunderstand the topics, invoke the authorities at random and without the use of reason; and finally bring out a false result. A peasant who merely says, "I have five pigs; if I kill one I shall have four pigs," is thinking in an extremely simple and elementary way; but he is thinking as clearly and correctly as Aristotle or Euclid. But suppose he reads or half-reads newspapers and books of popular science. Suppose he starts to call one pig the Land and another pig Capital and a third pig Exports, and finally brings out the result that the more pigs he kills the more he possesses; or that every sow that litters decreases the number of pigs in the world. He has learnt economic terminology, merely as a means of becoming entangled in economic fallacy. It is a fallacy he could never have fallen into while he was grounded in the divine dogma that Pigs is Pigs.

—*G. K. Chesterton*

Tangled Thought *August 19*

We think a short length of the untangled logical chain is better than an interminable length of it that is interminably tangled. It is merely that we prefer a man to do a sum of simple addition right than a sum of long division wrong.

Now what we observe about the whole current culture of journalism and general discussion is that people do not know how to begin to think. Not only is their thinking at third and fourth hand, but it always starts about three-quarters of the way through the process. Men do not know where their own thoughts came from. They do not know what their own words imply. They come in at the end of every controversy and know nothing of where it began or what it is all about. They are constantly assuming certain absolutes, which, if correctly defined, would strike even themselves as being not absolutes but absurdities. To think thus is to be in a tangle; to go on thinking is to be in more and more of a tangle. And at the back of all there is always something understood; which is really something misunderstood.

—*G. K. Chesterton*

Youth *August 20*

It is the sceptics who are the sentimentalists. More than half the "revolt" and the talk of being advanced and progressive is simply a weak sort of snobbishness which takes the form of a worship of Youth. Some men of my generation delight in declaring that they are of the Party of the Young and defending every detail of the latest fashions or freaks. If I do not do that, it is for the same reason that I do not dye my hair or wear stays. But even when it is less despicable than that, the current phrase that everything must be done for youth, that the rising generation is all that matters, is in sober fact a piece of pure sentimentalism. It is also, within reason, a perfectly natural piece of sentiment. All healthy people like to see the young enjoying themselves; but if we turn that pleasure into a principle, we are sentimentalists. If we desire the greatest happiness of the greatest number, it will be obvious that the greatest number, at any given moment, are rather more likely to be between twenty-five and seventy than to be between seventeen and twenty-five. Sacrificing everything to the young will be like working only for the rich. They will be a privileged class and the rest will be snobs or slaves. Moreover, the young will always have a fair amount of fun under the worst conditions; if we really wish to console the world, it will be much more rational to console the old.

—G. K. Chesterton

Orthodoxy *August 21*

I have been asked to explain something about myself which seems to be regarded as very extraordinary. The problem has been presented to me in the form of a cutting from a very flattering American article, which yet contained a certain suggestion of wonder. So far as I can understand, it is thought extraordinary that a man should be ordinary. I am ordinary in the correct sense of the term; which means the acceptance of an order; a Creator and the Creation, the common sense of gratitude for Creation, life and love as gifts permanently good, marriage and chivalry as laws rightly controlling them, and the rest of the normal traditions of our race and religion. It is also thought a little odd that I regard the grass as green, even after some newly-discovered Slovak artist has painted it grey; that I think daylight very tolerable in spite of thirteen Lithuanian philosophers sitting in a row and cursing the light of day; and that, in matters more polemical, I actually prefer weddings to divorces and babies to Birth Control. These eccentric views, which I share with the overwhelming majority of mankind, past and present, I should not attempt to defend here one by one. And I only give a general reply for a particular reason. I wish to make it unmistakably plain that my defence of these sentiments is not sentimental. It would be easy to gush about these things; but I defy the reader, after reading this, to find the faintest trace of the tear of sensibility. I hold this view not because it is sensibility, but because it is sense.

— *G. K. Chesterton*

The Protector   *August 22*

When God creates man, the performative force of His word overcomes the threat of meaninglessness represented by the Biblical image of sea and darkness. This gives a way of looking at one's own existence as in a parable. I see God protecting me from the chaos of a meaningless life. I adopt an attitude and I understand it in so far as I live in accordance with it, and thus grow in relation with God.

A grave weakness in contemporary explanations and expressions of faith is the absence of what really makes up true religion, namely awe and worship. God is reduced to being a factor and a language-word in the struggle for man's better existence. He gives man a pointer as to how to make the best of this world, how to be engaged in it and self-committed. What is subsidiary in the Gospels is given the chief role.

— *Martin D'Arcy*

Scoffers

In the good old days of Victorian rationalism it used to be the conventional habit to scoff at St. Thomas Aquinas and the mediaeval theologians; and especially to repeat perpetually a well-worn joke about the man who discussed how many angels could dance on the point of a needle. The comfortable and commercial Victorians, with their money and merchandise, might well have felt a sharper end of the same needle, even if it was the other end of it. It would have been good for their souls to have looked for that needle, not in the haystack of mediaeval metaphysics, but in the neat needle-case of their own favourite pocket Bible. It would have been better for them to meditate, not on how many angels could go on the point of a needle, but on how many camels could go through the eye of it.

— G. K. Chesterton

Christh *August 23*

I took my life in my hands and committed it to Christ, the Son of God. This was not, however, in any way an irrational act, for my mind saw Christ as "the way, the truth, and the life," all three. The process preceding the assent was like what happens in all processes of understanding and appreciation. One reads Plato, for instance, and at first suspects that Socrates is just playing with words; then a sense of the seriousness of the discussion develops and appreciation grows. Some reach such a degree of acceptance as to call themselves Platonists. Now the language and message of Christ are, let us assume, divine, and that message contains the good news of eternal life, our ultimate concern. Our human understanding boggles at it, but with the help of grace we reach at length what St. Paul calls "the mind of Christ." Then it is we cry out: "To whom shall we go? Thou hast the words of eternal life." This analysis, as it seems to me, is not far removed from those I have just summarized. But I do what the modern philosophers abhor, namely, appeal to supernatural grace as that which enlightens the mind to see and sets the will to act, and I treat the act as falling within the category of knowledge. In so doing, I have in agreement with me, as I think, the vast majority of those in the past who have considered this form of assent and others kindred to it. A good word here is "mindful," for it "reminds" us that as human beings the mind is immanent in almost all we do.

—Martin D'Arcy

Insight *August 24*

I saw, as every Catholic sees, staring me in the face, what I thought to be the expression of God's mind. But I had to learn to digest it, consciously or unconsciously, in my own way. Most of us, I suppose, who have had to lead a life of study would fancy that there were some important stages or crises in their thinking which revolutionized their outlook. Where the change was not total, it might be a matter of swapping ideas with another or exchanging systems as a Cartesian might turn over to Kant. But we each have, I discovered as I searched for my own Credo, an inner impulse or fate, a kind of Ariadne thread, that together with our free will, shows us the way to go. We each have our own inner impetus or fate, as we can discover when we look back. When we are old, we know exactly what we can do, and our reading is dictated by these specific and personal needs. In early manhood most of us read widely and might, as we think, have followed up various lines of thought. Gradually, ideas coalesce and take their individual shape and direction and become as distinctive as a highland tartan. In late years we may think we have new ideas, but if we look back on more youthful efforts we shall be surprised and rather ruffled to find these same ideas peeping out, even if they were only fledglings.

—Martin D'Arcy

Jesus *August 25*

The Christian view of life did provide a uniquely complete view of life, one in which every individual counted. Created by a living God; watched over by a loving Providence; possessed of free will with a world in which to win my spurs; offered the means of grace and the society of the new covenant, the Church of God; brought into union with Christ, God made man; presented with a vision of utter felicity, unless through one's own fault one lost one's soul; life for me had a purpose, and time seemed to be God's contrivance to allow me to grow and play my part in a vast drama.

This was the kind of unity I was taught, and the interpretation put upon it. The clinching truth, however, in all this pageant of ideas came in the knowledge of Jesus Christ. The Gospels have been subjected to a higher criticism; they have been pulled to pieces and demythologized; but all such attacks leave the mystery of Christ intact. Indeed, if some of the criticism be true, the mystery is increased. It seems to me that there is no figure in history comparable to the Christ of the Gospels, and if four different writers, different in their mental gifts and artistry have succeeded in making such a unique and consistent character, more than a miracle has taken place. He belongs to this world. He is at home in Bethany and Capharnaum, and yet He does not belong to this world. His language in the Sermon on the Mount and at the Last Supper is of a visitor, one who has come with a message, the bloodstained message of good news. The Gospel writers can narrate His fears and agonies and the most degraded form of death without lowering Him in our eyes. Far from that; He seems to grow in majesty in these records of Him.

—*Martin D'Arcy*

Chance   *August 26*

I always find it so hard to imagine how people can look at the order of creation around them and content their minds with the supposition that it got there by chance. Nothing but dead matter to start with, and then mysteriously arising amidst that dead matter living things, with the power of organic growth; and then amidst those living things, mysteriously again, conscious things, capable of feeling and of moving from place to place; and then amidst those conscious things, still more mysteriously, a self-conscious being, Man, with his mind capable of turning back upon itself and becoming its own object. The whole of creation leading up gradually to higher and higher stages of existence, with Mind as the last stage of all—and yet somehow Mind must have been there from the first, or how, from the first, did cosmos emerge from chaos; how, from the first, could creation have contained the germs of Mind, unless Mind had put them there? What do they make of it all, the materialists?

Oh, they say, that's all right; it's just a sort of accident, a sort of outside chance; after all, sooner or later these outside chances are bound to come off. Look at all the millions of worlds there are; is it very surprising that just a few of them, perhaps two or three, should have had the kind of climate which makes life possible? And since that happened, it was more or less bound to happen that in one of these at least the possibility should be actually realized, and life, followed by conscious life, followed by self-conscious life, should appear. I've never been able to find that argument very impressive; it starts all right, but it seems to flicker in the middle.

—*Msgr. Ronald Knox*

How? *August 27*

It's quite easy to see that with millions of worlds about you are likely to get one or two, and one or two only, with the kind of climate we have, on which, therefore, life is possible. But it's one thing to say the odds are on there being one or two bodies, like Mars and ourselves, on which life is *possible;* it's quite another thing to say the odds are on life actually *coming to exist,* here or in Mars or anywhere. As I wrote in a book somewhere, "if the police were to discover a human body in Lord Russell's Saratoga trunk, he would not be able to satisfy them with the explanation that, among all the innumerable articles of luggage in the world, it is only natural that there should be some few which are large enough to contain a body. They would want to know how it got there." How did life arise—just out of a particular lot of atoms happening to get jumbled together? If so, there is our second coincidence; those particular atoms happen to get jumbled up on a planet with a climate which happens to support life; and that life happens to survive. And later on, by a fresh accident, some of these plants happen to develop sensation, and these sensitive plants happen to survive and become animals; and then certain animals happen to develop the habit of reflective thought, and those particular animals happen to survive, and turn into men—altogether there is rather too much coincidence there. Accident is all right as an explanation at first, but there comes a point at which the thing begins to look like carelessness.

And, of course, even if you could prove that life (for example) arises automatically out of some particular arrangement of atoms—we haven't proved it, and we are no nearer proving it than we ever were—the question would still remain to be asked, what power it was which ordained that such an arrangement of atoms should result in the birth of a quite new order of existence.

—*Msgr. Ronald Knox*

Feast of Saint Augustine   *August 28*

I think of St. Augustine when in A.D. 410 the news was brought to him in Carthage that Rome had been sacked. It was a sore blow, but as he explained to his flock, "All earthly cities are vulnerable. Men build them and men destroy them. At the same there is the City of God which men did not build and cannot destroy and which is everlasting." Then he devoted the remaining seventeen years of his life to an exposition of the relation between the two cities in his great masterpiece, *The City of God,* thereby providing a basis for coping with the collapse of a spent civilization, lighting a way through the darkness that followed into a new civilization, Christendom, whose legatees and perhaps liquidators we are. Said Blake: "I give you the end of a golden string, and you wind it into ball. It will lead you in at heaven's gate, built in Jerusalem's wall." Let us then avert our eyes from the wrath to come, which would seem now to be upon us, and like

Augustine follow Blake's golden string beyond the impending darkness.

—*Malcolm Muggeridge*

Mind over Matter

People who like to use sham-scientific language will not be slow to tell you that the processes of the mind are only a function of the brain. That word "function" is a glorious piece of mumbo-jumbo; it means, in that connection, exactly nothing whatever. It may be true that each mental experience you have is connected with, nay, so far as our present experience goes, is inseparably connected with, some little groove inside one's brain; I wish I could ever learn how to talk scientific language properly. But that isn't to say that your thought is THE SAME THING as the groove in your brain, which would obviously be nonsense. And to say that the one is a function of the other is simply introducing a mathematical term to cover up the nonsense. What does happen, if you come to think of it, when a person goes mad; what do we really know about it? All we know is, that the mind can only receive its impressions, can only express itself, through a mysterious *liaison* with the material body which belongs to it. When that *liaison* is disturbed, I suppose you have the same kind of situation that you have when a deaf organist is playing on an organ in which all the stops are out of tune. He may be the best organist in the world, but the noise that comes out will be simply beastly, because the organ with which he is expressing himself is quite inadequate to his powers of performance. We simply don't know what has happened to the mind; all we know is that there has been an interruption in its sources of communication with the outside world.

... In so far as matter is important to the existence of mind, whereas mind is not important to the existence of matter, in that proportion we are emboldened to say that mind must, in the ultimate constitution of things, have a higher value and importance than matter has. For you can conceive of matter as existing for the sake of mind, whereas you cannot possibly think of mind as existing for the sake of matter.

—Msgr. Ronald Knox

The Mind

There is, of course, a . . . very simple and obvious consideration which asserts the priority of mind over matter; I mean the fact that whereas matter can only be the object of thought, mind can be its object as well as its subject. The mind of man, unlike brute matter, unlike even (unless we are strangely deceived in them) the consciousness of other sentient creatures, can turn back upon itself and become self-conscious, become aware of itself as thinking. That which can thus fulfil a double rôle in the scheme of existence must surely have a greater fullness of life and of meaning than that which is confined to a single rôle.

. . . It would be ridiculous to imagine that my thoughts exist for the purpose of making my tongue waggle, or your ears twitch. That which exists for the sake of something else must have less value, in the ultimate nature of things, than that for the sake of which it exists. Pills exist for the sake of health, not health for the sake of pills; which means that health is a more important thing than pills, and so on. And therefore, just in proportion as mind is useless to matter, in that proportion it claims to be a more worthwhile thing than matter. So the materialist's boomerang has come back and hit him in the face.

—Msgr. Ronald Knox

Thoughtless Philosophers

We have never read or heard of any age that had so high an opinion of its own acquisitions, that believed so firmly in its own intelligence, and that so little questioned its own immense superiority over all preceding ages, as the eighteenth century. It believed itself enlightened, highly cultivated, profound, philosophic, humane, and yet the doctrines and theories that it placed in vogue, and over which the upper classes grew enthusiastic in their admiration, are so narrow, so shallow, so directly in the face and eyes of common sense, so manifestly false and absurd, that one finds it difficult to believe that anybody out of a madhouse ever entertained them. What think you of a philosopher who defines man—"A digesting tube, open at both ends"? and of another who ascribes all the difference between a man and a horse, for instance, to "the fact that man's fore limbs terminate in hands and flexible fingers, while those of a horse terminate in hoofs"? Yet these philosophers were highly esteemed in their day, and gave a tone to public opinion. We laugh at them as they did with the disciples of Epicurus, at the superstitions of past ages, the belief in sorcery, magic, necromancy, demons, witches, wizards, magicians, and yet all these things flourished in the eighteenth century, are believed in this nineteenth century in our own country, in England, France, and Germany, by men of all professions, and in all ranks of society. Wherein, then, consists the progress of our enlightment?

—*Orestes Brownson*

Liberalism   *September 1*

The great misfortune of modern liberalism is, that it was begotten of impatience and born of a reaction against the tyranny and oppression, the licentiousness and despotism of governments and the governing classes; and it is more disposed to hate than to love, and is abler to destroy than to build up. Wherever you find it, it bears traces of its origin, and confides more in human passion than in divine Providence. The great majority of its adherents, even if they retain a vague and impotent religious sentiment, and pay some slight outward respect to the religion of their country, yet place the state above the church, the officers of government above the ministers of religion, and maintain that priests have nothing to do with the affairs of this world. They forget that it is precisely to introduce the elements of truth, justice, right, duty, conscience into the government of individuals and nations in this world, as the means of securing the next, that institutions of religion exist, and priests are consecrated. Politicians may do as they please, so long as they violate no rule of right, no principle of justice, no law of God; but in no world, in no order, in no rank, or condition, have men the right to do wrong. Religion, if any thing is the *lex suprema,* and what it forbids, no man has the right to do. This is a lesson liberalism has forgotten, or never learned.

—*Orestes Brownson*

The Upright Life   *September 2*

Political and economic physicism has really poisoned modern culture. In opposition to it the traditions of the *philosophia perennis* may once more teach us a specifically human conception. Such a conception—it is certainly not the invention of St. Thomas; all the superior minds of antiquity, even pagan antiquity, shared it, but St. Thomas, following Aristotle, clearly formulated the principles of it—considers politics and economics not as physical sciences, but as branches of ethics, the science of human actions. However immense the part played therein by conditions determined by the nature of material things and their automatic action, such a science is, nevertheless, defined by reference to the use which our freedom makes and ought to make of such conditions. Its end is the upright life, the good *human* life on this earth: a system of life worthy of man and of what is of most importance in man, that is to say, the spirit. Political and economic laws are not purely physical laws, like the laws of mechanics or chemistry, they are laws of human action, investing in themselves moral values. Justice, humanity, unswerving love of one's neighbour, are essentially part of the very structure of politics and economics. An act of treachery is not merely a thing forbidden by individual morality, but a thing *politically* bad, tending to ruin the political health of the social body.

—*Christopher Dawson*

A Better World

There is an idea of the hierarchy of values far different from the industrialist conception, wholly concentrated on production, which the modern world forms of civilisation. We see to what an extent the supremacy of the economic, itself derived from a system based on the fecundity of money—a fecundity which, like everything that transgresses the conditions laid down by nature, knows no limits—to what an extent the materialist or capitalist or Marxian conception of culture is at variance with the mind of the common Doctor of the Church.

The Christian idea is opposed to the modern world, I agree, to the extent that the modern world is *inhuman.*

But to the extent that the modern world, in spite of all its defects in quality, involves a real growth of history, no, the Christian conception of culture is not opposed to it. Rather the reverse: it would endeavour to preserve in the modern world and bring back to the order of the spirit all the riches of life the modern world contains.

The anguish, the great anguish, which rends the modern world, whence does it proceed if not from all the inhumanity it involves? That is to say that it aspires unwittingly to a civilisation of a Christian type, a civilisation like that of which the principles of St. Thomas give us an idea.

—Christopher Dawson

Religion

From the earliest times God willed to bring to the knowledge of men things far in excess of the requirements of any nature that ever was or ever could be created. He revealed to them the depths of His divine life, the secret of His eternity. And to guide their footsteps to such heights, to prepare them, on this earth already, for the vision of such splendours, He spread over the world, like a tablecloth, grace which was capable of divinising our knowledge and our love. God makes such divine advances to all men at all times; for He is the light "which enlighteneth every man." He will have all men to be saved, and to come to the knowledge of the truth. His advances are accepted or rejected.

This is the reason why none of the religions recorded in history is the simple natural religion contemplated in the abstract by philosophers. There are, no doubt, many features to be found in such religions answering the natural religious aspirations of the human being, but all in fact derive from a more remote origin, all retain some vestige of the primordial revelations and ordinations, and have all, with the exception of the religion of Christ, declined from the supernatural order and more or less deviated consecutively from the natural order.

The piety of pagan antiquity admirably perceived the vital need the State has of religion; its great misfortune was that it absorbed religion into civilisation, into a particular local civilisation, by confusing the State and religion, by deifying the State.

—*Christopher Dawson*

Words   *September 5*

I have always had a sort of mania about words—it's the only consistent and abiding passion I have ever had. For that reason if for no other, Pascal made an immediate appeal. I think the most wonderful sentence ever penned is in the first chapter of St. John's Gospel, "In the beginning was the Word . . . ". What a marvellous sentence that is. How tremendous are its implications. "In the beginning was the Word. . . ." It had to be the Word. It couldn't be, for instance, "In the beginning was video tape . . . ", "In the beginning was celluloid . . . ", or "In the beginning was a microphone . . . "—none of that. In the beginning was the Word, and one of the things that appalls me and saddens me about the world today is the condition of words. Words can be polluted even more dramatically and drastically than rivers and land and sea. There has been a terrible destruction of words in our time.

Let me give a striking example. Perhaps the most beautiful of words, the subject of that marvellous thirteenth chapter of the

Epistle to the Corinthians, is the word "love." Just think of how that word has been polluted and corrupted so that one scarcely dares to use it. Similarly with words like "freedom" and "liberation." The truth is that if we lose the meaning of words, it is far more serious in practise than losing our wealth or our power. Without our words, we are helpless and defenceless; their misuse is our undoing.

—*Malcolm Muggeridge*

The Power of Words   *September 6*

We speak of reforming our marriage laws, when we mean creating facilities for breaking more and more marriages. Jesus himself said that heaven and earth would pass away, but his words would not pass away. I believe that is true, and I think that our more sacred treasure today is the word of the Gospels, which we should guard at all costs, for it is most precious. Now Pascal is a master of words.

I was in Darwin, Australia, and I got a message that there was a man in a hospital there who had listened to something that I had said on the radio, and had expressed a wish that I should visit him. So I did. He turned out to be an old, wizened man who had lived in the bush and who was blind. I can never forget him. Wanting to think of something to say to him that would light him up and cheer him up, I suddenly remembered a phrase in the play *King Lear*. You may remember that Gloucester, commiserating with Lear on being blind, uses five words. I remembered them then: "I stumbled when I saw." I said this to the old man in the Darwin hospital. He was utterly enchanted. He got the point immediately. As I left the ward, I could hear him saying them over and over to himself: "I stumbled when I saw." That is what I mean by the marvellous power of words when they are used with true force in their true meaning.

—*Malcolm Muggeridge*

Our Confused World

Next to this genius of Pascal's words I would draw your attention to the beautiful lucidity of his mind, the wonderful clarity of his thought. Like all true believers, he was deeply skeptical. His intelligence was wonderfully astringent and critical. It is one of the fantasies of the twentieth century that believers are credulous people, sentimental people, and that you have to be a materialist and a scientist and a humanist to have a skeptical mind. But of course exactly the opposite is true. It is believers who can be astringent and skeptical, whereas people who believe seriously that this universe exists only in order to provide a theatre for man must take man with deadly seriousness. I believe myself that the age we are living in now will go down in history as one of the most credulous ever. How could anyone look at television advertisements without reaching that conclusion? All those extraordinary potions that are offered to make your face beautiful, those things you can swallow to make your breath fragrant, are all apparently believed in to the extent that people buy the products.

— *Malcolm Muggeridge*

Credulity

I have often thought that if I were a rich and adventurous man instead of an old and rather broken down one I should bring over a witch doctor from Africa and subject him to a course of television advertising and see how he would react. I think he would be green with envy. To think of all that weary slogging from African village to African village to dispose of his love potions and his jujus, while here, in the Western world, the most highly educated, the most progressive, the most advanced part of the earth, there is a reservoir of credulity beyond his wildest dreams.

— *Malcolm Muggeridge*

Faith

Faith does indeed tell us what the senses do not tell, but does not contradict their findings. It transcends but does not contradict them. Pascal repeats, "Faith is the gift of God." I think it is also the same thing that the poet William Blake, whom I so admire, calls the imagination. You know, we have got, as it were, mind blocks. So much has been achieved by human intelligence that we have got lost in it. Whereas this other dimension that Blake calls the imagination and that Pascal calls faith is the thing that we most desperately need.

—*Malcolm Muggeridge*

Modernists   *September 9*

The Modernists were peculiarly unfortunate when they said that the modern world must not be expected to tolerate the old syllogistic methods of the Schoolmen. They were proposing to scrap the one mediaeval instrument which the modern world will most immediately require. There would have been a far better case for saying that the revival of Gothic architecture has been sentimental and futile; that the Pre-Raphaelite movement in art was only an eccentric episode; that the fashionable use of the word "Guild" for every possible sort of social institution was affected and artificial; that the feudalism of Young England was very different from that of Old England. But of this method of clean-cut deduction, with the definition of the postulates and the actual answering of the question, is something of which the whole of our newspaper-flattered society is in sharp and instant need; as the poisoned are in need of medicine. I have here taken only one example which happened to catch my eye out of a hundred thousand that flash by every hour.

—*G. K. Chesterton*

The Intellectual September 10

What we call the intellectual world is divided into two types of
people—those who worship the intellect and those who use it.
There are exceptions; but, broadly speaking, they are never the
same people. Those who use the intellect never worship it; they
know too much about it. Those who worship the intellect never
use it; as you can see by the things they say about it. Hence there
has arisen a confusion about intellect and intellectualism; and, as
the supreme expression of that confusion, something that is called
in many countries the Intelligentsia, and in France more especially,
the Intellectuals. It is found in practice to consist of clubs and
coteries of people talking mostly about books and pictures, but
especially new books and new pictures; and about music, so long
as it is very modern music; or what some would call very unmusi-
cal music. The first fact to record about it is that what Carlyle said
of the world is very specially true of the intellectual world—that
it is mostly fools. Indeed, it has a curious attraction for complete
fools, as a warm fire has for cats. I have frequently visited such
societies, in the capacity of a common or normal fool, and I have
almost always found there a few fools who were more foolish than
I had imagined to be possible to man born of woman; people who
had hardly enough brains to be called half-witted. But it gave
them a glow within to be in what they imagined to be the
atmosphere of intellect; for they worshipped it like an unknown
god.

—G. K. Chesterton

The Thoughtless September 11

Anyhow, it is in this intellectual world, with its many fools and
few wits and fewer wise men, that there goes on perpetually a sort
of ferment of fashionable revolt and negation. From this comes all
that is called destructive criticism; though, as a matter of fact, the
new critic is generally destroyed by the next critic long before he
has had any chance of destroying anything else. When people say

solemnly that the world is in revolt against religion or private property or patriotism or marriage, they mean that *this* world is in revolt against them; or rather, is in permanent revolt against everything. Now, as a matter of fact, this world has a certain excuse for being always in that state of excitement, apart from mere fuss and mere folly. The reason is rather an important one; and I would ask anyone who really does want to think, and especially to think freely, to pause upon it seriously for a moment. It arises from the fact that these people are so much concerned with the study of Art. It collapses into mere drivelling and despair, because they try to transfer their treatment of art to the treatment of morals and philosophy. In this they make a bad blunder in reasoning. But then, as I have explained, intellectuals are not very intellectual.

The Arts exist, as we should put it in our primeval fashion, to show forth the glory of God; or, to translate the same thing in terms of our psychology, to awaken and keep alive the sense of wonder in man. The success of any work of art is achieved when we say of any subject, a tree or a cloud or a human character, "I have seen that a thousand times and I never saw it before."

— *G. K. Chesterton*

The Gospels   *September 12*

Over thirty years ago now, I was one evening in a room with about a dozen other philosophers. It was on the occasion of an International Congress of Philosophy. The talk turned to religion, its nature, its forms and titles, its deeds and faith. After a time a philosopher from the north of Europe said that he had lost his Lutheran faith as a young man and been attracted to Leibniz and then to Kant and others. Finally out of curiosity he had gone back to the Gospels to pass a new judgment upon them. To his amazement, however, he realized after a time that it was not he who was the judge. He was himself being judged and by one whose standards were so absolute and final that he had to go on his knees. When he had finished, a Swiss philosopher proceeded to tell a story of himself with an identical ending, though he had had a different, Calvinistic, upbringing and had sworn by other philosophical masters.

If this be the impression made upon two thinkers by the Christ of the Gospels, and by impression I do not mean feelings so much as the light which accompanies the discovery of a truth, life will consist in seeing more and more of reality magnetized, as it were, like iron filings round this living truth. One could see that this happened to St. Paul and to the Apostolic writers. Taken together, the writings of the New Testament already present a theological unity so closely-knit, so living, and so novel that it seems beyond human construction.

—*Martin D'Arcy*

Our Holiness

September 13

Christ gives me the impression of being at home in ... far-off spiritual regions. The heights of the spiritual life are so familiar to Him. He climbs the spiritual Himalayas, leading us on, as if the ascent were as well-known to him as a hill in Galilee. This is the decisive point of His revelation of Himself to the individual, for He makes clear to us the vision of holiness—and is in a sense Himself our holiness; and at the end of the vision is love laid bare more lovely than any human dream. The Pauline letters articulate the Gospels, acting like a fan, which, when it is opened up reveals what is hidden in the folds. St. Paul does more; he gives us the cosmic Christ against the setting of the powers of nature and the forces of the shining ranges of the firmament. He opens our eyes so that they are like to "eyelids of the morning." This vast universe, after the stories told of it by the astronomers, crushes us by its indifference as well as its size. The influence of the cosmic Christ is however so strong that we too become at home and we walk at ease and look with joy at the wonders of our God (*mirabila Dei Nostri*). I said that Christ is himself in a sense our holiness. This is so because he is more to us than we are to ourselves; he is, too, within the self, in the "crypts" as the Gospel says, or depths, as a co-conscious worker, for, as it is written in lines attributed to King Alfred:

> To see Thee is the end and the beginning;
> Thou carriest me, and Thou dost go before.
> Thou art the journey and the journey's end.

> —*Martin D'Arcy*

Truth

My Oxford studies made me certain that the intellect was a sure passport to reality. There could be no denying the mind's claims; it does not make the object; it apprehends it. This gave me certitude, but it did not help me much with discovering the nature of truth. My training was a hindrance for it lacked that sympathetic understanding which is so imperative if I were to make, in my mind, a kind of ecumenical peace among my philosophers and philosophies and arrive at a full, satisfactory system and view of life.

My interests at the time were philosophical, and it was only with time that they became more theological. Rousselot had provided a key which could open doors in his theory of how knowledge and love can be combined. Rousselot had leaned on St. Augustine; so it was natural to turn to him. Augustine had been an ardent Neoplatonist and he imbibed from them the idea of love as an attraction for, and an assimilation to, the highest. When he became a Christian, he found it easy to combine love and knowledge, for to him God was not only the paradigm of truth but also of goodness. The truths of this life were but shadows or images of His perfection, and the mind took satisfaction in looking upon God *modico ictu cordis,* "with a gentle stirring of the heart," and seeing all as dependent upon him.

> —*Martin D'Arcy*

God was and is the one object who is supremely lovable, and He draws all to Him, as Aristotle said, by desire. Aristotle's God, however, had no interest outside himself and was not the Christian God Augustine had fallen in love with. Even the Platonists saw truth only "from afar off." The Christian God is the initiator of our human loves, for it is through God's antecedent love that we rise up to love him back. "I would not be searching for you if I had not already found you"; in this view Pascal and Augustine were at one. Knowledge and love, therefore, went hand in hand when it came to loving God. "Think you that wisdom is other than truth, in which the supreme good is beheld and possessed?" "The happy life consists of joy in truth; for this is a joying in Thee, who art the Truth, O God, health of my countenance, my God." Holding such a view, he was able to describe love as a kind of bias of the soul—"my weight is my love"—towards living truth. Where our heart is, there is our treasure, and a secret love within us dictates to us where to look and what to find.

—Martin D'Arcy

God Is Central

Let me suggest this point to you—that God, not man, must be the measure of the Universe, must be the standard by which we are to judge all our experience. If we make man the centre of all our experience, then the riddle of existence becomes insoluble, and we had far better give it up.

—Msgr. Ronald Knox

About God

All the attributes of God, his simplicity, his immutability and so on, are not something which we learn from the Bible, or from the tradition of the Church, they are something which we learn from reason itself, learn from that same process of reasoning by which we prove that God exists. It is no good asserting the existence of a Creator who is not omnipotent; for if he is not omnipotent he is limited—who or what is it that limits him? You will have to fall back on assuming the existence of some power greater than that of the Creator himself. It is no good asserting the existence of a God who is not simple, who is in any way composite; for if so you will have to fall back on assuming the existence of some power which produced that fusion of elements in him. And so on all through; the proofs from which we learn the existence of God give us some idea, necessarily, of his Nature.

We have been talking about natural theology; that is, about the knowledge of God which man can reach for himself, if he will trust his own reason and his own conscience. The next stage in apologetic is to establish, on historical grounds, the fact that our Lord came to earth and that he claimed to bring a fuller revelation from God; the grounds, too, on which he justified that claim.

—*Msgr. Ronald Knox*

We Need Help

First of all let's get this point clear—that God wasn't *bound* to reveal himself to man. In spite of our dual nature, in spite of the Fall, man has got enough apparatus left to serve God, if he wants to, without any direct supernatural assistance. His reason will tell him that God exists, if he will only think. His conscience will tell him that God ought to be obeyed, and, in general outline, what are the laws which God wants him to obey, if he will only listen to it. We believe, in fact, that it is possible for a man brought up altogether remote from Christian influence and therefore, through no fault of his own, a heathen or practically a heathen, to reach heaven if he will make use of the actual graces God sends him, by being sorry for his sins and so on. And we should have no grievance against God, in strict justice at least, if all of us were in the same position; if you and I had never been brought up in the Catholic faith, if (for that matter) there had been no Catholic faith for us to be brought up in.

That's all perfectly true, but it doesn't need a very profound study of human nature to discover that most men, left to the light of their natural reason and conscience, don't, at least to all appearance, put up much of a show. The human reason is curiously apt to get warped in such a way that it only thinks what it wants to think; the human conscience is even more prone to accommodate itself, so that a man comes to approve of himself for doing exactly the thing he wants to do.

—*Msgr. Ronald Knox*

God's Ambassador   *September 18*

I always like that phrase in the *Imitation of Christ* which compares our natural reason to a spark left among the ashes—you know, that irritating bit of live coal which makes it *look* as if it ought to be possible to get the fire going again by just drawing it with a newspaper, but when you've tried it for about half an hour you find that you have to ring for the housemaid and get her to lay the fire afresh after all. That, as we know, is what our Lord's Incarnation meant, the *remaking* of our nature. And, so far as our reason is concerned, he did that in the first place by making to us a revelation of the Divine Nature; by telling us and showing us more about God than we knew, more than we ever could have known, by any philosophical speculation.

More than we ever could have known—whereas reason merely teaches us that God is One, revelation informs us there are three Persons in one Godhead; whereas the doctrine of Purgatory was something the human reason might have guessed at (and indeed, some of the pagans, notably Virgil, made an uncommonly good shot at it) only revelation could have established its truth, and so on. To bring us such information, we need a Messenger from God; an Ambassador, and one who can present credentials to us, so that we can be sure he comes from God. Remember, it is not logically necessary for us, at this stage in apologetics, to prove that Jesus Christ was the Son of God; all we want to be sure of at this stage is that he is God's Ambassador to man.

—*Msgr. Ronald Knox*

Humility

September 19

... We shall find that all our efforts to convey the reality of our existence are just so much children's scribble in the light of what it really is. The scribbles that have come nearest to conveying it are those of the artists rather than those of the philosophers or the theologians or the scientists. Let me express that in one rather grotesque image. Imagine a savage abasing himself before a painted stone. Because that primitive act conveys faith of a kind, that savage is nearer to the realities of things than, say, Einstein. This is what Jesus meant with his sayings about how children and fools understand things that are hidden better than do the learned and the wise. We today need faith more than any other thing on the earth. In the writings of Pascal you will find faith expressed.

Pascal was also a very proud man. But he put aside his pride to bow himself down at the altar rail with his fellow Christians, whomsoever they might be, in perfect brotherliness. This was an important aspect of Pascal. Before scientists became as arrogant as many of them are today, he, a superlatively great scientist, practised true humility, which is the greatest of all virtues. Indeed, as he points out, humility is the very condition of virtue. Because he understood how important humility is and because he could recognize the arrogance that was growing up among scholars and learned people, he foresaw the dangers that the Enlightenment would bring.

—*Malcolm Muggeridge*

Pride

It is in vain oh men that you seek within yourselves the cure for your miseries. All your insight only leads you to the knowledge that it is not in yourselves that you will discover the true and the good. The philosophers promised them to you and they have not been able to keep their promise. They do not know what your true good is or what your true state is. How should they have provided you with a cure for ills which they have not even understood. Your principal maladies are pride, which cuts you off from God, and sensuality, which binds you to the earth. And they have done nothing but foster at least one of these maladies. If they have given you God for your object, it has been to pander to your pride. They have made you think you were like him and resemble him by your nature. And those who have grasped the vanity of such a pretension have cast you down in the other abyss by making you believe that your nature is like that of the beast of the field and have led you to seek your good in lust, which is the lot of animals.

—*Blaise Pascal*

The Fall of Christendom

First and foremost I should put a sort of death wish at the heart of it, in the guise of what we call liberalism. It goes back, as Solzhenitsyn suggested in his recent Harvard address, to the Enlightenment and gained a great impetus during the period of American dominance in the world in this century, culturally and economically, if not militarily. Previous civilizations have been overthrown from without by the incursion of barbarian hordes. Christendom has dreamed up its own dissolution in the minds of its own intellectual elite. Our barbarians are home products, indoctrinated at the public expense, urged on by the media systematically stage by stage, dismantling Christendom, depreciating and deprecating all its values. The whole social structure is now tumbling down, dethroning its God, undermining all its certainties. All this, wonderfully enough, is being done in the name of the health, wealth, and happiness of all mankind. That is the basic scene that seems to me will strike a future Gibbon as being characteristic of the decline and fall of Christendom.

I could go on giving details, but you can very well fill in for yourselves.

—*Malcolm Muggeridge*

TV   *September 22*

The average Western man looks at television for four hours every day, which means that he spends ten years of his life looking into a television screen, something that precludes reading, conversation, and other exercises in literacy. About twenty years ago there was the twenty-fifth anniversary of the invention of television, a day that should have been signalized by wearing black and muffled bells and flags at half mast. However, the BBC decided in its wisdom to make a program showing men looking at television all over the world. Around the world this television crew went, filming people looking at television. It had no difficulty whatever finding them, in the deserts, on the tops of mountains, in the jungle—everywhere it went there was the little screen and people gathered round it. But what they discovered was that everybody was looking at the same programs: *I Love Lucy* and *Wagon Train.* So you had the ironic spectacle of the whole human race preoccupied with these great masterpieces of our civilization.

—*Malcolm Muggeridge*

Moral Vacuum   *September 23*

Another area of the moral and spiritual decline of Christendom is the abandonment of Christian mores. The movement away from Christian moral standards has not meant moving to an alternative humanistic system of moral standards as was anticipated, but moving into a moral vacuum, especially in the areas of eroticism. Christendom has also retreated from freedom. In the much talk today about human rights, we forget that our human rights are derived from the Christian faith. In Christian terms every single human being, whoever he or she may be, sick or well, clever or foolish, beautiful or ugly, every single human being is loved of his Creator, who has, as the Gospels tell us, counted the hairs of his head. This Creator cannot see even a sparrow fall to the ground without concern. Now it is from that concept that our rights derive. You will find as we move away from Christendom that whatever declarations may be made and agreements may be concluded, these basic human rights depend ultimately on the Christian concept of man and of his relationship to his Creator.

The West is also on a quest for security and plenty. The quest for security has given us a weapon so powerful that it can blow us and our earth to smithereens.

—Malcolm Muggeridge

Before Becoming a Catholic *September 24*

"Does God exist?" That question at least I could answer with an unhesitating affirmative, and with no fears for the results. If, however, I were asked, "Is the Pope infallible when he speaks *ex cathedra* on faith and morals?" I should have been tempted to reply, "Will you please give me notice of that question, as I should like to review once more the arguments which have convinced me on this point, but if you insist on an immediate reply, I can only answer, 'Yes, I believe the Pope to be infallible.' "

I am inclined to think that this attitude is more common among converts than is usually believed. "You must make a venture," said Newman. "Faith is a venture before a man is a Catholic. You approach the Church in the way of reason. You enter it in the light of the spirit."

A letter from another convert lies before me as I write. "I have no doubt at all that God exists, from which two things follow. Either he wishes us to worship him as Catholic, in which case it is clearly right to become a Catholic, or he doesn't mind whether we are Catholics or not, in which case one may as well be a Catholic as anything else."

—*Arnold Lunn*

Joining

I accepted the claims of the Church not by faith but as the logical conclusion of a reasoned argument. My darkness was illumined by reason rather than by anything in the nature of an "inner light." This perhaps explains a certain vague disquiet which Father Knox began to register on the very eve of my conversion. He wanted to know whether I was sound on this or that article of the Catholic faith—Hell for instance—and whether I understood what the Church meant by such and such a doctrine. Now times are still hard, and I had not spent the best part of a pound on a ticket to Oxford only to return as a Protestant to Paddington, so I insisted that I was prepared to accept all that the Church proposed for my belief and to reject with conviction what the Church condemned.

It was, however, some little time before Father Knox ceased to regard me with faint distrust. A few months later I visited him at Oxford, and asked him rather shyly if I might serve his Mass. He seemed dubious. Was I sure, he asked me, if I had really mastered the technique. I insisted on my competence.

—*Arnold Lunn*

Reasonable

In those distant days when doubts came I wondered whether they would ever go; now I only ask myself when they will go. In those days I used to worry as to whether Catholicism was true; now I only worry as to how most effectively to demonstrate Catholic truth. There are still unsolved difficulties, to which I have yet to find a satisfactory answer, but I have discovered a key which unlocks nine locks out of ten, and it is not the fault of the key but my wrist that the tenth lock proves rather sticky.

I have never been a great believer in the reasons of the heart; it is for the head to reason and for the heart to affirm. Those who have done what they could to justify at the bar of reason the credo with which they enter the Church may perhaps be forgiven if some years later they confess not only their faith but their love. Two years is a short period of probation, but it is long enough for the convert to discover a wholly personal significance in those words . . . from the psalms:

Lord, I love the beauty of your house and the dwelling-place of your glory.

— *Arnold Lunn*

Reformation *September 27*

It is perfectly true that we can find real wrongs, provoking rebellion, in the Roman Church just before the Reformation. What we cannot find is one of those real wrongs that the Reformation reformed. For instance, it was an abominable abuse that the corruption of the monasteries sometimes permitted a rich noble to play the patron and even play at being the Abbot, or draw on the revenues supposed to belong to a brotherhood of poverty and charity. But all that the Reformation did was to allow the same rich noble to take over *all* the revenue, to seize the whole house and turn it into a palace or a pig-sty, and utterly stamp out the last legend of the poor brotherhood. The worst things in worldly Catholicism were made worse by Protestantism. But the best things remained somehow through the era of corruption; nay, they survived even the era of reform. They survive today in all Catholic countries, not only in the colour and poetry and popularity of religion, but in the deepest lessons of practical psychology. And so completely are they justified, after the judgment of four centuries, that every one of them is now being copied, even by those who condemned it; only it is often caricatured. Psychoanalysis is the Confessional without the safeguards of the Confessional; Communism is the Franciscan movement without the moderating balance of the Church; and American sects, having howled for three centuries at the Popish theatricality and mere appeal to the senses, now "brighten" their services by super-theatrical films and rays of rose-red light falling on the head of the minister.

— G. K. Chesterton

Narrow Minds

Most men would return to the old ways in faith and morals if they could broaden their minds enough to do so. It is narrowness that chiefly keeps them in the rut of negation. But this enlargement is easily misunderstood, because the mind must be enlarged to see the simple things; or even to see the self-evident things.

I feel above all, this simple and forgotten fact; that whether certain charges are or are not true of Catholics, they are quite unquestionably true of everybody else. It never occurs to the critic to do anything so simple as to compare what is Catholic with what is Non-Catholic. The one thing that never seems to cross his mind, when he argues about what the Church is like, is the simple question of what the world would be like without it.

That is what I mean by being too narrow to see the house called the church against the background called the cosmos.

— G. K. Chesterton

Philosophies

It is quite obvious that there are three or four philosophies or views of life possible to reasonable men; and to a great extent these are embodied in the great religions or in the wide field of irreligion. There is the atheist, the materialist or monist or what-ever he calls himself, who believes that all is ultimately material, and all that is material is mechanical. That is emphatically a view of life; not a very bright or breezy view, but one into which it is quite possible to fit many facts of existence. Then there is the normal man with the natural religion, which accepts the general idea that the world has a design and therefore a designer; but feels the Architect of the Universe to be inscrutable and remote, as remote from men as from microbes. That sort of theism is perfectly sane; and is really the ancient basis of the solid if somewhat stagnant sanity of Islam. There is again the man who feels the burden of life so bitterly that he wishes to renounce all desire and all division, and rejoin a sort of spiritual unity and peace from which (as he thinks) our separate selves should never have broken away. That is the mood answered by Buddhism and by many metaphysicians and mystics. Then there is a fourth sort of man, sometimes called a mystic and perhaps more properly to be called a poet; in practice he can very often be called a pagan. His position is this; it is a twilight world and we know not where it ends.

—G. K. Chesterton

Told How to Think   *September 30*

These modern people mean by mental activity simply an express train going faster and faster along the same rails to the same station; or having more and more railway carriages hooked on to it to be taken to the same place. The one notion that has vanished from their minds is the notion of voluntary movement even to the same end. They have fixed not only the ends, but the means. They have imposed not only the doctrines, but the words. They are bound not merely in religion, which is avowedly binding, but in everything else as well. There are formal praises of free thought; but even the praises are in a fixed form. Thousands who have never learned to think at all are urged to think whatever may take their fancy about Jesus Christ. But they are, in fact, forbidden to think in any way but one about Abraham Lincoln. That is why it is worth remarking that it is a Catholic who has thought for himself.

—G. K. Chesterton

Mind and Matter

When I talk about mind and matter, I am not going to attempt any precise definition of those terms; I am going to use them in a popular sense, the good, old-fashioned sense in which they were used by late-Victorian journalists. In that loose sense, the two terms between them exhaust our experience; everything of which we are conscious falls under one head or the other. Matter stands for all those things other than oneself, outside oneself (if I may use such grossly popular terms), which form the object of one's experience; it is the brute fact which you can't get away from, the rude reality which obtrudes itself into your thought. If you are in the dentist's chair and shut your eyes and try to imagine that you are in a hot bath or in a punt on the river, that relentless drill comes buzzing round and having fun with your nerves, the symbol of matter triumphing over mind, insisting on making itself felt and being taken into consideration. The pleasant kingdom of the mind has no real frontiers to defend it; our thought cannot just select its own objects, as it would like to, they force themselves upon it; there is a something not ourselves which we cannot control or organize at will; let that serve for our very inadequate definition of matter.

But matter doesn't cover the whole of our experience; there can be no experience unless there is a mind to do the experiencing.

—*Msgr. Ronald Knox*

Fantasy

Twentieth-century man has created his own fantasy through science which has enabled him to explore as no other generation of men have the structure and mechanics of his own environment. What fantastic achievements have thereby been made possible in the way of moving faster, growing richer, communicating more rapidly, mastering illnesses, and altogether overcoming the hazards of our earthly existence. But all the achievements have led to a growing arrogance, a widening separation from the true nature of our being; in other words, an alienation from God. If it were possible to live without God, it would not be worth living at all. It was in a labour camp, Solzhenitsyn has told us, that he learnt what freedom meant and became free. So, amidst the shambles of a fallen Christendom, I feel a renewed confidence in the light of the Christian revelation with which it first began. I should hate you to think that his view that I've put before you is a pessimistic view. Strangely enough I believe it to be the only way to a proper and real hope.

—*Malcolm Muggeridge*

The Media   *October 3*

A strange thing I have observed over many years in this business of news gathering and news presentation is that by some infallible process media people always manage to miss the most important thing. It's almost as though there were some built-in propensity to do this. In moments of humility, I realize that if I had been correspondent in the Holy Land at the time of our Lord's ministry, I should almost certainly have spent my time knocking about with the entourage of Pontius Pilate, finding out what the Sanhedrin was up to, and lurking around Herod's court with the hope of signing up Salome to write her memoirs exclusively. I regret that this is true. Ironically enough, as the dramatization of the public scene gains impetus, so we move farther and farther from the reality of things and become more and more preoccupied with fantasy.

If when I was a young correspondent in Moscow in the early thirties you had said to me that it would be possible for the Soviet regime to continue for sixty years with its policy of doing everything possible to extirpate the Christian faith, to discredit its record and its originator, and that after this there would emerge figures like Solzhenitsyn speaking the authentic language of the Christian, grasping such great Christian truths as the cross in a way that few people do in our time, I would have said "No, it's impossible, it can't be." But I would have been wrong.

—*Malcolm Muggeridge*

Revelation

Revelation might have come to us through an angel; might have come to us, even, through the granting of special illumination to an ordinary human being. That God's Ambassador should be God himself is an extra, something we could not have claimed or covenanted for. But the Ambassador must have credentials; we must be able to distinguish the revelation which he brings from all the bogus revelations which are splashed across the pages of history; Mahomet with his book, Joanna Southcott with her sealed box, Joseph Smith with his gold plates, and so on. Nay, we must be able to distinguish it from merely private revelations, such as those given to St. Theresa and St. Margaret Mary, which, though we believe them to be divine in their origin, were nevertheless *private* revelations, not imposing belief on anybody except the persons themselves to whom they were made. There must be evidence for all to see.

. . . Revelation is not something to which we could have laid claim as a right, *a fortiori* we have no right to say we want a revelation of this or that kind, in excess of the bare logical minimum. To be sure, a revelation which was incapable of producing conviction would be almost worse than nothing; it would be a continual worry to us without in any way enabling us to make up our minds. But to say that we will not look at any revelation which does not come to us with headlines, so to speak, all across the page, shouting its message at us, compelling attention and forcing conviction on us—that would be presumptuous, seeing what we are. Beggars, after all, cannot be choosers.

—*Msgr. Ronald Knox*

The Claim

We are to examine the question, what it was that our Lord claimed to be. The evidence we shall use is that of the Gospels, used simply as historical documents compiled by people who lived within a short lifetime of the events. I shall not use the fourth Gospel, because, as you will know if you read the letters in *The Times,* a lot of fantastic stuff is still talked about the date and authorship of that Gospel, so that if I used it I might seem to be begging the question. I say, "what our Lord claimed to be," namely, the Son of God in a unique sense. I do not intend to prove, what revelation itself teaches us, that he was the Second Person of the Blessed Trinity, that he united a human with a divine Nature under one Person, or that he came to make atonement for our sins. All that is beside our present point; our present business is to determine whether he claimed to be a fully-accredited ambassador from Almighty God, revealing the things of God to us; and that will be sufficiently established if we prove that he claimed to be the Son of God in a sense so intimate that it is impossible for any creature to share that title with him. If we prove that he *claimed* to be the Son of God, that does not as yet prove that he *was.* We have still to reckon with the possibility that he was deceived, or that he was deceiving us. We shall not have eliminated those possibilities until we have considered what credentials he offers for our inspection.

—Msgr. Ronald Knox

A Mystery

First, let us get this clear—that our Lord's identity was a mystery, to the men of his time no less than to those historians, not of our faith, who have written about his life since. And it was a mystery, you may say, of his own making. There was no doubt at all that he behaved and spoke like a prophet, to say the very least. He didn't set out to be a philosopher, appealing to human reason. Nor yet did he set out to be one of the scribes, that is one of the doctors of the Jewish church, handing on the tradition of the elders. He corrected the tradition of the elders; he was always saying "Moses told you this, but I tell you that," and when you think what the *ipse dixit* of Moses was and still is among the Jews you will realize what a break with tradition that was. One of the first impressions he made upon his audiences was that he taught them as one having authority, and not as their scribes. What sort of authority could that be? To the Jewish mind there was an obvious answer, he must be a prophet, like one of the Old Testament prophets. But, here again, he was a puzzle. The Old Testament prophets had never spoken in their own name. They always began their utterances with the rubric, "Thus saith the Lord"; or they would describe how they had seen a vision, how the Lord God of hosts had spoken to them, and how he had sent them to deliver a message from him. In our Lord's preaching there was never a word of all that.

—*Msgr. Ronald Knox*

Feast of the Rosary   *October 7*

Bernadette [at Lourdes had] the first of the historic apparitions which have so directed, one might almost say dominated, the character and quality of contemporary devotion to Mary. From that simple scene have increasingly come devotions which have brought the rosary into the homes, streets, factories, and public places of remote hamlets and mighty cities in every corner of the modern world. Block rosaries in Detroit and in New England towns; the rosary recited by groups of sailors on American battleships; the rosary that is the pause that truly renews workers in a French factory of which I read not long ago; the rosary repeated in the cars of a train carrying Irish, English, and Scottish pilgrims to Lourdes; the rosary that gave one soul to the bodies of several score Italian sick in the Lourdes asylum which I visited two years ago; the rosary led on the radio by Hollywood stars at Christmastime; the rosary said in the privacy of so many Christian homes.

—*Cardinal John Wright*

With Authority October 8

[Jesus] spoke as one having authority, but the authority seemed somehow to belong to him personally, he never referred the credit of it elsewhere. And as he spoke, so he acted; he told devils to go out of men who were possessed without adjuring them by the name of God; he forgave sins, although the forgiveness of sins belonged to God only; he dispensed people from keeping the Sabbath; he cast the merchants out of the temple; he came into Jerusalem riding on an ass, in evident reference to an old prophecy which was always interpreted as describing the Messiah who was to come. He behaved, not as a prophet, but as something more than a prophet.

. . . He was dropping out hints all the time, such as would lead on those who heard him to the conclusion that he was an ambassador from God, without saying so in so many words. Take, for example, his constant use of the title "Son of Man." It was probably a title connected in Jewish minds with the idea of the Messiah; and he himself talks freely about the day when the Son of Man will come in judgment. But I think he showed a preference for that title just because it emphasized his humanity; and what was the point of emphasizing his humanity unless he were something more than an ordinary human being?

—Msgr. Ronald Knox

Divine October 9

Was it only to his friends, then, that he admitted who he was? No, to his enemies too; but only when their agreed determination to crucify him had made it unnecessary to spare their feelings any longer. The high priest, at his trial, adjures him by the divine name to say whether or no he is the Christ, the Son of the living God. And he answers openly, "I am." Now, observe how impossible it is to take this as anything but a confession of his most intimate convictions about himself. He was on oath; to accept the statement in any false sense was perjury. He was being tried for his

life, and the answer he gave meant certain death; he could have saved himself by withholding it. They were plunging into the guilt of shedding innocent blood; and he was abetting them, if he accepted the title loosely, recklessly, without supplying necessary qualifications. If, then, when he called himself the Son of God, he meant no more than that he was a man like themselves, but distinguished from themselves by the enjoyment, in a unique degree, of prophetic gifts, why did he not say so? Is it credible that he should *not* have said so, when he knew that the alternative was a charge of blasphemy from which he could not defend himself?

—*Msgr. Ronald Knox*

The Empty Tomb   *October 10*

Take the story of the empty tomb by itself. Could you have circumstantial evidence more complete? The body had disappeared; is there any possible motive to assign for its removal by any human agent using natural means? There is absolutely none. Even if you refuse to believe that the Jews took special precautions to keep the tomb safe, you must still recognize that the story of their doing so is true to life. It was in their interest to keep the body, and to be able at any moment to produce it, should any claim be made that Jesus of Nazareth had risen from the dead. If they removed it from the grave, why did they not produce it afterwards? Nor had Pilate, the Roman governor, any reason for wishing to smuggle away the body of the man he had crucified; its presence might conceivably lead to rioting and disturbance, but its disappearance was far more likely to have that effect. The women cannot have stolen it, for they were not strong enough to move away the stone, let alone to overpower a military guard. Did the guard, then, desert their posts, and some other human agent remove the body before the women came? That was the only possibility which presented itself to Mary Magdalen. Could Joseph of Arimathea have carried it away, or Nicodemus? But, in any of these events, why did not the agent who had removed the body give any sign, afterwards, of what he had done? If he were friendly disposed towards the disciples, to the disciples; if he were ill disposed, to the Jews?

—Msgr. Ronald Knox

Penance

It should be remembered that in all great religions the call for self-denial is to be found—in some, indeed, in a far more unqualified way than in Christianity. To judge from past experience, man can get to no heights, physical, artistic, or moral, without it. In such a well-known philosophy of life as the Neoplatonic, there are, as in the east, techniques for changing the self into the likeness of what is One and Perfect. It could be argued that the spirit of asceticism in the first centuries of Christianity was partly due to this Neoplatonic influence. I do not think, however, that any such influence worked upon the Celtic Church in its love for fasts and penances in Ireland and Lindisfarne! There are, besides, all the "hard sayings" in the New Testament to be taken into account. No, a solution, if there be one, must be sought in the very center of the Christian faith.

To get the proportion right we must go back to essentials. Human living itself is such an obstacle race that philosophers like Hegel and Marx have declared its very law is a dialectic. No sooner do we say or do something than its contrary is aroused and, by overcoming this, we arrive at a new unstable synthesis, which will straightway give rise to its opposite. St. Paul calls the Christian life a warfare and bids us always be in arms against the spirit of this world and the enemy within.

—Martin D'Arcy

Self-Discipline

[Life] is not static; we can improve or deteriorate; and wise, saintly persons have handed down to us means and techniques for attaining holiness. Some of these techniques can produce startling results; but I am not thinking of those who acquire extraordinary powers over their bodies, nor again of the mystics who suffer ecstasies and may be raised above the ground. The quintessential improvement lies in the emancipation of the will and in the mastery of our passions, so that we can love without compromises or self-consciousness and hold steadfastly to the truth; and this is a lifetime's hard work.

Here then is one form of self-denial, which most would accept as necessary. But we have to go further than this. Take this dialectic already mentioned, which comes from our nature being in discord with itself; take saws and proverbs and aphorisms as evidence: "All power corrupts . . ."; "the fascination of trifles obscures the good"; the rich man and the eye of a needle. This discord shows itself in the conflict between concupiscence and gentle love, animal and spiritual tastes, and the selfish and unselfish impulses. In the more ancient schools of education, the use of the rod may have been exaggerated, but it testified to the unruly element in the young.

—Martin D'Arcy

Relationship

If there be a God, and if what is presupposed in the language about Him and in the forms which worship takes be true of Him, then the relationship between the self and God must be so intimate and so special as to defy a fully adequate description. The theologian who is relying on reason and not on the help given by the Christian revelation is forced back on general terms which hold for all existent relationships, terms such as cause, necessity, existence. They carry the mind along, but only as heavy oars can move a speedboat. A less metaphysical or logical way might be to lay out for all to see by illustration what this relationship involves. Words like cause and contingency and effect are so common in our experience; they are used for public and private occasions, for turning on the gas, consuming food, writing books, and improving the birthrate. As a result we feel that they fall deplorably short of what we want to say when we pray to God as the sustainer of life, as providence and as lover of the self, this God "in whom we live and have our being." If we are so bound up with Him that we cannot do without Him, then by examining the experience of those who deny God in their lives or the generations which subsist on secular principles, we may be able to discern more vividly the nature of this relationship. When the idea and significance of God slip from the mind, and no one bothers about His judgments or Providence, there ensues perhaps at first a sense of release and independence; but there follow . . . danger [and destruction].

—Martin D'Arcy

Put on Christ   *October 14*

Christianity means . . . that by grace we do have the mind of Christ and begin the unending story of life with and in Him. We "put on" Christ; we wear his mask and impersonate him. Everything here is drawn together, or, what comes to the same thing, in following the Christ, we discover the way and the way is the way of truth, and it is in the way of truth that a philosophy of life can be lived.

The panorama opened by faith is, in short, this: a living God creating all but, in particular, man out of love, so as to get the best out of man and crown him with supreme happiness. This stands out by contrast with an immense dead universe to which we can assign neither beginning nor end, and human beings, like phosphorescent flies, flitting about in it. Such a cold picture is hardly to be borne; so all manner of idols have been set up, abstract absolutes and wholes, progress and humanity to make do and pacify the inquiring and restless soul of man. Those who, in reaction against too human idols, turn to some power for good or a spiritual principle or Absolute Spirit or Superconsciousness are making declarations out of weakness; for the habit of thinking in abstractions and with the help of the impersonal is a congenital weakness of the human mind and not a strength.

—Martin D'Arcy

Happy?

"That's all very interesting," said the naval officer, "but has Catholicism made you any *happier*? That's the point. That's what I want to know."

"But is that the point?" I asked. "Supposing one of your junior officers came to you and told you that he had discovered a new formula for hitting a moving target at sea. You would not ask him if this formula had made him happier, but you would want to know whether the formula enabled him to hit the target. Surely the thing that matters about Catholicism is not whether it makes Lunn happy, but whether it hits the target. Happiness is not necessarily a test of truth. Indeed, the realization that Catholicism was true might make a man very unhappy if the discrepancy between his own behaviour and the Catholic code were too glaring."

My naval friend's question was symptomatic. In this subjective age we are losing all sense of objective truth. "Objective truth," as my friend Mr. Joad remarks, "being regarded as unobtainable, what alone is thought interesting are the reasons which lead people to formulate their particular brand of error." Mr. Joad might have added that modern people tend to assess creeds solely by the degree of pleasure which they afford to those who embrace them.

—Arnold Lunn

Thank You *October 16*

Only a poet could do justice to this theme, but I who am only a controversialist must be at least allowed to say "Thank you." Among the moments for which I am most grateful is one which I shall always associate with my first Easter as a Catholic.

A few months after I had been received I spent Palm Sunday at Sestrières, the famous ski-ing centre in the Italian Alps. The congregation had struggled along a trench between walls of snow six feet in height into a little church decorated with disconsolate palms which remembered the Eastern sun. I decided to spend Easter Sunday at some lower level, where it would not be necessary to consult the calendar in order to convince myself that April had arrived.

I have spent many winters among the mountains, and for me Easter will always be associated with the feet that are beautiful upon the mountains for the good tidings that they bring of Resurrection. In Mürren, where I lived continuously for two years, the first snows often come in October, and the ground is sometimes white until the end of April. In the lowlands, winter gives place without a struggle to spring, and the few sparse snowfalls are only a memory when the buds begin to burgeon. But there is no such gradualness about the Alpine spring. Winter puts up a desperate resistance, and every yard of advance is sternly contested. The premature jubilation of a meadow gay with crocus and anemone may be turned into mourning by a sudden smother of snow. The destructive avalanche is no less characteristic of spring than the tender soldanella. Spring in the lowlands is a lyric, in the Alps an epic.

—Arnold Lunn

Deo Gratias *October 17*

On my way to Orta I found myself with an hour to spare at a wayside town. I went along to the church to discover if I could make my Easter confession and found an obliging priest. After sampling my Italian, he asked me if I could speak French. I replied in the affirmative, and then wondered whether I ought to include this misstatement in the list of sins to be confessed. But his French was no better than my own. He concluded by an odd question. What penances was I accustomed to get in England? I answered, "Oh, trois *Ave Maria,*" to which he replied, "Alors, un suffit." Charmed by this attractive specimen of the genial Catholicism of the south, I emerged into the April sunshine, and slept that night at Orta.

The next morning I heard Mass in a little hill chapel overlooking the lake. I came out just before the last prayers to link the Easter Mass with the Easter loveliness of the lake. The mountain wind was weaving delicate patterns on the water and the lake darkened where the wind touched it. The northern hills were still white, but the slopes which fell away from the terrace and which faced the sun were blue with gentians, and I saw quite plain that the visible beauty of the hills which I had loved as a boy was linked by a kind of necessary connection with the invisible beauty which I had discovered as a man. And the words of the psalm rose to my lips,

QUID RETRIBUAM DOMINO PRO OMNIBUS QUAE RETRIBUIT.[1]

—Arnold Lunn

Golden Mean   *October 18*

"Truth is not falsehood," said St. Augustine, "because spoken with untuneful accent." (*Nec eo falsum quia incomposite sonant signa labiorum.*) You will find this sentence in a passage in which St. Augustine describes his recoil from the academic heresies of the Manichees towards the broad humanity of the Faith. But St. Augustine not only condemns by implication the aesthete who attaches too much importance to, and also the low-brow who affects to despise culture; he insists that a thing is not necessarily

---

[1] What shall I give to the Lord for all He has given me?

true because it is crudely, nor necessarily false because it is gracefully expressed.

"Just as good and bad food may be served up in graceful or in ugly vessels, so truth and falsehood may be expressed either in beautiful or in uncouth phrases."

In this as in all other things the Catholic family preserves the golden mean. You are wrong, says the Church to the critical prig, to despise the old woman because she thinks the waxen doll beautiful. Piety is more important than good taste. You are wrong, says the Church to the puritan, to despise beauty, for beauty is a mirror which reflects, however dimly, an aspect of the eternal God.

— *Arnold Lunn*

Our Absurdity

We have been vouchsafed in the confusion and complexities of today an amazing sign that the promises Christianity enshrines are valid promises. Far from this faith's being, as the media here would have us believe, something that is over and done with, it represents on the contrary, in the desperate circumstances that Solzhenitsyn describes, the only possibility of being released, being liberated, being reborn.

Of course, it's all too easy to ridicule the absurdities and contradictions of our present way of life, issuing denunciations in the mode of some twentieth-century Jeremiah. To do so is highly satisfying to the ego but should be resisted. Here I am speaking to myself.

Built into life is a strong vein of irony for which we should only be grateful to our Creator. It helps us to find our way through the fantasy that encompasses us to the reality of our existence. God has mercifully made the fantasies — the pursuit of power, of sensual satisfaction, of money, of learning, of celebrity, of happiness — so preposterously unrewarding that we are forced to turn to him for help and for mercy.

— *Malcolm Muggeridge*

The Incarnation

[Is there an] interminable soap opera going on from century to century, from era to era, whose old discarded sets and props litter the earth? Surely not. Was it to provide a location for so repetitive and ribald a performance that the universe was created and man came into existence? I can't believe it. If this were all, then the cynics, the hedonists, and the suicides would be right. The most we can hope for from life is some passing amusement, some gratification of our senses, and death. But it's not all.

Thanks to the great mercy and marvel of the Incarnation, the cosmic scene is resolved into a human drama. God reaches down to relate himself to man, and man reaches up to relate himself to God. Time looks into eternity and eternity into time, making now always and always now. Everything is transformed by this sublime drama of the Incarnation, God's special parable for fallen man in a fallen world. The way opens before us that was charted in the birth, ministry, death, and resurrection of Jesus Christ, a way that successive generations of believers have striven to follow. They have derived therefrom the moral, spiritual, and intellectual creativity out of which has come everything truly great in our art, our literature, our music. From that source comes the splendour of the great cathedrals and the illumination of the saints and mystics.

—Malcolm Muggeridge

Divine

In some ways the most remarkable sentence in the New Testament is: "And the Word was made flesh and came to dwell among us; and we had sight of his glory, glory such as belongs to the Father's only begotten son, full of grace and truth." Here is a declaration by one who had seen this man and perhaps had rested on his breast; and of this man he, a Jew acquainted with the doctrine of the Presence of God, the Glory or Shekinah (the word for "was made flesh" in the Greek is "eskenosen," "pitched his tent," with a play on the word "Shekinah") dared to say that he had sight of this Glory and spoken with the divine Word. Had not the truth of Christ's divinity impressed itself upon them so strongly, the Gospel writers could never have been able to give a consistent portrait of a man who could be both God and man at the same time. Let one detail suffice to bring this out: novelists and biographers have much greater difficulty in describing a good man than they do in describing a man in whom good and evil are mixed. In the case of Christ, the writers had not only goodness before them, but divinity as well. Now the good can so easily look condescending or too aloof or too single-hued to be described. The saints, the more perfect they become, the less do they attribute virtue or value to themselves. In their modesty their universal cry is as in the presence of a sinner: "There but for the grace of God go I." The figure in the Gospels, on the other hand, speaks with an absolute authority: "I say to you." He commands the sea to obey Him; He cures the sick and raises the dead and forgives sins.

—Martin D'Arcy

Truth Eternal   *October 22*

God has no place; He is everywhere, and heaven is not a locality in space, as we understand these terms. Lastly there is an agony, the greatest a human being can suffer, which consists in the loss of God's love and consequent bitter loneliness. It was to save mankind from such a possible fate that God redeemed man, not by bargaining or buying back, but by identifying Himself with us, taking our name, and becoming the head of a new race. It is this mysterious love-act which is shadowed forth in the sacrificial rites of tribes and peoples. If this be once grasped, then it can be understood how time and again members of the Christian religion have almost caricatured the truth and, by their overdevotion and obstinate clinging to images and icons, led to the kind of protests we have just quoted. It might then be wise, in a world which is so apt to look upon ancient and medieval man as credulous and unscientific, to remove some of its more antique furniture and replace it with what is modern and acceptable. That would require a new investigation into which are now the favorite images and a glance at new expressions in our daily languages, expressions drawn from scientific devices, examples of speed and of distance overcome, depth psychology and new modes of communication. A genius might even write a new Apocalypse.

—Martin D'Arcy

The Proud Oppose   *October 23*

The man of 2000 A.D. will live by the same truths as the authors of the New Testament, Augustine, Aquinas, Copernicus, and the Abbé Mendel, but he will see them revarnished, with a patina of time and in new settings which reflect their truth. The early Christians started with what their contemporaries considered a fatal handicap. Their ideas were not contemporary; they sounded uncultured especially when expounded by obscure provincials in a kind of argot. St. Paul, when he spoke at the Areopagus was laughed out of the assembly, and his later admission that what he taught was to the Jews a stumbling block and to the Gentiles folly did not promise well for the success of Christianity. Celsus, one of the intellectual opponents of the new cult, accused it of frivolous novelty and of upsetting the great tradition which had made the Greco-Roman civilization the envy of the world. In Hellenistic circles, it seemed nonsense to mix the divine and the human, the unchanging and necessary with what was changeable and therefore radically imperfect and half unreal. That time could be important to the gods, and that God could enter time belonged to the world of fancy and fairy tale.

—Martin D'Arcy

Reasonable

If man were completely a god, it might be true that all aspects of his bodily being were godlike; just as if he were completely a beast, we could hardly blame him for any diet, however beastly. But we say that experience confirms our theory of his human complexity. It has nothing to do with the natural things themselves. If red roses mysteriously maddened men to commit murder, we should make rules to cover them up; but red roses would be quite as pure as white ones.

In most modern people there is a battle between the new opinions, which they do not follow out to their end, and the old traditions, which they do not trace back to their beginning. If they followed the new notions forward, it would lead them to Bedlam. If they followed the better instincts backward it would lead them to Rome. At the best they remain suspended between two logical alternatives, trying to tell themselves, as does Dean Inge, that they are merely avoiding two extremes. But there is this great difference in his case, that the question on which he is wrong is, in however perverted a form, a matter of science, whereas the matter in which he is right is by this time simply a matter of sentiment. I need not say that I do not use the word here in a contemptuous sense, for in these things there is a very close kinship between sentiment and sense. But the fact remains that all the people in his position can only go on being sensible. It is left for us to be also reasonable.

—G. K. Chesterton

Slavery

I have chosen the subject of the slavery of the mind because I believe many worthy people imagine I am myself a slave. The nature of my supposed slavery I need not name and do not propose specially to discuss. It is shared by every sane man when he looks up a train in Bradshaw. That is, it consists in thinking a certain authority reliable; which is entirely reasonable. Indeed it would be rather difficult to travel in every train to find out where it went. It would be still more difficult to go to the destination in order to discover whether it was safe to begin the journey. Suppose a wild scare arose that Bradshaw was a conspiracy to produce railway accidents, a man might still believe the Guide to be a Guide and the scare to be only a scare; but he would know of the existence of the scare. What I mean by the slavery of the mind is that state in which men do not know of the alternative. It is something which clogs the imagination, like a drug or a mesmeric sleep, so that a person cannot possibly think of certain things at all. It is not the state in which he says, "I see what you mean; but I cannot think that because I sincerely think this" (which is simply rational): it is one in which he has never thought of the other view; and therefore does not even know that he has never thought of it. Though I am not discussing here my own religion, I think it only right to say that its authorities have never had this sort of narrowness. You may condemn their condemnations as oppressive; but not in this sense as obscurantist. St. Thomas Aquinas begins his inquiry by saying in effect, "Is there a God? it would seem not, for the following reasons"; and the most criticized of recent Encyclicals always stated a view before condemning it. The thing I mean is a man's inability to state his opponent's view; and often his inability even to state his own.

— G. K. Chesterton

Our Religion *October 26*

Ours is at this moment the most rational of all religions. It is even, in a sense, the most rationalistic of all religions. Those who talk about it as merely or mainly emotional simply do not know what they are talking about. It is all the other religions, all the modern religions, that are merely emotional. This is as true of the emotional salvationism of the first Protestants as of the emotional intuitionalism of the last Modernists. We alone are left accepting the action of the reason and the will without any necessary assistance from the emotions. A convinced Catholic is easily the most hard-headed and logical person walking about the world today. But this old slander, of a slimy sentimentalism in all we say and do, is terribly perpetuated by this mere muddle about words. We are still supposed to have a silly sort of devotion, when we really have the most sensible sort.

Freethinkers are occasionally thoughtful, though never free. In the modern world of the West, at any rate, they seem always to be tied to the treadmill of a materialist and monist cosmos. The universal sceptic, in Asia or in Antiquity, has probably been a bolder thinker, though very probably a more unhappy man. But what we have to deal with as scepticism is not scepticism; but a fixed faith in monism. The freethinker is not free to question monism. He is forbidden, for instance, in the only intelligible modern sense, to believe in a miracle.

— G. K. Chesterton

Christ's Church October 27

On two occasions at least he called it his congregation or assembly; and the Greek word for that, *ecclesia,* is, of course, the word by which we know it, his Church. That became, from the first ages, its common appellation; you will find the term used no less than fifty times in the writings of St Paul. Of course, it was to be something more than the mere word "kingdom" implies; our Lord told his followers that he was the Vine and they were the branches, that is, that there was a spiritual unity which was to bind each of them to the others and all of them to him. He told them that the Holy Spirit was to come and dwell in them, to guide them into all truth. But the point to notice here is that, deliberately, he left behind him a Church.

Everybody who has studied the Gospels seriously admits that; all Christians, you may say roughly, admit that. But then, what kind of fact is this Church, of which he speaks in such glowing terms, to which he makes such glorious promises? Is it a definite body of people, united together by external marks, by a common worship and a common faith, with its own definite boundaries, so that you can say with certainty So-and-so is a member of the Church, So-and-so does not belong to the Church?

—*Msgr. Ronald Knox*

The Apostles   *October 28*

Our Lord did more than found a Church; he founded a hierarchy. Of course, one expects any religious teacher to have his own group of chosen disciples; a few who go about with him everywhere and see more of him than the generality of his contemporaries do. But if you come to think of it, all through the record which the Gospels give us our Lord is more concerned with the instruction of twelve men than with all the rest of the Jews. He must teach the multitudes and heal their sick, because they will not leave him alone; but when he sees the chance, he will steal away into a desert place with his disciples. And after his Resurrection, though we are told that on one occasion he appeared to more than 500 brethren at once, it is evident that for the most part he was closeted with his twelve apostles, speaking to them of the things which pertain to the kingdom of God, that is, his Church. They were not, then, merely witnesses whom he must always have about him, they were something more important than that; the nucleus round which his Church was to grow. And so it is to them he speaks in words such as he never uses in his public discourses: "As the Father hath sent me, I also send you . . . all authority is given to me, going therefore teach ye all nations . . . whose soever sins you remit, they are remitted unto them, and whose soever sins you retain, they are retained"; and to St Peter above all he gives the privilege of immovable faith, and the power to bind and to loose.

—*Msgr. Ronald Knox*

His Church

Our Lord made certain promises, of vast moment, to his followers and to their successors. If there are to be two bodies of people, each claiming with plausible arguments to be the true Church, then one must be right and the other wrong; otherwise we could not be certain that our Lord's promises had descended to both, or to either. If, therefore, schisms happen within the body of Christendom, the result of such schism is not to produce two Churches of Christ; what you have left is one true Church of Christ and one schismatic body; otherwise, after all these centuries, we should no longer be certain that our Lord's promises held good.

He has further laid it down, that his Church should be distinguished by sanctity. Not in the sense that all Christians are holy, however desirable that might be; or even that the rulers of the Church should at all times be recognizably holy people; he will not interfere with the freedom of our wills to that extent. But his true Church will always be *productive* of saints. These signs shall follow them that believe; in my name they shall cast out devils, they shall lay hands on the sick, and they shall recover, and if they drink any deadly thing, it shall not hurt them. Those special graces with which our Lord delights his saints to honour will not be the property of one age, they will appear in all ages, and the true Church will always be able to point to them as an element in her sanctity.

And again, our Lord insists that his Church is to be Catholic; "Going, teach *all* nations."

—Msgr. Ronald Knox

Human

In her broad humanity the Church is infinitely more human than the humanist. The humanist complacently conscious of his culture is a prig, and pride, which is only an acute form of priggishness, heads the list of mortal sins. The Church, indeed, never tires of reminding her most gifted sons that culture is not an asset which entitles them to put on airs, but a debit which they can only cancel by services to God, a talent for which they will have to render account. "All evil," said St. Thomas Aquinas, "is a mistaking of means for an end."

The Church has always insisted that bad belief breeds bad conduct, and that right belief is a help to right conduct, but none the less the Church has never lost sight of the distinction which Protestantism tends to blur. *Credo* means "I believe"; it does not mean "I behave." Catholicism is often a test not only of character but of intelligence, and there is no reason why a man should cease to be intelligent because he has ceased to be good. There is no reason why he should stop believing because, for the moment, he has stopped behaving.

The Church has always regarded the sins of the mind as more serious than the sins of the flesh, for there is always hope of a return of the prodigal so long as his mind still recognizes the Church as his home. There is hope for the man who says, "I'm weak, and I can't resist sinning," but far less hope for those who say, "What the Church calls sin is really the new morality approved by the best progressive thinkers." It is this type of intellectual dishonesty which is at the root of most modern maladies.

—*Arnold Lunn*

Curiosity

The bankruptcy of materialism is responsible for the growing curiosity about the one Church which has never compromised in its witness to the supernatural, and which has never attempted to adapt its beliefs to the foolish fashion of the moment. Many of those who reject our exclusive claims as too fantastic to deserve examination are inclined to believe that we are in possession of some occult truths.

Those who have come to the conclusion that "there's something in Catholicism" are prepared to give us a hearing. The world is slowly beginning to discover that the Catholic is prepared to defend his belief without appealing to faith, to religious experience or to authority. People who would run a mile to avoid an emotional revivalist will listen with eager curiosity to a Catholic who is prepared to summarize the reasoned evidence for the Resurrection or for modern miracles at Lourdes, and to argue his case in the tone and in the manner of a barrister in a court of law.

Ignorance about Catholicism is still profound, but it is no longer complacent ignorance. Curiosity is conquering complacency. People are beginning to ask questions, silly questions perhaps, but a silly question marks an advance on a silly statement.

—Arnold Lunn

Feast of All Saints   *November 1*

Writing to the Ephesians, Saint Paul described how the Church is one with Christ and therefore is holy: holy in her Founder, holy in her doctrine, sacraments, and work, holy in her members.

The exemplary members of the Church are the saints. We, with all our faults and even our grave sins, are the fellow citizens of the saints, so long as we strive, with the aid of God's grace, to make good our salvation, to preserve unity with the saints, with one another, and with Jesus in the living temple of God which is the Holy Catholic Church.

All these things Saint Paul said in words which perfectly fit the circumstances of our gathering this afternoon. You come together from more than one hundred parishes and almost one hundred and fifty clubs of every type. You include the descendants of a score or more of nationalities and races. Every state of life is represented among you. Your divisions, personal, temperamental, social, and group, are almost as many as yourselves.

And yet, to you with perfect truth I may apply the words of the Apostle to the Catholic Christians of Ephesus: "You are now no longer strangers and foreigners, but you are citizens with the saints and members of God's household: You are built upon the foundation of the Apostles and prophets, with Christ Jesus Himself as the chief cornerstone. In Him the whole structure is closely fitted together and grows into a temple holy in the Lord; in Him you too are being built together into a dwelling place for God in the Spirit."

Ours is the Church of the Saints, and we are the brothers and sisters of the saints. It is most important that we never permit ourselves to forget this.

— Cardinal John Wright

The Search   *November 2*

The search for God may take many forms. Every scientist who devotes himself to the disinterested search for truth is a theist, conscious or unconscious, for God is truth. Every man who consecrates his life to the service of his fellow-men has enrolled himself in the service of God, even though God is hidden from his sight. "Then shall the just answer Him, saying: Lord, when did we see Thee hungry . . . and the King answering, shall say to them: Amen I say to you, as long as you did it to one of these My least brethren, you did it to Me."

Happiness is a by-product of a life devoted to other ends than pleasure-seeking. A truism, but a truism which, as Mr. Joad observes, few people believe till they have found it out for themselves. "You cannot take the kingdom of pleasure by storm."

The disquiet of the soul to which St. Augustine refers may be dispelled for a time by crowd gaiety. And it is, indeed, the unconscious realization of this fact which accounts for that hatred of solitude which characterizes your true hedonist. Dr. Buchman displayed his well-known understanding of modern psychology when he pivoted his movement round the magic word "group," for the young people of to-day are essentially groupminded. Christianity is individualistic in its insistence on the infinite value of the individual soul, and on the supreme importance of the relation between the individual and God.

— Arnold Lunn

Welcomes Sinners

The Catholic Church is not a group but a family, and this family includes not only the saints who practise what the Groups preach, but also a motley collection who would be very ill at ease at one of Dr. Buchman's house parties. The Church spares no effort to keep the erring within the fold, and to maintain contact with sinners who do not even pretend to aim at those high standards of absolute truth and absolute purity on which the Groups insist, but who none the less have souls to be saved. The Church which makes no concessions to human sin is always ready to make concessions to human weakness.

If a man is too unintelligent to appreciate the overwhelming evidence for the existence of God, he may at least be credited with sincerity and cannot be excused of snobbery for attaching no importance to the things of the spirit, but the man who believes in God is a snob if he attaches more importance to social and cultural than to spiritual standards. Snobbery, however, is fortunately not incurable. Reason is the best doctor, for reason, if we accept its guidance, will in time force even the most snobbish of moderns on to his knees.

—Arnold Lunn

The Tyranny of Fashion

The tyranny of fashion is responsible for more serious evils than the top hat and painted toe-nails. Fashion is the prolific mother of heresy, for most heresies are inspired by the hope of reconciling timeless truth with the passing fashions. A weekly paper which lies before me as I write announces that a well-known Anglican will contribute an article on "A Faith for To-day." But why *"a"* Faith and why *"To-day"*? Nothing dates more rapidly than modernism and nothing dates less than *the* Faith which in St. Augustine's memorable phrase is "ever old and ever new."

There are modernists whose scholarship and whose sincerity command respect, but there are others who remind me of timid scholars at a public school pathetically anxious to conciliate the athletic "bloods." To the man in the street the "popular scientist" is a "blood," and there are parsons who seem to think that they can lure the man in the street into the pew by posing as the friends and allies of these great men. Such parsons are a little ashamed of their clerical collars and anxious to convince the scientists that whatever may be the case with their collar studs, their hearts, at least, are in the right place.

—*Arnold Lunn*

Snobbery   *November 5*

Mental snobbery might be defined as the uncritical acceptance of beliefs merely because they are modish, and it is undeniable that for every man whose disbelief in miracles or whose belief in evolution is the outcome of examining the evidence, there are a hundred whose views on these questions are determined by the mental fashions of the age in which they live. But perhaps snobbery is too harsh a word. Our lives are crowded, and a range of amusements unknown to our forefathers crowds out our leisure moments. We have very little time to read and still less time to think. It is simpler to take our views about these high matters from the experts, and since the so-called experts whose views reach the public through the medium of the popular press or the wireless are still under the influence of Victorian secularism, it is not surprising that Strube's "Little Man" should be losing the uncritical faith in Christianity which consoled his grandfather and acquiring in its place a no less uncritical faith in the dogmas of popular scientists.

—*Arnold Lunn*

Becoming A Catholic

The step which I took in 1917 is one which I have never had the wish, never even the velleity, to retract. I do not adduce this fact as a piece of startling evidence in favour of the Petrine claims. It is open to anybody to say that I feel like that because I am that kind of person. I am only putting on record the answer of one convert to the question, "Are you sorry you left the Church of England?" It is often said of us converts—a friend of mine heard it said of me, years ago, on the top of an omnibus, "He realizes, now, that he's made a mistake". But in fact I have never experienced a mood of discouragement or of hesitation, during these last thirty-three years, that has suggested, even on the horizon of my mind, the possibility of going back where I came from. Faith is a gift, and may be withdrawn; when people whom I know lose (or seem to lose) the faith, I remind myself that there, but for the grace of God, went I. But on the two or three occasions when converts whom I knew have gone back to the Church of England, I found it quite impossible to follow the workings of their mind. Revealed theology is something which I can only see as an integral whole; only by an abuse of the mind could I abandon one tenet without abandoning the rest.

I have not yet answered the further question, "Did the Church of Rome come up to your expectations?" It would give me great pleasure if I could cut short the discussion by returning a simple "Yes". But a truer analysis demands the more complicated answer, "No, thank God it didn't. Because I was expecting the wrong things."

—Msgr. Ronald Knox

Learning About Catholics

Earlier in the summer I paid another visit to Belgium, this time with my brother, who now shared my religious views, with Mr Wickham, of St John's, Bovey Tracey, and Mr Lyon, of Middlecot —a house overlooking Bovey from the edge of the moor. If I have not already mentioned my friendship with Mr Lyon and my visits to Middlecot, it is because I made them so often that they had become almost a part of my everyday experience: I cannot remember any topic in religion, politics, society, literature, or (Heaven help me) art which I have not discussed with Mr Lyon or his guests, sprawling before a wood fire in that ample chimney corner. Once again, my fellow-travellers were as ready as myself to appreciate not only the religion of Belgium but the forms in which it expressed itself. We made the same round—Bruges, Ypres, Brussels, Antwerp, Namur, Dinant, Bruges again and always Bruges; if I had lost any of my fervid belief in the religion of Belgium as a working religion which must be transplanted to English soil, this visit revived it. It was Benediction at St John the Baptist's, Namur, that I described to my Plymouth congregation when I tried to paint them the picture of what the Church of England was to be.

—*Msgr. Ronald Knox*

State Took over Religion   *November 8*

The Reformation was the usurping by the Crown of the administrative rights previously enjoyed by the Papacy. The circumstances of the change were atrocious on both sides; the effect was that a large spiritual "connection" (as we talk of "a business connection") changed hands. More and Cranmer did not die for the sake of two separate churches respectively, but for the sake of this single spiritual connection—each of them for his idea of what it ought to be. The Reformation did not unchurch the Church; it merely put the Church into a state of Babylonish captivity under the Crown. In order to keep the peace, Queen Elizabeth and her advisers botched together a series of provisional formulas—doctrinal and liturgical—midway between the two parties in tendency. These formulas, which we call the "Reformation settlement," were a *pis aller*, a *faute de mieux*; nobody wanted them, everybody hoped they would change when a monarch of more decided views came in. It was the seventeenth century, with its Puritan persecution, which made Englishmen think of the Reformation settlement as an end in itself. It was the eighteenth century, with its combination of Latitudinarianism and Erastianism, that made the Church of England "inclusive" of divergent doctrines. It was the nineteenth century, with the gradual abandonment by Parliament of its legal claim to tyrannize over the Church, which unconsciously and as it were by accident put administrative power into hands it was never meant for—the hands of the Bishops.

—*Msgr. Ronald Knox*

A Satiric Book   *November 9*

The argument of the book was a simple *reductio ad absurdum*. If (as the British public seemed to think) it was the duty of all *Christian* bodies to unite for worship, sinking their differences on each side, why should the movement be confined to Christians? What about the Jews, from whom we were only separated by the Council of Jerusalem? And if the Jews, why not the Mohammedans? We could always split the difference between monogamy and tetragamy by having two wives all round. The Brahmins presented few difficulties: the worshippers of Mumbo-jumbo only needed a passing reference. At this point the spirit of satire carried me away, and I suggested with every appearance of misgiving that perhaps after all, given proper precautions, charity should demand of us that we should accept the submission of the Pope. After making arrangements for the suitable degradation of the Roman hierarchy, I went boldly forward to the case of the atheists, and suggested that we might join with them in a common definition of the Divine Nature, which should assert it to be such as to involve Existence and Non-existence simultaneously. Here, with a few exhortations to the public, I left my argument to my readers.

—*Msgr. Ronald Knox*

Against Mediocrity   *November 10*

My sermon[1] was, generally speaking, an attack on those moderating influences in the Church of England which I had hated so
long. The Bishops were engaged in an effort to make a Procrus-
tean bed out of the Establishment, levelling up in some places and
levelling down in others so as to reduce us all to a single standard
of mediocrity. The characteristic marks of this standard I defined
as "green stoles and bad brass and the Church of England Men's
Society, and the Holy Eucharist at eight and Matins at eleven, and
Confession if you happen to feel like it"; and even if this standard
should come to be raised a little, the official religion would bear
the same marks of pointlessness and restraint. Against this policy
of repression at both ends I raised quite frankly the standard of
revolt; the Bishops had (as I had already shown) no right to dictate
the policy of the Church according to their own fancy; they must
act as legal officials or not at all. And meanwhile a real enemy was
creeping into the Church, which I described vaguely as Modernism.
Our great danger was the absence of a living authority to deal
with this, and I asserted boldly that if and when the Church of
England either gave up the recitation of the Creed *Quicumque vult*
(the strongest mark of her orthodoxy), or tampered with the
marriage laws so as to countenance divorce, or officially admitted
Nonconformists to Communion, it would be a church to which
neither I nor my supposedly sympathetic audience could conscientiously continue to belong.

—*Msgr. Ronald Knox*

An Anglican Retreat   *November 11*

It is extraordinary to me to reflect that this was the only formal
retreat I made between my Anglican ordination and my conversion.
   . . . I had a chapel where I could celebrate daily, with the
Blessed Sacrament reserved, and, so far as the terrors and distrac-

---

[1] At the time that this was written Msgr. Knox was an Anglican priest.

tions of the time allowed, I found in my hermit existence an extraordinary peace. I passed the whole three weeks in this way.

One of my friends told me afterwards that he had imagined my retreat (to which I sacrificed several rival attractions) to be a sign of uneasiness about the "Roman question." As a matter of fact, even when I was interrogating my conscience most strictly, I was wholly without qualm of this kind; I turned to my own religion for spiritual comfort and, however little progress I may have made, never once found it shallow or unsatisfactory. I went to the Catholic Church at Stroud when the Sacrament was exposed there, merely because there was exposition: I had no doubt of my own sacraments.

—*Msgr. Ronald Knox*

Leaning Toward Rome   *November 12*

I had Howell's words in my ears all the way back to Shrewsbury, "Don't break all our hearts." Certainly I must do nothing precipitate, avoid taking myself too seriously, above all "carry on" as if nothing had happened. Yet I knew, I think, that I had seen the ghost: the Polar bear (if I may use the less elegant parallel) had vanished, and I was straining my eyes over the heap of clothes. It was at this time that Wilfrid Moor became my chief confidant, and I his: it was in a letter to him that I enclosed a curious document I still preserve. It contained thirty-one reasons why I should remain an Anglican, and thirty-one reasons why I should become a Roman Catholic, *and all wrong reasons.* My vanity, my ambition, my cowardice, my inertia, all the vices I knew to be in my nature were called in evidence in this diabolic controversy: whatever I did, I maintained, it should not be for these reasons.

... In the first place I wrote to my father, to suggest that I was uneasy in my mind about the Anglican position, though I did not wish to discuss the subject in detail until I should meet him in the summer holidays.

—*Msgr. Ronald Knox*

A Coincidence?   *November 13*

The term came to an end, and one of my first visits was to
Hickleton; Lord Halifax, at Mr Howell's suggestion, had asked me
to come and talk over my difficulties with him. I had looked upon
him as my religious leader for ten years past, and I went gladly to
avail myself of that large-hearted sympathy and long experience.
Maurice Child, who all through this time and right up to my
conversion was continually my confidant and support, came with
me. We came down to dinner in the fading light of the August
evening, both dressed in cassock and ferraiuolo, priests, it was
impossible not to feel, in a Catholic household. The first figure I
saw in the hall was a familiar one; it was Father Martindale.

There was no reason why he should not have been there. He
was engaged upon Mgr Benson's Life, and had come to Hickleton
for material in connection with the Anglican part of it. (I imagine
Hugh Benson had been to Hickleton, in my own errand, twelve
years before.) But to meet in this way one of the very few
Catholic priests I knew, one for whose powers I had already the
utmost respect, seemed too good to be a coincidence.

—Msgr. Ronald Knox

War Nerves?   *November 14*

Before I went back to Shrewsbury I applied for advice in one
other quarter. Mr Mackay, of Margaret Street, had done me many
kindnesses, and I knew that the loss of Wilfrid Moor would make
him sympathetic. His advice was psychological and practical: the
war, he said, had put all our nerves on the stretch, and we did not
realize at what a high pitch of tension we were living. Might not
my own case be simply one of "war-nerves"? And, for fear of that,
would it not be best to wait till the end of the war? I made the
obvious answer, and he said, "Surely two years from now." If I
took nobody else's advice, I was faithful to his. My brother also
inclined to the "war-nerves" theory, and urged that I ought to take
up parish work to occupy my mind. Mr Kilburn, of St Saviour's,

Hoxton, was good enough to suggest my going there and trying the effect of seeing my old religion at work. The same advice, it will be remembered, was given to Hugh Benson. "He might equally well have told me to go and teach Buddhism." I did not feel so strongly as that, but I was quite certain that I could not hear confessions, and ought not to preach. My last preaching engagement I fulfilled that September at Froyle, near Alton: the Vicar of St Martin's, Cardiff, had already been kind enough to release me from my promise to conduct the Three Hours on Good Friday. I would seek, at Shrewsbury, for spiritual rest and for work which could not trouble my conscience.

—*Msgr. Ronald Knox*

Teaching at a Boys School   *November 15*

I despair of being able to convey any impression of the next fourteen months, up to the Christmas of 1916. If I try to give any full picture of my life, it will necessarily be irrelevant to my main topic: if I simply follow up the history of my inward developments I shall give a quite false because arbitrarily selected picture. The truth is that I lived in two distinct compartments at Shrewsbury: in my relations with those around me, I must have appeared simply as a clergyman of eccentric views, taking a long holiday from most of the official practices of religion, and thinking of nothing except how to make himself agreeable; nor was this hypocritical, for while I was with other people this was exactly what I was. But give me half an hour by myself, with no work pressing, and I would plunge at once into self-questioning, brooding, and something not unlike despair. The headmaster, as I have said, was in my confidence, and I imagine that Mrs Alington suspected something of what I felt; only one of the masters, to my knowledge, realized the situation: the others may or may not have guessed something, but I never said a word. Not even in the holidays did I unbosom myself to anybody except a few trusted friends.

—*Msgr. Ronald Knox*

Waiting

Father Martindale once suggested, in writing to me, that if you did not find yourself arriving at "getting-up point" in the morning by natural process, it sometimes became necessary to put force upon yourself and bring yourself up to scratch; I think he was afraid that I might be waiting about listlessly for a divine illumination. I told him that at least I was not conscious of going back; my ears were still strained to catch any call: I think this was quite true, even when I was busiest. But what troubled me at Shrewsbury was not so much the material comfort of my surroundings, or the immense happiness (from a human point of view) I was deriving from my work, as the sense that by persevering in this attitude of uncertainty I was shirking the strain of "mental fight" to which I had been accustomed. It was so easy to be charitable to people of other beliefs, when you were not sure that they were false. It was so easy to be tolerant of other people's misdemeanours, when you were not quite sure that a fixed standard existed for judging right and wrong. When I was at Balliol, we used to adapt the phrase "I hold no brief for So-and-so" in a positive way: thus we said that Charles Lister held a brief for Socialism, Julian Grenfell a brief for sport, and so on. At that time (having several "briefs" of my own) I used to argue that to hold no briefs was to be less than a man. Ever since then I had been fighting for a cause, ready to argue a point, eager to make converts. Now I found myself briefless: I did not know what cause I wanted to win.

—*Msgr. Ronald Knox*

Praying

I had not, of course, given up my own prayers. I never abandoned the recitation of the Divine Office; often I had to read it while I was invigilating over the work of my pupils, but I was not fearful of scandalizing them, for at the worst they would probably be no wiser than the Trinity undergraduate, who said that when he came into my room he always found me learning the Prayer Book by heart. But beyond this, whenever my work allowed, I did my best to make a half-hour meditation, grievously distracted as a rule by the troubles that exercised me, but devoted to the intention of obtaining light. It was the Psalms of David I chiefly used, and found extraordinary comfort in certain phrases of them: *"Exspecta Dominum, viriliter age, et confortetur cor tuum, et sustine Dominum," "Deus meus es tu, quoniam bonorum meorum non eges," "Spera in Domino et fac bonitatem, et inhabita terram, et pasceris in divitiis eius,"*[1] and so on. But, with all the grace then given me, I did not find it easy to win satisfaction in prayer.

I had little time for reading during the term, and what reading I did during odd half-hours was mostly of a quite light type, not calculated to affect my religious views. (Evelyn Southwell had a principle that everybody ought to read Belloc's *Path to Rome* every autumn; I reread it twice at Shrewsbury.)

— *Msgr. Ronald Knox*

Reading   *November 18*

I do not think I can be accused of "cramming myself up with Jesuit stuff." (I did, however, read Father Martindale's Life of Hugh Benson in the summer.)

From . . . this reading I derived a wealth of impressions, but I think the only sudden access of illumination I got was from a phrase in Milman's (soundly Protestant) *History of Latin Christianity.* I cannot remember it well enough to quote it, but the gist of it is this; he comments upon the extraordinary precision with which, time after time, the Bishops of Rome managed to foresee which side the Church would eventually take in a controversy, and "plumped" for it beforehand. The Church fixes the date of Easter, the Church decides that heretics need not be rebaptized, the Church decides that the Incarnate combined two Natures in one

[1] "Wait for the Lord, act manfully, and let your heart be strengthened; wait for the Lord"; "You are my God, for You have no need of any good I might give You"; "Hope in the Lord and do what is good, and you will enjoy its riches."

Person; but each time Rome (like Lancashire) thinks to-day what the world will think to-morrow. This uncanny capacity for taking the pulse of the Church is ascribed by Milman partly to the extreme cunning of the early Pontiffs, partly to their geographically central position, and so on. And then it occurred to me that there was another explanation. I could have laughed aloud.

— *Msgr. Ronald Knox*

The Arians
November 19

Strange as it may seem, I had always assumed at the back of my mind that when my handbooks talked about "Arian" and "Catholic" bishops they knew what they were talking about; it never occurred to me that the Arians also regarded themselves as Catholics and wanted to know why they should be thought otherwise. "Ah! but," says my Church historian, "the Church came to think otherwise, and thus they found themselves deCatholicized in the long run." But what Church? Why did those who anathematized Nestorius come to be regarded as "Catholics" rather than those who still accept his doctrines? I had used this argument against the attitude of the Greek Orthodox Church when it broke away from unity, but it had never occurred to me before that *what we mean when we talk of the Catholic party is the party in which the Bishop of Rome was, and nothing else*: that the handbooks had simply taken over the word without thinking or arguing about it, as if it explained itself; but it didn't.

I am desperately afraid here of not stating my meaning clearly: what it comes to is this. I had been in the habit of supposing that the Nestorians were wrong because East and West agreed that they were wrong; I now felt that "the East" had no right to condemn the Nestorians, it was merely a matter of "hard swearing"— except in so far as the Easterns, when they did so, had the Pope in their own boat.

— *Msgr. Ronald Knox*

The Pope

If you ask "Who are the Orthodox?" you will be told "The people who hold the Orthodox Faith." If you ask them how they know it is the Orthodox Faith they say "Because it is held by the Orthodox Church." And the Nestorians will say exactly the same of themselves—and who is to choose between them? Each say that they have the *consensus fidelium* behind them, and if you ask who the *fideles* were you are referred back to the very formula which the *consensus fidelium* was to prove. But if you ask a Catholic "What is the Catholic Faith?" and are told it is that held by the Catholic Church; if you persevere, and ask what is the Catholic Church, you are no longer met with the irritatingly circular definition "the Church which holds the Catholic Faith"; you are told it is the Church which is in communion with the Bishop of Rome.

When I had got so far, my solution of the difficulties was this. If you did not believe in authority at all, but only believed in the "experience of Christendom," the Papacy seemed to be *the* thing which mediaeval Christendom was certain about, and the loss of which Christendom (if you use the term in a wide sense) had been largely engaged in mourning for ever since.

—*Msgr. Ronald Knox*

The Necessity for a Pope

If you took your authority from the Councils, you were faced with the fact that the Councils were only decided by majorities, and the obvious majority of Christendom came to believe (if it did not believe already) in the Pope. If you took your stand on the *consensus fidelium,* you must either despair of defining the *fideles,* or else define them as the people who kept touch with the centre of Unity, that is, with the Pope. If you took a Gallican view of the Church, and wanted the Papacy to be a constitutional monarchy, your church became a philosopher's dream instead of a living reality: in ordinary real life you must have the Pope as he is, or no

Pope at all. All these efforts which men have made at various times to invent a substitute for the full Petrine claims were simply zigzag paths which came to the same thing in the end; they all led to Rome. Modernism, and Tractarianism, and Consensus-fideliumism, and Gallicanism all demanded a Pope.

—Msgr. Ronald Knox

No Sensible Attraction

Meanwhile, the Church of Rome held out to me no sensible attraction whatever. I do not merely mean that her ritual and ceremonial, with all their dignity and beauty, could not act as a bait: this must have been true at any time for anybody of my school. In Tractarian days the historic worship of the Church may have been an allurement; but we had been accustomed to so accurate a reproduction of it all that it had lost the charm of novelty, and lacked besides the excitement of being illicit. Picture the schoolboy, who after terms of surreptitious smoking, when the necessity of precaution and the consciousness of being a "sportsman" were elements in his pleasure as real as the fragrance of the tobacco itself, presented by an aunt, on going up to a university, with a new pipe and tobacco-pouch. Something of the same blasé appreciation makes itself felt in the mind of the modern Anglican extremist when he is invited to admire Catholic services; he has not merely done all this before, he has done it defiantly, deliberately, with the joy of contest to encourage him.

—Msgr. Ronald Knox

Don't Wait

Gradually, the question narrowed itself down; I was conscious that I *could* not force myself back into my old position, and it only remained to ask, could I conscientiously join the only institution which looked like the Church of Christ, or must I remain outside, retaining perhaps in myself some half-light of faith, but unable to teach, to proselytize, or to assert? Catholics who find such an alternative even abstractly unthinkable should take note of Shane Leslie's article on Florence Nightingale in the *Dublin Review* of October, 1917. They will see there that it is possible for a soul to become dissatisfied with Anglicanism through long turning of the eyes Romewards, yet find herself unable to enter into that rest for which (St. Augustine tells us) her struggles are evidence that she was created.

It was in this frame of mind that I talked to Father Martindale again, when I went to Oxford at the beginning of Lent, and he now told me that I had nothing to gain by waiting; I ought to go away for a day or two and be received at Easter. My answer was that I could not hope to resolve my difficulties so suddenly; I must go properly into retreat.

— *Msgr. Ronald Knox*

In the Hands of God
November 24

I had burnt my boats, and felt that from the worldly point of view I could simply throw myself on Providence. Yet, up to the last week or so, I had such a dread of discussing my affairs and inflicting myself on others that I hardly unburdened myself to anybody, even to Catholics. Nor did I attend Catholic places of worship, except that as the summer drew on I used occasionally to stop at the Cathedral on my way back from the office and pray there in the Chapel of the Blessed Sacrament. The Cathedral had always exercised a kind of spell over me, and I found now in that extraordinary sense of spaciousness which is communicated to the mind by half-lights and by the muffled sound of distant footfalls, a welcome sense of detachment. But I could not yet pray easily; I only asked that God's will might be done, and that he would give me purity of intention.

It remained to arrange for my retreat. Father Talbot, of the Oratory, to whom I turned at the last moment for this practical advice (for I wanted to consult somebody on the spot) suggested with penetrating wisdom that the most important thing was to get away from the atmosphere of controversy.

—*Msgr. Ronald Knox*

Seeking Authority

During those two years and more of spiritual exile I did come to wonder whether I had a right to believe in anything—to believe, that is, without being in visible Communion with that one visible Body of faithful people of whom the prophet foretold, "All thy people shall be taught of God." For authority played a large part in my belief, and I could not now find that any certain source of authority was available outside the pale of the Roman Catholic Church. Once inside, I should not care how the authority came to me; I did not crave for infallible decrees; I wanted to be certain I belonged to that Church of which Saint Paul said proudly, "We have the Mind of Christ." I was by this time unable to believe that I was already in the Church—it was not that I had ceased to believe anything, but that I had a more exacting idea of what "being inside the Church" meant. Now, either I must accept this fuller idea, with all the corollaries it involved in the way of spiritual submission and worldly resignation, or I must give up all positive basis for my religion.

—*Msgr. Ronald Knox*

On Retreat

My feeling was this. I had by now become so tired with my buffeting against the waves of difficulty that I hardly knew whether I believed in anything; whether I must not embrace my second alternative, and give up asserting supernatural religion altogether. That first Sunday morning, for example, I read some chapters of Faber's *Creator and Creature,* and my spiritual appetite seemed to revolt against it. "That," I told myself, "is the real trouble: it is not the Pope, or Indulgences, or Infallibility: you do not really believe in God as the Catholics do. If you can steadily face all this mountain of assertion about the greatness of God in comparison with man, you may be a Catholic yet—but can you?" Now, my retreat should be my *experimentum crucis.* If my acts (of resignation especially) during my retreat should result, as they well might, in revulsion from the whole thought of religion, then, for this time at least, I would own myself defeated. But if in the making of them I found that religion was still a real world to me, that my soul still functioned (after two years of vague aspiration and spiritual numbness) as a soul made to serve its Creator and to no other end, then it was all right. Then I would enter the Kingdom of Heaven as a little child; it was close to my hand.

—*Msgr. Ronald Knox*

Grace Triumphed

Well before the end of my first week, I knew that grace had triumphed. I neither expected nor received any sensible supernatural illumination: I did not have to take my spiritual temperature, "evaluate" my "experiences," or proceed in any such quasi-scientific manner. I turned away from the emotional as far as possible, and devoted myself singly to the resignation of my will to God's Will. *Attulit et nobis aliquando optantibus aetas Adventum auxiliumque Dei;*[1] in the mere practice of religion, in the mere performance of these (very informal) exercises, I knew that it was all right.

I am not trying to explain it, but I must try to illustrate it by an example. It was as if I had been a man homeless and needing shelter, who first of all had taken refuge under a shed at the back of an empty house. Then he had found an outhouse unlocked, and felt more cheerfulness and comfort there. Then he had tried a door in the building itself, and, by some art, found a secret spring which let you in at the back door; nightly thenceforward he had

[1] At last, time brought even to me what I longed for: the presence and help of God.

visited this back part of the house, more roomy than anything he had yet experienced, and giving, through a little crack, a view into the wide spaces of the house itself beyond. Then, one night, he had tried the spring, and the door had refused to open. The button could still be pushed, but it was followed by no sound of groaning hinges. Baffled, and unable now to content himself with shed or outhouse, he had wandered round and round the house, looking enviously at its frowning fastnesses. And then he tried the front door, and found that it had been open all the time.

—*Msgr. Ronald Knox*

Reconciled

That is a very crude allegory,[1] and not meant to represent the actual facts—merely to give some idea of the extraordinary feeling, partly of relief, and partly of incredible stupidity in the past, which accompanied my discovery. I told the Father Abbot that I felt quite certain, but, to test myself, would wait till Tuesday before I definitely asked to be received. From twelve till one on Tuesday I was in the chapel, asking the Holy Spirit to show me my error if I had let any wrong motive or false calculation mislead me. All through the midday meal I was conscious of little except a strong desire to laugh—not hysterically, but in sheer happiness at feeling the free exercise of my spiritual faculties. After the meal, I asked the Father Abbot to write to the Bishop, and arrange for my reception on the Saturday.

During those last few days, I did ask one or two questions of Father Conway, the acting guest-master, not with any desire of "making terms" for my conscience, but merely to set my mind at rest and persuade myself that I had not underestimated one or two claims of the Catholic religion. During my leisure time I read a few Catholic novels, especially *Come Rack! Come Rope!* Hugh

[1] See reading for November 27.

Benson, who had set my feet on the way towards the Church, watched over my footsteps to the last.

—Msgr. Ronald Knox

Why? *November 29*

I suppose it is inevitable that, after the question "Why did you become a Roman Catholic?" Anglicans and others should proceed to the question "What does it feel like?" In answer to this, I can register one impression at once, curiously inconsistent with my preconceived notions on the subject. I had been encouraged to suppose, and fully prepared to find, that the immediate result of submission to Rome would be the sense of having one's liberty cramped and restricted in a number of ways, necessary no doubt to the welfare of the Church at large, but galling to the individual. The discouragement of criticism would make theology uninteresting, and even one's devotions would become a feverish hunt after indulgences (this latter bogey is one sedulously presented to the would-be convert by Anglican controversialists).

As I say, I was quite prepared for all this: the curious thing is that my experience has been exactly the opposite. I have been overwhelmed with the feeling of liberty—the glorious liberty of the sons of God.

—Msgr. Ronald Knox

Peace *November 30*

It was not till I became a Catholic that I became conscious of my former homelessness, my exile from the place that was my own. . . .

It was not that, as an Anglican, I had been over-scrupulous about other people's disapproval: I always rather enjoyed being disapproved of. It was simply that I now found ease and naturalness, and stretched myself like a man who has been sitting in a cramped position.

For the Church of England as an institution, my chief feeling is one of unbounded gratitude to God for having been born in circumstances where I had a schoolmaster to bring me to Christ. Or rather (for "schoolmaster" is too cold a term) I feel as if I had been left in charge of a foster-mother, who reared me as her own child. Was it her fault if, in her affection for me, she let me think I *was* her own child, and hid from me my true birth and princely destiny?

And if at last I have found my true parentage, as I now think it, can I forget the kindnesses she showered on me, her care and my happiness in her arms? Such is not my intention; God forgive me if through any fault of mine it should become my act.

"And so," they go on, "you have found peace?" Certainly I have found harbourage, the resting-place which God has allowed to His people on earth.

—*Msgr. Ronald Knox*

About Prayer   *December 1*

Prayer becomes self-conscious and sentimental when we cease to believe in its practical importance. Nothing has been more fatal to devotion outside the Catholic Church than the thesis which we owe to Modernism, that it is of little value to pray for anything but a change in one's own character. It was unscientific, so we were told, to pray for good character. The scientist was prepared to condone "Please make Tommy a good boy," but refused his *imprimatur* to "Please make Sunday a good day."

It is not surprising that those who regard prayer as a sentimental form of auto-suggestion common among people who are morbidly interested in their own characters should be shy of being classed among those who pray. It is more embarrassing for a Protestant than for a Catholic to plead guilty to praying, since a Catholic on his knees is not necessarily indulging in character culture, but may be offering up a petition for practical and tangible benefits. Disreputable Catholics in fiction or the drama are often represented invoking the intercession of Our Lady. All of which is vaguely reassuring and helps to create among our pagan friends a genuine tolerance for the prayers of Catholics which they are not prepared to extend to the orison of Protestants.

—*Arnold Lunn*

We Must Pray   *December 2*

Long before I became a Catholic a friend of mine, who had been born in the Church, explained to me that Catholics might be divided into praying Catholics and non-praying Catholics. He was a non-praying Catholic; not, mark you, a non-practising Catholic, for he kept the faith on one Low Mass a week, and one confession and Communion every year. I was impressed, and I decided that if ever I became a Catholic, I would join the non-praying part of the Church. But a careful study of the texts from which the Church derives her charter suggested the melancholy conclusion that the founder of Christianity had made no provision for people who do not pray. I am now inclined to suspect that my friend prays with difficulty rather than not at all. "Ask and ye shall receive." If Christ meant what he said, it is foolish not to ask.

Here, as so often, faith represents not only the triumph of courage over cowardice but the triumph of reason over emotion, for it is reasonable to take a chance of death in the crevasse rather than to await certain death passively.

—*Arnold Lunn*

Petitions   *December 3*

Fifty years ago England was Christian in theory if no longer in practice, and it was from the ranks of Protestants who practised their religion and in whose life prayer had played an important part that the Church made most of her converts in this country. To-day the situation is very different. An increasing proportion of converts are men or women who gave up their religion either at school or shortly after leaving school. Such converts have to overcome an immense prejudice against prayer, which lingers in a modified form long after they have been received into the Church.

The convert who tries to resume the lost habit of prayer usually feels self-conscious and embarrassed on his knees. He is troubled by a vague association in his mind between pseudo-piety and sanctimonious smugness. The embarrassment which a modern convert from scepticism suffers when he is discovered on his knees is the product of doubt. People whose faith is unaffected and who are convinced that petitions are always heard, and often granted, bring their needs before God in the same matter of fact, unembarrassed fashion as they ask a request of a friend or patron in this world.

—Arnold Lunn

The Spirit of Rebellion   *December 4*

We are not God and God is not incarnate in us. We can, however, become partakers of His divinity through the sacraments. The barrier between God and man is not the flesh, nor is the flesh intrinsically evil, for the flesh was the tabernacle of God Himself when God became incarnate in man. It is not the body but the abuse of the body which separates man from God. The true conflict is not between spirit and body but between the spirit of truth and the spirit of rebellion.

Pantheism evades the problem of God's relation to man by a lazy substitute. The Church faces this problem, recognizes that no complete solution is possible in our present state of knowledge, but by her partial solution throws a beam of light across the darkness of ultimate mystery.

Most of the great heresiarchs have been men who have lost this Catholic sense of proportion, and who, in consequence of this loss, have tried to simplify Christianity by reducing the faith to a single formula. Luther reduced Christianity to the single formula, "Justification by Faith"; the Puritans eliminated the complication of Free Will, and simplified salvation by predestinating themselves to Heaven and other people to hell; the Quakers rejected all authority save the single authority of the Inner Light; Protestantism is tending to simplify apologetics by eliminating every argument excepting the argument from religious experience.

—Arnold Lunn

Catholicism   *December 5*

Catholicism, which is as rich and complex as life itself, differs from the academic over-simplification of the great heresies much as Sussex differs from a map of Sussex. The universal Church is the home of all mankind, whereas every heresy is an artificial simplification with a limited and particular appeal to a particular mentality.

At this point the Protestant may object that those who simplify doctrine are merely following the precedent set by Our Lord, who summed up the duty of man in two commandments, the love of God and the love of our neighbour. True, but Our Lord developed the implications of these two great commandments in the Sermon on the Mount and in the teaching which is recorded in the Gospels. If our Protestant critics continue by reminding us that God's teaching and language is very much more simple than many of the definitions of the Catholic Church and the commentaries of theologians, we may reply that Our Lord, for the most part, was speaking to simple people, and He used language that simple people can understand. Let us also remember that the child Jesus when twelve years of age was discovered by His parents in the Temple, "sitting in the midst of the doctors both hearing them and asking them questions, and all they that heard him were astonished at his understanding and his answers."

—Arnold Lunn

Apostolicity

In order to be apostolic a Church must have continuity, not only of life but of faith. People sometimes accuse us Catholics of having added to the faith; of having foisted in doctrines which were no part of the original deposit, that of the Immaculate Conception, for example. But nobody seriously accuses us of having subtracted from the faith; of having dropped any article of belief which was an integral part of theology as theology was understood by the early Fathers. And that's important. The apostles, you see, were in the first instance witnesses; people who could bear testimony to certain things they had seen and heard, and hand on that testimony to those who came after them. Every Catholic bishop is the repository of a tradition which he took over from his predecessor and is bound to hand on, undiminished, to his successor. That's why, if he has time and opportunity, a Catholic bishop on his death-bed calls his canons together and makes a solemn profession of faith; he wants to make it clear that, in his time at least, the deposit of tradition has not been tampered with.

Continuity of life, continuity of faith—there you have the essentials of that mark of apostolicity by which we distinguish the true Church.

—Msgr. Ronald Knox

Tenacity

If for a moment I may assume the airs of a bishop on his death-bed, and throw back my regard over the past, I would say that this instinct of tenacity marks us off, us Catholics, from all that I have known of non-Catholic religion in Oxford, since I knew Oxford. As a member of this University, I have the age of Christ; it is thirty-three years since I matriculated. During the first nine of those years, I knew Oxford as a Protestant; during the last thirteen as a Catholic; and during all that time, the modern religious debate has been constantly the subject uppermost in my thoughts. I can remember, when I was an undergraduate, a sermon from the

Bishop of London, I mean the one who is just retiring, then at the height of his remarkable influence. He preached about the faith, and gave us a parable, probably from some incident in the South African War, about a wounded soldier with a flag in his hands, "slipping . . . slipping." And then, of course, he told us that we mustn't let the faith slip like that. But I'm afraid it is what we were doing, and what those who followed us have been doing ever since. The instinct of holding on to a religious tradition which you have received, handing it on undiminished to others, where is it now, outside the Catholic Church?

—*Msgr. Ronald Knox*

Feast of the Immaculate Conception   *December 8*

The Holy Spirit of God impels the teaching Church to put before us the figure of the Immaculate Conception. As Cardinal Newman points out, in the figure of the Immaculate Conception we have a sure vision of what human nature is when it is free from sin and therefore a vision of the beauty and strength of the nature we ourselves possess when finally we dominate by God's grace the sin which cripples it. Cardinal Newman wrote beautifully of the Immaculate Conception and its lessons for us, discouraged by our own weakness. He asked us to suppose that Eve had stood the trial instead of succumbing to the temptation, to suppose that she had kept the grace that was hers and ours in the beginning, and then to suppose that she eventually had children. Those children from the first moment of their existence would, through divine bounty, have received the same privileges that Eve had possessed. As she was taken from Adam's side clothed, so to say, in a garment of grace, so her children in turn would have received what may be called an *immaculate conception.* We, her descendants, would have been conceived in grace as in fact we are conceived in sin.

Mary is placed before our eyes as a daughter of Eve unfallen, and thus she shows us what our nature would have possessed supernaturally and by privilege if Eve had not fallen. When we speculate on this in these days of discouragement it should occur to us that, although we do not have the privileges that were Mary's or that were Eve's, nonetheless ours is still the nature that was elevated in Eve. It is deprived but not depraved, wounded but not intrinsically corrupted. Ours is the same human nature that Mary possessed and, therefore, in the splendor of Mary we have a promise of something of what we yet may be if we cooperate with the grace of God that is restored to us, but was hers from the beginning.

—*Cardinal John Wright*

We Believe

December 9

Our belief in the authenticity of the Christian revelation is based on man's expectation of Christ, on the evidence of Christ's power, and on the evidence of his goodness. We would not claim belief for a Christ who enjoyed miraculous powers, but offered no moral inspiration, nor yet for a Christ who claimed our moral sympathy, but showed no powers which exceeded those of our common nature. So we base our argument partly on his miracles, but partly on his character, on the atmosphere which surrounded him, that fragrance which breathed from him, so that men came away from listening to his simple direct methods of preaching with the feeling, "never man spoke like this Man." What wonder, then, if his saints in every age have caught and handed on in their measure, the kindling enthusiasm of his appeal? The saints, after all, are the best advertisement the Christian religion ever had. And we know that the saints are really the characteristic products of Christendom, its natural fruit, when we have looked back at the life of Jesus of Nazareth, to find all their inspiration centred, and all their light focused, in his.

—*Msgr. Ronald Knox*

Our Lord

Our Lord Jesus Christ was both God and Man. As you all know, the formula in which Catholic theology enshrines that notion, the polish which Catholic theology gives to that rough jewel of truth, is the formula of the Hypostatic Union. We all learned to repeat those words before we had the foggiest notion what they meant; they tripped so easily off our tongues that the first word got shortened down into *haipstatic*, and perhaps became vaguely connected in our minds with the meaningless sort of shout we used to hear on the parade ground. However, we know a little more about it now; at least I hope we do. The doctrine of the hypostatic union is that in the historical figure of Jesus of Nazareth we have to distinguish two natures, a human and a divine Nature; but that those two natures belong to a single Person, and that Person is wholly divine.

The Christian mysteries transcend human thought. But they do not contradict human thought; they cut across our experience just at those points where it is impossible to say "This or that is impossible" because human thought, even in interpreting ordinary human experience, finds in it, at those points, an insoluble mystery.

—Msgr. Ronald Knox

The Incarnation

The Incarnation of our Lord is a mystery. And wherever it deals with mystery, you will find that Catholic theology is a middle way between two extremes. That is natural, because a theological mystery always involves something which seems to our minds a contradiction; we are expected to hold simultaneously two truths which are apparently irreconcilable. And there is an obvious temptation for the incomplete theologian, when he is up against that kind of situation, to explain away one of those truths in the interests of the other. It's like cheating at patience, one can see in a moment that it is wrong, because it makes the thing too simple.

So here, in the mystery of the Incarnation. Fr D'Arcy, I expect, told you last Sunday about Nestorianism and those more modern views, all tainted with Nestorianism, which explain away the mystery of the Incarnation by explaining away the statement that our Lord was God. This morning, we have to deal with the opposite error; with the ideas of the Docetae, and Apollinarians, and Monophysites, and Monothelites, who tried to explain away the mystery of the Incarnation by explaining away the statement that our Lord was Man.

—*Msgr. Ronald Knox*

The Reformation *December 12*

We shall deceive ourselves if we think of the Reformation as merely a matter of doctrinal differences, or merely a conflict between the new nobilities and the old tradition of Europe. In part, at least, the Reformation was a genuine protest against the corrupt state of morals which followed on the Renaissance. And where the Reformers got the upper hand, uncontrolled by secular princes, they overdid their part by trying to introduce a discipline far stricter than the discipline of the Catholic Church had been before them. In Scotland, for example, a person guilty of adultery who refused to submit to the discipline of the Kirk was put under the greater excommunication, solemnly given over into the power and hands of the devil, and outlawed from Christian society. If the Reformation had really succeeded, the sinners of Europe would have lived under conditions of intolerable oppression.

The Reformation did not succeed; kings and courts were too strong for it, and it made terms with the world after all. But it left its mark on society by creating, among certain classes, a tradition of Puritanism which has not yet died out.

—*Msgr. Ronald Knox*

After the Reformation   *December 13*

In England and Scotland, at any rate, a system of rigorism in
morals commended itself to, and imbedded itself in, the mentality
of the lower middle class. I am not saying that contemptuously,
though you will often find such terms used in contempt. A class
that has to be frugal, has to maintain a certain standard of
respectability, that is excluded from the freer activities of the
landed gentry, easily develops and clings to a tradition of Puritanism.
There is no room for it in the theatre; it is too poor for the dress
circle, too refined for the pit. It has no money to waste on racing
or on gambling; it is too superior to join in the rough dances of
the countryside, too provincial to acquire the manners of the
ballroom. Finally, in England, though not in Scotland, it loses the
tradition of drinking intoxicants, because it is too proud for the
public houses and cannot afford to belong to clubs; so a temperance movement rounds off the completeness of the Puritan
mentality. That mentality ruled England yesterday, and is making
a hard struggle against defeat at this moment. It still wants to
enforce a stricter morality by law, in the same spirit in which
Calvin and John Knox made the attempt three and a half centuries
ago.

—Msgr. Ronald Knox

Morality   *December 14*

In Catholic countries, and in a Catholic society which manages to
maintain itself, as ours did for more than two centuries, quite
outside the general life of the nation, this Puritan ideal has never
ruled. You get approaches to it; the tendency in our own Church
is labelled, rather loosely, by the seventeenth-century nickname of
Jansenism. The Curé d'Ars at the beginning of last century was
not satisfied until he had banished dancing altogether from his
parish; and even to-day, where the influence of the priesthood is
strong, as in Ireland or in French Canada, you will find it exercised,
sometimes, in a rather rigorist spirit. But it is an influence that

remains personal; a Catholic society, however strict in its views, has no itch for moral legislation, such as Puritanism has. It will only frame laws for the repression of vice where it is necessary to preserve the whole structure of social life, as, for example, in the matter of legalized divorce.

We Catholics have not only to do our best to keep down our own warring passions and live decent lives, which will often be hard enough in this odd world we have been born into. We have to bear witness to moral principles which the world owned yesterday, and has begun to turn its back on to-day. We have to disapprove of some of the things our neighbours do, without being stuffy about it.

—Msgr. Ronald Knox

Reaction *December 15*

Now, when a society goes pagan, as our society is going pagan hand over hand—that is not pulpit rhetoric, it is plain fact for anybody who takes the trouble to think—you get [a reaction] on the part of Christian thought.

The Catholic reaction is this. You cannot call it Puritan, even when it protests against the age; for it distinguishes between the importance of the various issues; it is not clouded by a mist of middle-class tradition, does not mistake indulgence as such for sin. Nor yet does it deserve to be called Victorian, because evidently it does not reflect the fashion of a single century. It is strong in controversy, because it takes its stand on unalterable moral principle; not mere ecclesiastical legislation, but the law written in men's hearts. Only, that does not mean that as Catholics we shall avoid all the bother of argument and find ourselves universally respected. We shall find that people are for ever trying to persuade us that our outlook is mediaeval, because we stand apart from the sex-madness of our generation. And it makes us unpopular; people laugh at the Puritan but they do not laugh at the Catholic, they feel they are up against something too hard and too formidable for that. A quite new hatred of the Catholic religion is growing up, has grown up within my own lifetime; a hatred of its strict principles on certain points, which our neighbours, though their own liberty of action is not in the least interfered with, dislike as being a criticism of their own conduct, and a criticism which in their heart of hearts they know to be just.

—*Msgr. Ronald Knox*

How to Live December 16

It is the nature of the undergraduate to discuss all things in heaven and earth with the utmost seriousness and sometimes with very slight information. And I suppose that those interminable conversations which go on, year after year, in these venerable buildings don't vary much from year to year in their character.

. . . Nowadays I fancy that the subjects which command general attention are more self-centred, and very pardonably so. The modern question is "How am I to live?" . . .

. . . The fun of living, can be found only in regulating your life according to fixed principles of conduct. Third, that there is one single standard of morality, ideally for all people, and practically for all Christian people. And fourth, that if you are really a Christian, the irksomeness of merely obeying negative rules is exchanged for the positive joy of trying to live so as to please our Lord Jesus Christ.

First, there are such things as right and wrong. Whatever else in our human judgments is merely convention, this at least is a fixed principle, that some courses of action deserve to be rewarded, and others deserve to be punished.

—*Msgr. Ronald Knox*

That whole notion of reward and punishment, of praise and blame, is an elementary notion, born in us, otherwise it could never have got into us. Every attempt to explain away our moral judgments as merely aesthetic or merely utilitarian has completely broken down. It's quite possible to mistake a wrong action for a right one, like the man who assassinates a tyrant. It is quite possible to mistake a right action for a wrong one, like the people who think it is wicked to fight for your country even in a just quarrel. But if right and wrong didn't exist, it would have been quite impossible for such a mistake to arise as to suppose that they did. The human mind has no creative power to have invented for itself such phantasies.

Second, the art of living depends upon living by a rule of conduct, and it is that, really, which lends zest and interest to the performance. Of course, it's true that we've got to make a living, and that struggle lends a certain zest and interest to life; but so far we are no better off than the beasts—they too must struggle for their daily food. But Man, as an intellectual creature, is meant to have a fuller life than this; he has a character to form of which, under God, he is the architect. And any form of art demands rules that you are to work by, laws of harmony, laws of proportion, and so on. To be the artist of his own character, Man must have laws, outside of himself.

—Msgr. Ronald Knox

Laws of Conduct *December 18*

The Christian sets before himself the highest of all ideals of character, to imitate as far as possible the life of our Lord Jesus Christ. *He* is the Hero, the Model, whose lineaments we want to translate, with however faltering a hand, on to the canvas of our own lives. A man who is entirely unmoral, if such a creature could exist, would be one who has never tasted life at all.

Next, this law of conduct is the same ideally for all mankind.

People talk sometimes about the difference between heathen and Christian morality, and wonder whether perhaps pagan morality wasn't a finer thing. But, of course, in their broad outlines there *is* no difference between Christian and pagan morality at all. The Christian Church didn't suddenly impose on the world a set of moral sentiments of which it had never heard before, a set of moral sentiments with which it violently disagreed. How could Christianity have spread so suddenly and so easily if it had not found a response in the consciences of those to whom it was preached? No, the pagans knew well enough what was right in theory, valued fidelity in married people, continence in young people, even virginity as a form of self-devotion; they knew it was wrong to lie and steal and quarrel and all the rest of it, just as we do. It is possible, of course, for the human conscience to grow blunted, it is possible, therefore, for false standards of morals to prevail, for people to get wrong ideas about the importance of this virtue or that. But the human conscience does admire virtue when it sees it.

—Msgr. Ronald Knox

Heirs of the Apostles   *December 19*

Apostolicity means being in a position to trace your history, by a continuous tradition, back to the apostles. I say by a continuous tradition, because, of course, in a general way every Christian denomination can trace its history back to the apostles. The Quakers, for example, go back to George Fox in the early part of the seventeenth century; and, of course, George Fox didn't have to invent Christianity himself, he'd learned it from other people, and those other people had learned it from other people, and those other people had learned it from Catholics. But the point is that George Fox deliberately broke away from the main current of Christian tradition, and regarded the Anglican churches as temples of Baal, and the Anglican clergymen as priests of Baal. So that Quaker history doesn't date from the apostles, and doesn't pretend to date from the apostles, it dates from George Fox. Whereas we

Catholics do not trace our history back to Edmund Campion at the end of the sixteenth century or to St Augustine of Canterbury at the end of the sixth century; we trace it back to the apostles themselves, to whom our Lord's promises were made, and we wouldn't claim to be the inheritors of those promises unless we could show that we are the heirs of the apostles.

—Msgr. Ronald Knox

Continuity *December 20*

A continuous spiritual history means, not merely deriving certain supernatural powers from that fountain of grace which was committed to the apostles, but by deriving from that same apostolical tradition the *right* to minister in God's Church, and to minister in this or that part of God's Church. Our Lord said to his disciples, "As my Father hath sent me, even so send I you"; he commissioned them to act in his name, and this commission to act is something which you must derive by legitimate descent from them, no less than the power to perform spiritual acts. Ever since our Lord said that, the Church has been sending people, commissioning them to minister in this or that place, in this or that capacity, and to minister without her commission is an act of schism.

Our submission is, then, that whenever there has been a schism in the history of Christendom one side was in the wrong, not merely because it broke away from that Catholic, world-wide unity which the true Church must possess, but because it tried to go back upon that apostolic, age-old continuity by which the true Church is equally marked. If you look at the schism which has most to do with controversies which affect our own country, the English Reformation, you can see at once that it was a schism between the supporters of an old, continuous tradition, and the supporters of a new order of things.

—Msgr. Ronald Knox

True Revelation *December 21*

We . . . claim that the Christian revelation is true because [Jesus'] miracles, culminating in the unique miracle of his Resurrection, can neither be disregarded on historical grounds, nor yet be philosophically explained, unless they were meant to set the seal upon an authentic mission from God to man. The lame walk, the deaf hear, the lepers are cleansed, the dead are raised up— so our Lord himself appeals to his wonderful works to bear testimony of him. What manner of man is this, his followers asked themselves, that the wind and the sea obey him? What wonder, then, if we find his Church in history capable of the most extraordinary conquests, meeting and vanquishing paganism in no strength but that of her own inherent vitality, assimilating and taming the barbarian elements that flooded into Europe in the Dark Ages, holding her own against the stubborn nationalisms of mediaeval Europe? What wonder if she, who lives with the life of her Risen Master, dies so many deaths and achieves so many resurrections; survives the Mahomedan attack, survives the Reformation, survives the French Revolution, seems to gain strength, even in our own day, from all the efforts that are made to disintegrate the civilization which she gave us? "I have power to lay down my life, and power to take it again." Wherever faith in the miracle of the Resurrection strikes deep root, the miracle of the Resurrection repeats itself.

—Msgr. Ronald Knox

On the Road *December 22*

While on the road we cannot help wondering about God. What is He like? What does He want for us? What does He expect of us? And sometimes we ask whether He exists at all. So many of our fellow pilgrims have decided that there is no God; others just go through life doubting or not knowing. But the important questions still require answers. What happens after death? Nothing? Has life no meaning? Are we only part of an absurd situation devoid of sense and purpose?

If only we could see God, life would be very different; our uncertainties would go and we should take each step in life, clear about the direction and firm in our tread. There would be no faltering, no confusion. But it is not like that. Furthermore, apart from our inability to see God with our eyes or hear His voice with our ears, there is, in addition, the problem that, as pilgrims, we are weak and wounded. We do not function as we should.

There are times when we seem to respond to what we know is expected of us. There are other times when we falter badly. We get tied up with all kinds of things that distract us from thinking about the end of the journey, or delay us on the way, indeed entice us to go in the wrong direction altogether. We are sinners, always in danger of going wrong.

Moreover, there is a great deal of pain and suffering. That can slow the pace. Many simply cannot cope and many, indeed, suffer so much that they cannot believe that here is someone who loves them.

—Cardinal Basil Hume

We Are Pilgrims   *December 23*

There were many travellers in Judea and Galilee on that first Christmas night, for a census of the people had to be made. Places to lodge were scarce. Some, the poor ones, had no more than a cave or a stable in which to shelter and rest from the fatigue of their long journey. Others were still on the road, they were men in search. Three men, pilgrims these, were in search of a king— one, they said, who would be born at this time and to whom they would be led by a star. Where that star would lead them and what exactly they would find, they were none too certain. They asked questions and sought guidance. The light from the star in the heavens would be their guide, and they sought too that inner light which is what wise men will always seek.

The pilgrim through life's journey needs light for guidance along the road that leads to our true and final home. That pilgrim is you, and that pilgrim is me, often confused and often wounded.

Life is a pilgrimage. We are on the march, and sooner or later we shall reach our destination. That destination we call heaven. There we shall see God as He is, and that experience will be the cause of a happiness which will be complete and have no end. We are made for that.

—Cardinal Basil Hume

God Is with Us   *December 24*

It is good to realise that God is present everywhere. In Him we live and move and have our being. His presence is manifested to us through His creation, and in our reflection and enjoyment of it we are in touch with Him. It is good to realise too that, at any moment, we may just rest in the thought of God's presence here and now. God speaks through His creation, but He speaks too through stillness and silence. And if we cannot find that silence because of the noise which surrounds us, we must look for it inside ourselves. In that silence He may invite us to pursue further our search for Him.

We do not see Him as He is. Crouched in the cleft of a rock we catch glimpses of His presence, when something of His glory is manifested to us in His creation. But for us to know Him more intimately, He must speak and tell us about Himself. In Old Testament times the people of God, His chosen people, meditated on Him and on His intervention in their affairs. All this is recorded, and is done so for our benefit. God uses these records and meditations as a way of speaking to us, they are God's Word. But if "in former days, God spoke to our fathers in many ways and by many means, through the prophets", wrote the author of the letter to the Hebrews, "now at last in these times He has spoken to us with a Son to speak for Him; a Son who is the radiance of his Father's splendour and the full expression of his being" (Heb 1:1–3).

—Cardinal Basil Hume

The Word Became Flesh

The Word has become flesh and dwelt amongst us. It is now no longer just a question of listening to the Word of God as contained in the Old Testament writings; a person has come among us, and that person is God made man. Hence the importance of that passage in St John's gospel which records a conversation between Our Lord and the apostle Philip. Jesus had said: "If you had learned to recognise me, you would have learned to recognise my Father too. From now onwards you are to recognise Him; you have seen Him"; Philip did not understand, so he said: "Lord, let us see the Father, and then we shall be satisfied". The Lord then said, and very solemnly: "Have I been with you all this time, Philip, and you still do not know me? To have seen me is to have seen the Father, so how can you say 'Let us see the Father'? Do you not believe that I am in the Father, and the Father is in me?" (Jn 14:6–10).

There are men and women all over the world who have dedicated their lives to obeying the teaching given in that twenty-fifth chapter of St Matthew. They are truly living the Gospel. There are many, too, who do not know the Gospel and yet devote themselves to serving the poor in their needs. Our Lord has a word for them. "When was it that we saw thee sick or in prison and came to thee?", they asked. "Believe me, when you did it to one of these my least brethren, you did it unto me" (Mt 25:39–40).

— *Cardinal Basil Hume*

The Shepherds

And there were shepherds in the same district living in the fields and keeping watch over their flocks by night. And behold, an angel of the Lord stood by them and the glory of God shone round about them, and they feared exceedingly.

And the angel said to them, "Do not be afraid, for behold, I bring you good news of great joy which shall be to all the people;

for there has been born to you today in the town of David a Savior, who is Christ the Lord. And this shall be a sign to you: you will find an infant wrapped in swaddling clothes and lying in a manger." And suddenly there was with the angel a multitude of the heavenly host praising God and saying,

"Glory to God in the highest,
    and peace on earth among men
        of good will."

And it came to pass, when the angels had departed from them into heaven, that the shepherds were saying to one another, "Let us go over to Bethlehem and see this thing that has come to pass, which the Lord has made known to us."

So they went with haste, and they found Mary and Joseph, and the babe lying in the manger. And when they had seen, they understood what had been told them concerning this child. And all who heard marvelled at the things told them by the shepherds. But Mary kept in mind all these words, pondering them in her heart. And the shepherds returned, glorifying and praising God for all that they had heard and seen, even as it was spoken to them.

— Saint Luke

Response   *December 27*

When we have acknowledged the existence of that "Someone" and learned that He has intervened in our affairs, we should begin to respond. We want to find out more about Him, try to be in touch with Him, and then discover that we should obey Him and serve Him. We have come to recognise that in God are to be found the ultimate meaning and purpose of all things, and especially of ourselves. This response is what we call "the spiritual life".

If we do not have a spiritual life, then our living is impoverished. Important questions remain unanswered; life itself will appear to be pointless, and we have no future to which to look forward. But we are made "to know God, to love Him and serve Him in this world, and to be happy with Him for ever in the next". This is the point of the pilgrimage.

Goodness, truth, beauty and power in the created universe are different manifestations of the glory of God, the Creator. He shows His power in many different ways, in the forces of nature, in the strength and skill of humans, in machines of every kind. He reveals His goodness and beauty in all that is lovely and desirable.

— *Cardinal Basil Hume*

We Can't See God   *December 28*

If only we could see God—that wish, deep in the hearts of countless men and women down the ages, inspired the prayer of a notable Old Testament pilgrim. Moses prayed: "Show me your glory, I beg you" (Ex 33:18). But he was told: "You cannot see My face, for man cannot see Me and live". "You must stand on the rock", Moses was told, "and when My glory passes by, I will put you in a cleft of the rock and shield you with My hand while I pass by. Then I shall take My hand away and you shall see the back of Me; but My face is not to be seen" (Ex 33:22–23).

We cannot see God, but we can catch glimpses of His "glory". What is that "glory"?, the Shekinah to which reference is made so often in the Bible?

. . . [God's] mind is explored as we go in pursuit of truth. C.S. Lewis explained it thus: "I was learning the far more secret doctrine that pleasures are shafts of the glory as it strikes our sensibility. As it impinges on our wills or understanding, we give it different names—goodness or truth or the like. But its flash upon our senses and mood is pleasure. But aren't there bad, unlawful pleasures? Certainly there are. But in calling them 'bad pleasures' I take it we are using a kind of shorthand. We mean, 'pleasures snatched by unlawful act'. It is the stealing of the apple that is bad, not the sweetness."

— *Cardinal Basil Hume*

Unreliable Emotions

Many years ago I was overtaken by night and storm while ski-ing alone among the Oberland glaciers. The storm was uncomfortable, but by no means unbearable, and my position was not so desperate as in the imaginary case which I have just quoted by way of illustration. Reason, indeed, insisted that I had nothing serious to worry about. The cold, though unpleasant, was by no means unendurable, and provided that I kept moving and did not lose heart, I knew that I would certainly survive the experience. Emotion disagreed, for to emotion the driving mist and snow and the black darkness were the only surviving realities in a world from which colour and warmth and light had vanished as for ever. Emotion sneered at my faith in the life to come, the life which would return with the dawn upon a frozen world. Emotion was quite convinced that this belief in the coming day was nothing more than a case of wish-fulfilment.

There are moments even in the lives of the saints when it is difficult to believe that the sun of faith will return and disperse the dark mists of doubt, and at such moments reason has to struggle hard against emotion. Many of those who succumb to exposure among the mountains die because they have lost the will to live, because their reason has proved weaker than their emotions, and because it is easier to die than not.

—Arnold Lunn

Longing for God

The longing for God may be smothered beneath successive strata of self-indulgence and sin, but there is no soul which has never felt the desire for God. Have you ever reflected on the fact that if this universal longing does not correspond to some objective reality, it is the only universal appetite which feeds on complete illusion? The hunger for God, like the hunger for food and the hunger for a mate, is a craving for something objectively real.

To argue that the hunger for God disproves the existence of God is as irrational as to maintain that the belief in the existence of cows is an example of "wish-fulfilment" because the thought of beef makes a hungry man's mouth water.

Nature employs pain as a warning and pleasure as an encouragement. The Creator has associated happiness with the physical processes necessary for the continuance of life, eating, drinking and mating, and with the spiritual processes necessary for the gaining of eternal life. And, if Nature be our guide, the fact that religion offers you happiness is evidence not of its falsity but of its truth. Manicheism, oldest of all heresies, adapts itself with chameleon-like skill to the changing fashions of the day. The pleasures of sex and wine have been condemned in the past. In our own age the neo-Puritans are concentrating on denouncing the happiness which is associated with religion. Do not, I beg of you, allow these Puritan complexes to deprive you of religious joy.

—*Arnold Lunn*

God Loves Us   *December 31*

We have to hang on to the fact of God's love for us. That demands courage and tenacity. There is so much in the world that seems to contradict the whole idea of a loving God; there is enough in our own lives to make us doubt it. No one has ever given a totally satisfactory explanation of why there is evil, and so suffering, in life, at least not to my way of thinking. But there are truths which point us in the right direction. They will indicate where a solution is to be found. First, we are sinners. We are free. We have to be free in order to be able to love truly. We misuse that freedom, individually and collectively, so there is tragedy, suffering and death. Secondly, there is the fact that God became man, accepted the human condition (except for sin) and gave it a new significance and value. Thirdly, we have to hang on all the time to the fact that God loves us, and this in every crisis and however much events and facts appear to contradict the truth. We must trust God. It is very easy to trust when the evidence for doing so is obvious; it is quite different when it is not. God asks us, sometimes often, to go on with the pilgrimage through life in the dark, but always trusting. Trust is a proof of love.

—Cardinal Basil Hume

Movable Fasts
and Feasts

Ash Wednesday

We have been told that we must love God. "Thou shalt love the Lord thy God with thy whole heart and with thy whole soul and with thy whole mind. This is the greatest and first commandment. And the second is like to this: Thou shalt love thy neighbour as thyself" (Mt 22:37–39). The spiritual lives of too many people are based on fear. Now I would not wish to minimise the importance of a wholesome filial fear of God. Fear of hell is, on occasions, no bad motive for avoiding sin. Furthermore, our task is to be pleasing to God and this means that we must keep the commandments, and do what He expects of us. Morality is important, and not only as an end in itself. It should be the test of our intent to love God and serve Him. We should be fearful lest in breaking His law we displease Him. There can be no serious spiritual life which ignores obedience to God. That is evident.

It would, however, be an impoverished spiritual life which was not based on trying to love God. After all, that is the first commandment. Fear is an exhausting emotion. Love must cast out fear, eventually. But I believe that it takes most of us quite a long time to learn about the love of God. It dawns slowly.

— Cardinal Basil Hume

Holy Thursday

The Master waiting on his servants—as if to assure his disciples that the Holy Eucharist was a foretaste of heaven, we know what our Lord did. At the last supper he knelt down and washed their feet. And when he came to St Peter—last of all, I suppose; that seems to have been the spirit of the occasion—St Peter made the obvious protest, "Lord, is it for *thee* to wash *my* feet?" The disciples, you will remember, had just been having a discussion among themselves, which should be the greatest. It seems an inappropriate moment, but St Luke assures us that it was so. And our Lord solved the difficulty by asking them, "Tell me, which is the greater, the man who sits at table, or the man who serves him?

Surely the man who sits at table, yet I am here among you as your servant." Then he suits the action to the word; girds himself like a slave and kneels with a basin at their feet. Oh yes, Peter is to be the greatest among them; but when he achieves that position, it will not be long before he realizes what it involves; to be the chief Christian is to be *servus servorum Dei*, slave of the slaves of God.

Our Lord does not say, "Look at me, watch what I am doing at this moment; see how, when need arises, I can abase myself." He says, "I am here among you as your servant"—it is not a mere momentary gesture; what he says of himself is true all the time. I am here among you, here on earth, among you men; there would be no point in God becoming Man, unless he who was fashioned in the likeness of men went further, and took upon himself the form of a slave. The whole process of the Incarnation, if you come to think of it, is a topsy-turvy kind of arrangement; it is God doing something for the sake of man, when man only exists for the sake of God.

—*Msgr. Ronald Knox*

Good Friday

He hung on the cross between two thieves. Perhaps that special touch of disgrace was added in the hope that the people whom He had loved and healed, comforted and forgiven would identify Him with these criminals; if so the hope was vain. Ever since, the world has talked of His cross with hardly a word for the other crosses; kings have searched for and found and carried His cross, particles of it are still adored throughout the world. The others? They have played their part. They clustered around that central cross as around a judgment seat and heard a divine sentence passed. They showed to all men that suffering can be a soaring flight direct to heaven, or a weight pressing us down deeper into hell; for it was from the vantage point of a cross that one criminal recognized the throne and royal robes of the King, while the others saw only a dying criminal who could be safely mocked.

Christ laid down His life in obedience to the command of His

Father; the obedience, like the command, was inspired by an infinite love for men. That obedience brought out the terrible severity of divine justice's refusal to forgive sin until the penalty had been undergone; at the same time, it revealed the infinite goodness of God Who sent His only-begotten Son into the world to die that men might escape the penalty of their sin. With the help of His own people, Christ was handed over to the Gentiles to be put to death; salvation follows the same course, from the Jews to the Gentiles, not for the destruction of God but for the happiness of man.

— Walter Farrell

Holy Saturday

The light was fading; they must make haste to finish, to remove the wedge and let the stone roll up and close the tomb. Then they went away, leaving the body in the silence of the tomb.

"Next day, the next after the day of preparation, the chief priests and the Pharisees gathered in Pilate's presence, and said, Sir, we have recalled it to memory that this deceiver, while he yet lived, said, I am to rise again after three days. Give orders, then, that his tomb shall be securely guarded until the third day; or perhaps his disciples will come and steal him away. If they should then say to the people, He has risen from the dead, this last deceit will be more dangerous than the old." They were taking no chances, these politicians. But the Roman was annoyed with them; how much longer was this affair to go on. "You have guards; away with you, make it secure as you best know how. And they went and made the tomb secure, putting a seal on the stone and setting a guard over it" (Mt 27:62–66). Such precautions do men take against the will of God!

In the darkness of the grave, Jesus was now no more than other men, a body of flesh awaiting corruption. So his unhappy disciples must have thought. So also has Holbein painted him and Philippe de Champaigne too, setting before us the anatomy of a man tortured to death: the mouth agape, the eyes upturned, the deathly hue of the flesh now that the blood of the wounds would flow no more. And yet, corruption, which in the natural order must follow inevitably, was not to be. "A grain of wheat must fall into the ground and die," said Jesus, "or else it remains nothing more than a grain of wheat; but if it dies, then it yields rich fruit." The seed lay in the fostering earth; the fruit would spring forth from the seed and the harvest was at hand.

— Henri Daniel-Rops

Easter

As a matter of fact, Christ had tried to ease the reception of the news of the miracle of His resurrection by what might be called the practice sessions or rehearsals: the resurrections of Lazarus, the son of the widow of Naim, and the saints who walked the streets of the Holy City after His death. He could not hope that men would accept the fact of a man walking from the tomb quite as nonchalantly as they do the fact of a man walking from the door of his house in the morning; but, at least, the shock of contact with divine power in meeting death might be eased enough so that the minds of men would not be numbed by it. Of course, these were merely rehearsals; these men who had risen from the dead had to die again, and men saw them die. Christ was the first Who rose from the dead immortal; He was the real conqueror of death. The rest of us are to share in that conquest but it was first accomplished by Him.

From the darkness of the narrow tomb, through the daylight of that first Easter morning, came the same Man Who had died on the cross, possessed of the same body and the same soul. The body, kept incorrupt in the tomb for three days by divine power, was now reunited to the soul; the identical body that had been laid in the tomb by others now came forth by itself. There was no point in an apparent or fantastic body being shown to men that morning; that would mean that Christ had not risen and, as we have seen, Christ had to rise from the dead. Lest there be any doubt of the reality of that body of His, Christ invited the terrified disciples to "Touch me and see, that a spirit has not flesh and bones as I have."

In Christ, life has conquered death. The air, the odor, the very color of life enter into the darkest corner of the tomb. Death is a gateway, as is life; a motion to high goals, as is life; a fulfillment of hope, an unveiling of faith, a consummation of charity, as life never is. Life's promises are fulfilled by death's opening up of enduring life. The rehearsal is over, death lifts the curtain, and the eternal play is on.

—Walter Farrell

The Ascension

Since the Ascension, we have found it easier to realize the love of God, because it is mirrored for us in the human sympathy of Jesus Christ. But there is something else—since the Ascension, it has been easier for us to imagine heaven as a desirable goal. Try as we will, the idea of heaven eludes us. Are we to think of it as a place, from which every element of unhappiness is excluded? But we know how much our love of places is conditioned by moods and sentiments, by the desire for change, by association and by history! Or are we to think of it as a state? But then, how are we to think of a state except in terms of selfish enjoyment? Or should we look forward to being reunited with those we have loved? But how frail they are, these earthly bonds; how time impairs them! No, when we have tried everything, we shall find no better window on eternity than St Paul's formula, "to depart and be with Christ". If he has left us, and gone to heaven, it is so that we may no longer be disconcerted by the barrier of cloud that stands between us and it. We are not concerned to "go" here or there, to be in this or that state of existence. We want to find him.

So little, and so much it is given us to know about the ascended Christ.

—Msgr. Ronald Knox

Pentecost

So the moment foretold had come. The Spirit who comforts had descended on them. His presence made itself felt in their very behaviour and in the supernatural joy which they experienced, a joy so evident that the first witnesses—local people, pilgrims, inquisitive onlookers attracted to the spot by the strange celestial roaring noise—grinned at them and thought that they were drunk. But a curious power emanated from them and made them apostles, bearers of the good news, thanks to the mysterious gift which they had received of being understood by all who listened, whatever their language, and thanks even more to the fresh courage which lifted up their hearts and was going to ensure that even those who had abandoned the Master when he was alive would defend him now that he was dead to the point of sacrificing their own lives.

Proof of this was given on the spot. The leader of the little group, the man whom the Master himself had marked out as such, Simon, surnamed Peter, had been no more heroic than the others at the time of the great test. Recognized by the curious on the night of the farcical trial when he was waiting about in fear and trembling for news, he had capitulated at once and proclaimed three times—with an oath—that he had nothing to do with the arrested man. Yet—and perhaps this is the first miracle in the whole story—this frightened man, ready to deny anything to save his own life, a man, in a word, like so many others, found himself completely changed when the Spirit had breathed on him.

—Henri Daniel-Rops

Trinity Sunday

Our God is the God of all things, the God of Heaven and earth and sea and river, the God of sun and moon and all the stars, the God of high mountains and lowly valleys, the God over Heaven and in Heaven and under Heaven. He has a dwelling both in Heaven and earth, the sea and all that are therein. He inspires all things, he quickens all things; he surpasses all things, he sustains all things. He kindles the light of the sun and the light of the moon. He made springs in arid land and dry islands in the sea, and stars he appointed to minister to the greater lights. He has a Son coeternal with Himself, and like unto Him. But the Son is not younger than the Father, nor is the Father older than the Son. And the Holy Spirit breathes in them. Father and Son and Holy Spirit are not divided. Howbeit, I desire to unite you to the Son of the Heavenly King, for you are the children of the King of the earth.

St. Patrick

And when Jesus had been baptized, he came up from the water. And behold, the heavens were opened, and he saw the Spirit of God descending as a dove and coming upon him. And a voice from the heavens said, "This is my beloved Son, in whom I am well pleased."

St. Matthew's Gospel

Corpus Christi

And at the window, behind the wall of partition that is a wall of partition no longer, stands the Beloved himself, calling us out into the open; calling us away from the ointments and the spikenard of Solomon's court, that stupefy and enchain our senses, to the gardens and the vineyards, to the fields and the villages, to the pure airs of eternity. Arise (he says), make haste and come. Come away from the blind pursuit of creatures, from all the plans your busy brain evolves for your present and future pleasures, from the frivolous distractions it clings to. Come away from the pettiness and the meanness of your everyday life, from the grudges, the jealousies, the unhealed enmities that set your imagination throbbing. Come away from the cares and solicitudes about the morrow that seem so urgent, your heavy anxieties about the world's future and your own, so short either of them and so uncertain. Come away into the wilderness of prayer, where my love will follow you and my hand hold you; learn to live, with the innermost part of your soul, with all your secret aspirations, with all the centre of your hopes and cares, in that supernatural world which can be yours now, which must be yours hereafter.

I wonder, is that why some of us are so frightened of holy communion, because we still cling so to the world of sense? It is certain that Catholics are most apt to neglect communion just when they most need it; in the spring-time of youth, when the blood is hot, and the passions strong, and ambition dominates us. Why is that, unless that we are more wedded, when we are young, to the desires that perish? I wonder, is that why so many of us who go often to communion find that it makes, apparently, little difference to us; that we are still as full of bad habits as we were ten or fifteen years ago, that our lives, if anything, compare unfavourably with the lives of others, who have not our opportunities for going to communion frequently? Is it perhaps because, all the time, we are shrinking from the act of confidence which would throw the whole burden of our lives on our Lord; do not want holy communion to have its proper effect on us, which is to make the joys and distractions of this world have less meaning and less appeal for us? We must not expect him to work the marvels of his grace in us, if we oppose its action through the stubbornness of our own wills, still clinging to self and to sense.

—*Msgr. Ronald Knox*

INDEX